Policing Football

KU-205-759

WITHDRAWN

LIVERPOOL JOHN MOORES UNIVERSITY
Aldham Robarts L.R.C.
TEL. 051 231 3701/3634

WITHDRAWN

Policing Football

Social Interaction and Negotiated Disorder

Megan O'Neill

© Megan O'Neill 2005

All rights reserved. No reproduction, copy or transmission of this
publication may be made without written permission.

No paragraph of this publication may be reproduced, copied or transmitted
save with written permission or in accordance with the provisions of the
Copyright, Designs and Patents Act 1988, or under the terms of any licence
permitting limited copying issued by the Copyright Licensing Agency,
90 Tottenham Court Road, London W1T 4LP.

Any person who does any unauthorized act in relation to this publication
may be liable to criminal prosecution and civil claims for damages.

The author has asserted her right to be identified as the author of this work
in accordance with the Copyright, Designs and Patents Act 1988.

First published 2005 by
PALGRAVE MACMILLAN
Houndmills, Basingstoke, Hampshire RG21 6XS and
175 Fifth Avenue, New York, N. Y. 10010
Companies and representatives throughout the world

PALGRAVE MACMILLAN is the global academic imprint of the Palgrave
Macmillan division of St. Martin's Press, LLC and of Palgrave Macmillan Ltd.
Macmillan® is a registered trademark in the United States, United Kingdom
and other countries. Palgrave is a registered trademark in the European
Union and other countries.

ISBN-13: 978–1–4039–4118–3 hardback
ISBN-10: 1–4039–4118–1   hardback

This book is printed on paper suitable for recycling and made from fully
managed and sustained forest sources.

A catalogue record for this book is available from the British Library.

Library of Congress Cataloging-in-Publication Data
O'Neill, Megan, 1974–
    Policing football : social interaction and negotiated disorder /
Megan O'Neill.
        p. cm.
    Includes bibliographical references and index.
    ISBN 1–4039–4118–1 (cloth)
        1. Soccer hooliganism–Great Britain–Prevention. 2. Police–Great Britain.
I. Title.

GV943.9.F35O54 2005   2005048571
302.3′3–dc22

10   9   8   7   6   5   4   3   2   1
14   13 12 11 10 09 08 07 06 05

Printed and bound in Great Britain by
Antony Rowe Ltd, Chippenham and Eastbourne

To the Man and the Bean

Contents

Part III

Acknowledgements

I would like to thank the following for their support (in its many forms), assistance and advice during the course of this research project and book preparation: the individual police officers and staff from the main police force I studied, without whose generous co-operation this project would not have happened, and especially my two gatekeepers there; Prof. Steve Bruce, Dr. Richard Giulianotti, Prof. Peter K. Manning and Prof. Dick Hobbs for reading numerous drafts and providing thoughtful comments; Dr. Christopher Wright for an ever-open door and his uncanny ability to help me see the way through the haze of my ideas, Prof. Simon Holdaway for the precious gifts of time and publishing guidance; the other police forces and football grounds I visited during the course of this research, especially their security advisors; the private security company at the football matches; the police officers and staff at Tulliallan Police College; the Football Intelligence Section of the National Criminal Intelligence Service; the British Schools and Universities Foundation; Prof. Christopher Gane in the Law Department at Aberdeen University; Ms. Lisa Burns; Dr. Christopher Bear; the members of the Sociology Department at Aberdeen University for their unwavering and ever-ready encouragement; Drs Kirsty Welsh, Gwen Robinson, Victoria Gosling and Garry Crawford for listening to me rant on many, many occasions; Bill and Carol O'Neill for all their support over the years; and most importantly Boab, Jackie, Bill and Molly without whose strength I would have many times lost my own.

Part I

Introduction: Football, Policing and the Excitement of Mundane Sociology

If you were to ask just about any British male what is significant about 3pm on Saturday afternoons outside of summer, you would probably get the same one-word answer: football.[1] A good portion of the female population would also say the same thing, and just about anyone who lives in Britain, even if he or she does not follow football, could probably name at least three major domestic clubs and maybe also the current league champions. However, what no one in this pop survey would say is that non-summer Saturday afternoons are also the moment when the largest national mobilisation of police officers occurs in British urban areas. Football supporters on their way to, during and back from the matches that they love are the subjects of constant and pervasive police supervision. This is not a new phenomenon and yet there has been no detailed sociological study of police involvement at domestic football. This book represents the first attempt to provide such a study.

For many, the police and stewards at a football match may seem to be a part of the backdrop to the main event: the match would not be quite right without them, but they are not the main focus of the action. While in a certain respect this is true, the police and stewards do indeed have a crucial role to play in the overall football match day experience. To whom would people with spare tickets give them to be passed on to eager kids? How would the 'hooligans' have any fun if the opposing group failed to turn up? Who would keep the (often sarcastic) banter going at the turnstiles during the long queues? Who would keep supporters safe from physical retaliation as they jeer at the opposing fans? Who would hold up lost children above the crowds to find their parents? How would 'wandering' coaches full of visiting supporters get back on the path home (and not towards the city centre where home supporters were massing)? I observed the police perform these and many other activities before, during and after football matches, and feel that their role is far from insignificant, both operationally as well as socially.

This project focuses on the interaction between police officers and supporters, using the work of Erving Goffman (1959) as a way to guide field observations. These observations were gathered through the ethnographic methods of participant observation and informal interviews. This is not an analysis of police crowd control tactics at football, but is instead a study of how the police and the supporters directly interact with each other during both the calm and the more disorderly moments in relation to a football match. Police operational tactics will be mentioned occasionally as they are part of the context in which this interaction occurs, but at all times the main focus will be on the personal relationships that have developed within this favourite national pastime between the agents of social control and the subjects of their work. This will at times include the football 'hooligans' (and what is implied by that term will be discussed later) but the majority of the interaction the police have is with non-violent football supporters. Before discussing exactly how these ethnographic research methods were used, this chapter will first look at the theoretical foundation of this book, referred to as the interpretive framework. It will then address the methods employed to gather the data and will close with an overview of the chapters to follow.

The interpretive framework

In order to develop my emphasis on relationships and interaction, the work of Erving Goffman (1959) formed the basis of my theoretical approach. Goffman's primary interest is 'the everyday, routine, and often trivial interactions which comprise the bulk of man's social experience' (Birrell 1978: 13). This proved to be useful in my research as I was examining interaction during all aspects of a football match: the mundane as well as the disorderly. His concepts, especially those in *The Presentation of Self in Everyday Life* (1959) and other earlier works, helped to organise the data and structure my analytical process.

According to Branaman (1997: xlv), 'Erving Goffman is the quintessential sociologist of everyday social life'. Instead of investigating the eventful and unusual aspects of existence, Goffman concerns himself primarily with the ways people keep encounters with others smooth and relaxed. He attempts to discover the unwritten rules of social order, 'the structure of face-to-face interaction, and the nuances of the interaction process' (Birrell 1978: 16). As the main focus of my work in the field was the structure of relationships and interaction between the police officers and football supporters, learning how they related to each other in mundane and calm situations was just as important as studying when things got heated and tensions rose. Goffman's focus on these routine aspects of life proved to be informative in that capacity.

Goffman's work can be grouped into four central theoretical ideas (Branaman 1997). The first concerns how the self is produced socially based on validation awarded or withheld by others. The second looks at what happens when the social arrangements that we use to organise ourselves are taken away. The third idea comprises his metaphors for social life: drama, ritual and game, which demonstrate that morality and manipulation are not as separate as we may believe. The fourth idea looks at how social experience is organised by frames that determine the meaning of social events (1997: xlvi–ii). Goffman's dramaturgic metaphor is probably his best known and comprises the bulk of the interpretive framework that I employ. It was introduced in *The Presentation of Self in Everyday Life* (1959). In this work, Goffman discusses social life by using the metaphor of the stage, which he calls the 'dramaturgic' approach. Goffman endorses the view that all social interaction is like a theatrical performance in which actors perform one of many roles available to them, depending on the situation (front stage) in which they find themselves. They must also provide the audience for another actor and determine whether his/her performance is believable. When away from the particular situation in the 'backstage' area, the role can be dropped because the previous audience will not usually be present, and the actor can relax into another role (Birrell 1978: 19–20). The model is more complicated than this, and explains the different ways the performance can be violated and the different kinds of people that can commit those violations (Manning 1992: 40–4). As Messinger et al (1962) point out, however, this is not to suggest that we consciously experience life as theatre, but that this is a useful metaphor that a social scientist can use to better understand interaction. It was useful to me in that I employed it to analyse the interaction I observed between police and football supporters at the matches. This helped to provide a deeper insight not only into how they relate to and are sometimes dependent on each other, but also into how the work of Goffman can be developed. This will be discussed in Chapters 3–7.

Whilst the beginning of *Presentation of Self* discusses the performance of the individual, Goffman uses the concept of 'teams' and how they perform in interaction through most of the book. This does not refer to football or other sports teams, but to 'any set of individuals who co-operate in staging a single routine' (Goffman 1959: 85). Goffman has observed that often the impression fostered by an individual is in fact part of a larger routine involving several individuals. These team members must work together in order to produce a coherent and unified definition of the situation. This concept of interaction teams proved to be useful in my data analysis. In the later chapters, I will organise my discussion of interaction at football matches around the behavioural rules and guidelines that apply to all individuals in this setting and then discuss how the interaction teams that can be identified there manifest and enact these rules. In addition, Goffman suggests that teams can also be comprised of only one member (this will be discussed in more detail with the senior officers on pp. 143–4), audiences of no members (e.g. when a social setting alone is particu-larly impressive), and that an actor can perform for his or herself (1959: 86). A fuller discussion of all the teams I identified will be saved for Chapters 3–7.

I am not the first to find the dramaturgic metaphor useful in my research. For example, Fielding and Fielding (1992: 205) discuss how the offensive comments male police officers have for females may be restricted to 'backstage' areas so that the women do not hear them very often. Winlow et al (2001: 541) in their work on bouncers describe the careful impression management these men cultivate through clothes, behaviour and even scar tissue to demonstrate their hyper-masculine role. Armstrong and Giulianotti (1998: 119) analyse the changing nature of football hooliganism and suggest that the football grounds went from being front stages where violence was enacted to becoming the backstages where stories of conquests outside the ground were shared. My analysis of football policing through the use of this dra-maturgic approach has highlighted not only some significant aspects of police and football supporter interaction, but has suggested a few possible developments of Goffman's ideas. These will be discussed more thoroughly in Chapters 3–7 and on pp. 198–9.

Other aspects of Goffman's work were also influential, especially from his earlier books, and those will be mentioned as well in the ana-lytical chapters to follow. One of the main advantages to Goffman's dramaturgic approach is that it highlights the order and routine in any encounter. This was especially important to establish when considering police and football supporters. What could easily be assumed to be a disorderly or even chaotic situation proved to have its own underlying structure and social order. As will be discussed in later chapters, both police officers and supporters have usually reliable expectations about each other's behaviour, based on years of interaction with each other. The dramaturgical approach revealed this.

In addition to illuminating the details of personal interaction at football, Goffman's dramaturgical approach is also useful for analysing the wider structure of football policing. Order, 'teams', and territory are just a few aspects of Goffman's work that have implications for general social structure. As police forces are major institutions in British culture, discovering how they interact with certain sections of the population is vital to developing a deeper understanding of them and our culture as a whole. Football supporters have also become visible members of society and these groups encounter each other several times a week at hundreds of football grounds around the country. Thus by using Goffman's dramaturgical approach we can gain a deeper microscopic and macroscopic insight into the structure of social interaction through this aspect of British culture. This is not to suggest that no other theorist affected this research. Other writers have influenced my study, such as Foucault and Bourdieu, and their contributions will be discussed in the analytical chapters. However, while there are some uses to be gained from them, Goffman still proved to be the one best suited to the task at hand.

Research methods

My research into football policing took place in Scotland during the 1998–99 football season. I also attended a few matches at the end of the 1997–98 season and continued contact with the police into the 1999–2000 and 2000–01 seasons. Scotland has a long history of addressing domestic football disorder, or 'hooliganism', and thus proved to be a rich location for this study. Football hooligan activity seems to have developed there in the 1930s, while only in England in the mid-1960s (Giulianotti 1996).[2] It was a Scottish ground, Aberdeen, which was the first football stadium in the UK to become all-seated and the sale and consumption of alcohol inside the ground has been banned in Scotland since the mid-1970s (Giulianotti 1996).[3] I visited three football grounds of the Scottish Premier League (the top level of competition in Scotland) during the course of my research and secured the assistance of three police forces.

Various forms of hooliganism still occur in Scotland today, including the casuals who emerged in the early 1980s. A casual is a type of hooligan who does not dress in the colours of the club he or she supports, but in designer casual clothing (Giulianotti 1996). Casuals can also be organised in their approach to football violence, as was seen during their peak in the late 1980s when up to 1,000 from each opposing side would meet in a pre-arranged place to fight. The term 'casual' is no longer in common use in England, but was still being used in Scotland at the time of my research. However, these behaviours attributed to 'casuals' in Scotland are similar to those of some of the current domestic 'hooligans' in England.[4] For the sake of continuity I will use the term 'hooligan' throughout this book, but as later chapters will show, what exactly is implied by this term cannot be assumed (Coalter 1985, Armstrong and Young 2000). Each police group I encountered had their own unique understanding of it, which I will explore in detail. As Dunning et al (2002: 1–2) have pointed out, 'hooliganism' is really a construct of the media and politicians and is not a definitive legal or sociological concept.

My primary method of research was participant observation. As the main purpose of this project is to investigate the relationships and interaction between police officers and domestic football supporters this ethnographic methodology proved to be most appropriate. Interaction among the police officers also developed as an interest during the work, and I spent three matches observing the football stewards and their interactions with football supporters and police officers. Participant observation was the main method I employed for all of these. I decided not to try to extend my inquiry to the football supporters themselves. Many works have already been conducted into their perspective (as will be discussed in Chapter 1) so I wished to focus on the hitherto under-researched police perspective at football. I also feel that my close association with the police would have prevented me from getting to know the supporters, as I was mistaken for a football spotter or detective on several occasions by both football fans and police officers. It would therefore have been impossible to build a true rapport with the supporters. Even if I could, I would then risk losing the trust I had established with the police. As Westmarland (2000: 36) discusses, getting to know the 'local' population is impossible for most police ethnographies, thus, I have focused my ethnography on the police and steward perspective and oriented my actions around their routines.

It is important to note that while I did attend two international football matches during the course of my fieldwork, the vast bulk of this research involves domestic football supporters. As has been discussed elsewhere (Giulianotti 1991, 1995), Scottish national supporters, nicknamed the 'Tartan Army', are a very different group from the supporters of the various domestic teams. The former group has cultivated a reputation of joviality and fun while the latter is often seen as violent and aggressive. Interaction between the police and national supporters is thus quite different from that with the domestic supporters. For simplicity's sake this analysis is largely restricted to interaction with domestic supporters and should not be assumed to apply to the national supporters as well. Observations that specifically involve national supporters will be noted in the text.

While my research was conducted at more than one football ground, I focused the bulk of my efforts on one particular police force and the stadium in its jurisdiction. By doing so it was possible to develop a detailed overview of the police tactics used and how interaction may vary among the different types of officers involved with the same match. I became very familiar with the layout of the ground, the different police procedures, and the informal routines that many of the officers had developed. The police agreed to give me complete access to their football policing arrangements for the year. I was able to gain this kind of access through utilising my prior acquaintance with one of their officers. This kind of access would have been difficult to obtain in another force without that initial connection. There were two subdivisions in the main force that I researched involved with football policing and I split my time between them.

My participant observation took place with the police before, during and after the matches. I was allowed to attend the police briefings, walk or drive with the officers while they worked, and sit (and eat) with them during their breaks. I was also with the stewards in the same way during three of the matches. Thus I experienced to a certain extent the 'social life and social processes' that were occurring in this setting as a participant (Emerson et al 2001: 352). I did not engage in policing activity directly but was able to empathetically share in their experiences. At times it was difficult to explain this position to the police and stewards, as they tried to incorporate me into a role that made more sense to them. For example, the steward supervisors would sometimes ask if I wanted a job with them, starting immediately. I had to politely decline, as being employed by the subjects of my study would have inhibited the professional distance I needed to maintain. I was an observer in that I was constantly taking mental notes about what was happening around me to write up for analysis later. I would watch unfolding events, observe how the people involved interacted with each other, what they said, and how they interacted with me.

During this mental notes stage I had to be calculating when I positioned myself, as I needed to make sure I experienced the many different aspects of football policing (the various positions in the ground, areas of the city, ranks of officers, etc.). My jotted notes were written when I had returned home so as not to draw too much attention to myself or make any of my participants uncomfortable by taking notes in front of them. I often used mnemonic techniques to remember lists of events that I found significant or else ran through the events of the day chronologically in my mind. I would then write down everything I could remember. On a few occasions, I would use the small notebook I carried with me during the matches to scribble down notes when I was in the toilet. Reiner notes that this latter technique comes with its own hazards as 'frequent visits to the toilet to jot down very brief reminders for subsequent report writing are helpful – but may raise concerns about the researcher's health' (2000b: 224). All these written notes were then later typed up in a more coherent and orderly form, often bringing to mind other events I had previously forgotten. Lewis (1982: 418) in his research of policing in English football matches also took unobtrusive notes but, unlike me, brought a small tape recorder to dictate observations to himself and to record crowd chants. Reiner (2000b: 224) has found that because of the physical circumstances of researching the police, most ethnographers take the approach I did as tape-recording and open note-taking are often impractical due to the sometimes physically active and noisy aspects of the job. These fieldnotes were essential to the final analysis as they formed the bulk of the data I collected, but they only provided the starting point. Like Van Maanen (1988: 109–15), I had to look beyond them, interpret them, and find the deeper meaning of the events at hand. I did this through the application of Goffman's approach in which I incorporated all the events I witnessed and so gained a holistic and sociological view of the project.

While participant observation followed by detailed note taking was my main method during the research, I also conducted interviews with the officers and stewards while they worked. If the supporters were calm or the police officers I was observing were on a break, I would talk to the officers about their job and their feelings about football policing. These were my informal interviews (similar to that described as informal conversation by Hammersley and Atkinson (1995: 139)). I did not use a set list of questions, but just chatted informally and tried to touch on certain topics, such as how they felt about policing games and the supporters themselves. I made sure to speak to officers in each of the main posts, duties and ranks involved in football policing. However, some were either too busy attending to their task or were just not very conversational. Thus my interviews were not conducted randomly in the scientific sense, but on more of an ad hoc basis with any officer willing to chat during the few quiet moments of a football day. As Hammersley and Atkinson suggest, it is not always possible or even necessary to obtain a representative sample of informants. The purpose will 'often be to target those people who have the knowledge desired and who may be willing to divulge it to the ethnographer' (1995: 137). They were all aware that I was speaking to them for the purposes of my research project, as the senior officer usually introduced me during the pre-match briefing. I used this same interviewing approach during my time with the stewards. This informal interviewing was also conducted without the use of my notepad, as I did not want to inhibit our discussions. Armstrong found this to be the better method as well and would also rely on his memory to write up notes later (1993: 22).

I conducted more formal interviews with two sergeants and an inspector who had specific roles to play in the administration of football policing (Westmarland [2001] also used this particular mixture of methods). These one-on-one interviews took place in their offices at a pre-arranged time outside of the football matches. On these occasions, I did have a list of questions to ask and usually got through them all, though not always in the order I had intended. I also brought along a tape recorder and asked their permission to record the interview (which all gave freely). After the interview, I typed up a transcript of the discussion to incorporate into the final data analysis.

As the subsequent chapters will show, the police officers most relevant to this research project were the uniformed constables, the plain clothes football spotters (who were also detectives at the time of my research), mobile unit officers, senior officers and women police constables. These were the individuals who had the most direct interaction with the supporters and so were best suited to fulfil the aims of the study. I decided not to extend this research to those officers who had more indirect contact with supporters, such as traffic wardens, traffic police, mounted police or canine units. While these kinds of officers may work at or in relation to football matches, their interaction with supporters is less direct. The first two groups are concerned with supporters' cars rather than the supporters themselves. The last two groups may have contact with supporters, but the police animal in question mediates that interaction and so the dynamic is altered. In any event, the use of police animals was not a usual tactic at the matches I attended so I decided to leave these officers out of the research.

In addition to attending football matches in three cities, I also visited the Scottish Police College twice and the National Criminal Intelligence Service (NCIS) once. I interviewed the officer in charge of the Senior Command Course at the police college that trains chief inspectors to be football match commanders (the police officer with ultimate authority over all the emergency services during a match). During my second visit there, I attended this one-day course as an observer. NCIS is the main intelligence gathering body in the UK, especially in areas such as international crime, counterfeiting and football hooliganism. I interviewed two detectives involved with its Football Intelligence Section (FIS). They showed me what role FIS plays in policing football hooliganism and how it coordinates information-sharing with the police forces in England and Wales. The football intelligence officers of each police force send the information they have gathered on hooligans to the FIS of NCIS. The FIS collates the information and passes to other forces the intelligence that is relevant to them. At the time of my research the FIS of NCIS was not directly involved with the intelligence processes for Scottish football matches, but was occasionally in contact with Scottish officers if the information gathered warranted it. Thus the work of NCIS does not feature in my findings to follow, but it is important to note that their role in England is much more prominent than that in Scotland.

I gained my access to the police through a friend at the university who was a part-time student and a full-time police officer. Like Punch's (1993: 183) initial contact, the link between academia and policing was probably advantageous as he could see things from my perspective and anticipate the best way for me to navigate the police system. He took me to my first match through the police entrance and let me see the Closed Circuit Television (CCTV) room as well as the holding area for people who had been arrested. Once I decided I wanted to make football policing the focus of my research, he put me in touch with a Sergeant who became my 'sponsor' in effect, and my first point of contact whenever I wanted to set up my observations for the following match. This latter person was the one who took my proposal to the appropriate senior officer for approval and he agreed to arrange whatever I wanted to do with the specific officers concerned. I never signed any agreement with the force about my obligations to them for allowing me access to their activities. All I gave was a verbal agreement to my sponsor that the police would get a copy of the manuscript and a condensed 'report' of the more practical findings. Due to constraints on time and funding, I had to restrict my direct contact with the police to primarily football match days. While this may mean that I had access to a limited range of the policing experience, I did not encounter many barriers to that access. I am sure that as my project revolved around football, a rather innocuous aspect of policing for the most part, there was probably little perceived threat to the interests of the police. The only real barriers I did experience were the occasional warning to 'stay in the car' or when I was put in the CCTV room for my 'safety'.

I was never with a police group long enough to necessitate the kind of bonding discussed by Norris (1993) and Westmarland (2000). The main football ground I studied is located very close to the boundary between two police subdivisions. This means that the 'Stadium' subdivision is responsible for the ground itself and the area to the north of it. The 'City Centre' subdivision has responsibility for policing all of the city centre and the supporters as they walk from the pubs, train station, and bus station to the match. Therefore, I had to split my research time between these two subdivisions to obtain a complete picture of a football match day. The stadium officers mainly policed the inside of the ground while the city centre officers were responsible for events outside of the ground. These two groups have a very different experience of football policing and both sides need to be considered, as well as how they relate to each other. This will be developed further in later chapters. However, as a consequence I was not able to develop a close rapport with any of the uniformed officers. Because I wanted to get as wide a picture of football policing as possible, I had to spread my time out among the various subdivisions and police units. Punch (1993: 187) and Rubinstein (1973: xiii) took a different approach in that they stuck to just a few officers for the duration of their study to build trust and understanding. Due to the focus of my project I had to sacrifice some quality for the quantity of the interactions I observed and experienced. However, the plain clothes detectives (football spotters) were the same two or three men each time I worked with them, so a deeper rapport could be established there. But as I only worked with them on about four occasions, this can only be a marginal difference. Overall though, I feel I was able to establish a degree of trust with the officers during the match. I was present at the pre-match briefings and so at least my face was seen frequently by many, even if I only had direct contact with a few. I became a routine part of the football landscape for that year.

Overview of chapters

Football disorder and violence have not gone unnoticed by academics, as Chapter 1 will discuss. Research began in the late 1960s and continues to this day. The methods used have ranged from analysis of largely secondary material to detailed ethnographic study of the hooligans themselves and their culture. What many of these studies focus upon, however, is the violent or aggressive side of football culture, the working class origins of some hooligans and the image of masculinity hooliganism presents. Football hooligans are a modern folk devil (to use the term of Cohen 1980) and have arguably been the source of moral panics in contemporary society (Marsh et al 1978). The research presented in this book, however, considers some of the more mundane and routine aspects of being a supporter, whether violent or not, and police interaction with supporters. The majority of football matches in the UK no longer experience any severe spectator disorder, so it is important to consider how this order is socially constructed and sustained as well as how it is disrupted. The existing writing on football supporters often neglects the role of the police in this culture and the effect they can have on the resulting events.

UK police departments have undergone a transformation of their managerial system in recent years. They now experience constant pressure to justify the funding they receive and to work as efficiently as possible (McLaughlin and Murji 1997). In this atmosphere, it could be argued that football and the football hooligan present a very interesting opportunity for the police. The matches are regular events with fairly predictable behaviour from the supporters as well as from the football hooligans. Thus the police have an opportunity to show their skills at tackling one of the contemporary social demons with a fairly probable chance of success. For a police force under scrutiny, this could be a welcome opportunity to demonstrate the force's overall competence and efficiency. The action of the government via their recent hooligan legislation supports the police in these endeavours, as Chapter 2 explores. In the 13 years since the Hillsborough Stadium disaster (15 April 1989), football supporters have been the subjects of legislation that strictly controls their movements and increases police power to deal with them. As Foucault (1977: 17) might suggest, this is punishment not for an act, but for a person. Many of the behaviours that fall under the 'hooliganism' umbrella can be dealt with under existing legislation. However, it seems that legislators and other agents of social control feel that this small section of the population deserves special consideration.

So just how do the police interact with supporters during a football match, considering all the public and legal support they have to exercise strict controls over supporters' behaviour? Chapters 3–7 are an analysis of my observations during (primarily) one football season with the police. Chapters 3–5 consider two main aspects of interaction between the police officers and supporters: the informal guidelines and rules that can structure interaction during a match day and how these rules are enacted within the various police teams. The first section details how the police present themselves and the situation to outsiders, the typologies they hold of supporters, and the informal rules that guide police actions. The second section considers how the various police interaction 'teams' can be identified and the way space and time are used in interaction. These are teams in the Goffmanesque sense of the word in that they may not be formally organised as such but they tend to interact with other people as a team. Chapter 3 applies the above structure to uniformed foot patrol officers. Mobile Support Units (uniformed officers in vans) and plain clothes detectives or football spotters are considered in Chapter 4 and senior officers are discussed within this structure in Chapter 5. As these discussions will demonstrate, informal negotiation and sanctions during the mundane moments often preclude the use of formal legislative police powers to control supporters' actions at football matches.

Chapter 6 departs from this structure described above in its analysis of women police constables. As will be shown, they present a unique development in the nature of team interaction. This discussion then links into my analysis of the 'underlying police community'. This term refers to the social ties that bind all police officers together in any one force (and even between different forces) despite the barriers of the interaction teams. However, this community is not always a supportive one, but it shows that the common-sense idea of *the police* is misguided. Chapter 7 is also a departure from the structure of the earlier chapters when it considers the non-police teams involved with the running of a match: CCTV operators and stewards. They are usually excluded from any kind of association with police teams, as their work is not deemed to be 'real' police work. Even some tasks performed by police officers themselves are not viewed as really being worth police time, and so this last chapter will also describe this unofficial hierarchy of 'real' police officers and police work.

The purpose of this book is not to find a cure for football hooliganism nor is it intended to bring about a change in policy and legislation.[5] Its impetus is a sociological one, its *raison d'être* to advance knowledge and add to academic debate in three main areas: the study of football hooliganism, the sociology of policing, and the continued utility of Goffman's work in understanding contemporary life. While these are three different academic projects, advancing the knowledge of each has been best served by exploring how they relate to and enhance each other, as will be demonstrated below.

Much has been said about football hooliganism already (see Chapter 1). We have learned how the thrill of a potential fight is often an end in itself and how understood rules of decorum usually prevent innocent bystanders from experiencing harm. My study of the police role in football events brings to light an entirely new side of the football hooligan. While it has been said before that hooligans are more ordered than they appear, it now seems that this order extends to their relationships with some police officers as well and is not restricted to themselves. After examining this from a Goffmanesque perspective, it will be suggested (Chapter 4) that the hooligan 'team' and the police 'team' often perform *with* each other (as actors in the same play), rather than *for* each other (as actors and audience). It was only through the analysis of the calm interaction moments that this was revealed. However, the resilience of these informal behaviour codes only goes so far. Once they are breached the police officer may have to resort to bringing in the formal sanctions available to him or her.

Since its beginning in the 1960s, research on the police has been growing steadily. Many writers have taken an ethnographic approach to this work and have produced intriguing reports of police culture and its internal social divisions (see the Conclusion for more on this). But by focussing on police work at football grounds and with Goffman in mind, I have found that the police are not only internally divided, but actually operate as small, independent teams. Often these teams are more concerned with how they present the situation to each other, rather than to the public at large or to the hooligans. An underlying police 'community' ties them together on one level and presents them to outsiders as united. This image of unity is not the reality, however, as my work will show (Chapter 6).

Erving Goffman is one of the most influential sociologists to date. His work has been applied to a wide variety of settings and is pervasive in modern sociological thought. I found his work extremely insightful for my research on interaction between police officers and football supporters, as Chapters 3–7 demonstrate. But my research has also been able to give something back to Goffman to aid in the continuing development of his work. It appears from my study of police and football supporters that interaction teams are more flexible than Goffman first suggested, as has been mentioned above. In addition, there can also be a power hierarchy among teams, something that Goffman does not really consider in depth. However, all these issues will be discussed more fully throughout the book and in its conclusion. I now turn to Chapter 1 to consider the main literature on football and football policing to date.

1
Previous Research

The study of football supporters, or more specifically, football hooligans, has interested academics and government ministers for many years. Police officers have also added their thoughts to this phenomenon and the result is a very large body of work on the issue. This chapter will discuss some of this research, but only that which shows how academics have constructed football supporters over the years, primarily through varying conceptions of masculinity, class, violence and identity, and thus will give an idea of whom it is the police are policing in football. It will also analyse the few academic works that have been done on football policing specifically, demonstrating the need for a book such as this. The final section will describe some publications and research by police officers themselves that reveal how football supporters and hooligans tend to be viewed by those policing them. Thus this chapter presents an insight into the various manifestations and interpretations of the football supporter identity. As the later chapters of this book will explore in detail police identities as expressed in football policing, it is important to develop an understanding of people with whom they are interacting and developing these identities. Government research and legislation will be discussed in the following chapter.

Football literature

The initial football-related academic literature focused on football hooliganism exclusively and tried to explain and thus eradicate football violence through examining issues of masculinity and class, which will be discussed first. Later, football followers were studied more closely in ethnographies for a better understanding of their culture, their internal differences (i.e. that not all fans are 'hooligans' and not all hooligans are the same) and what meaning their violence holds for them. The purpose was not to stop their violence but to establish its significance. This section will include a discussion of football 'casuals', identity formation of hooligans and fans, the importance of space, ideas of deviance and the current composition of football crowds. So the research to be considered here went from seeing all football supporters as inherently dangerous to understanding football hooligans specifically as a new type of sub-culture whose 'deviance' is not so certain. Football hooligans have their own rules, just as I will later argue that *football policing* has its own rules that may seem disturbing to outsiders.

Before beginning the discussion, it is important to mention one key event in the history of UK football. By requiring all-seated stadiums and the eradication on perimeter fences, Lord Justice Taylor's report (The Home Office 1990) after the disaster at Hillsborough stadium brought about drastic changes in the appearance of the grounds and the movements of supporters and police officers. While many agree that these measures have improved order within the grounds, police officers see 'the major issue of football-related crowd disorder as now being...outside the stadiums' (Coalter 1985: 117). Outside the structure of the ground, crowds may still exist, but the ability of the police to control them is reduced drastically.

While the Taylor Report and other football legislation will be covered in more detail in the following chapter, it is important to mention it here as a turning point in the evaluation of football disorder. Any research on the matter must first be considered as either pre or post-Taylor. While the Taylor report did not end football violence, it did coincide with a noticeable change in its nature, as will be discussed below. It was also after this event that the emphasis for authority figures changed from crowd management to crowd safety and comfort. Academic research also changed in that authors began to recognise the differences within football supporters. Their research started to focus more on the culture of football hooliganism and understanding the meaning it holds for its participants instead of looking for ways to eradicate it. What all these academic discussions do have in common is that they centre on one or a combination of the issues of masculinity, class and violence. It is to a fuller discussion of the various theories on football hooliganism that I now turn.

Early hooligan studies: issues of class, masculinity and violence

The culture of football hooliganism has been a growing area of academic debate since about 1971. In that year, Taylor offered a Marxist view that fighting among fans at football matches is due to their wider alienation from the development of the clubs. Football is becoming more and more a middle-class and multi-national interest, and they, the 'real' working class, masculine supporters, are losing their voice (Taylor 1971). Taylor later modified this view to state that disorder in football grounds is a form of release for the working class from the economic and political policies of the Conservative government that left labourers differentiated and isolated (1982). To quell violence in football and the fear that it invokes in others, Taylor (1987) believes that a new moral education is needed (Archetti and Romero 1994). While he once saw football supporters as resistance fighters, Taylor now sees them as dangerous and uncontrolled and thus in need of citizenship lessons to end their 'untutored masculinity' (Armstrong 1998: 16). Weed (2001: 416) finds fault in Taylor's argument in that the disorderly football fans are not seeking to fight with authority figures, but with other fans from opposing teams. In addition, Taylor's work was largely based on speculation rather than empirical research (Dunning et al 2002: 14) and he views these supporters as one homogenous working class unit.

In the 1980s, researchers from Leicester University criticised Taylor's argument for ignoring the fact that disorder at football matches is a far from recent development. Through archival research and the application of Norbert Elias' theory of the 'civilising process,' Dunning and his associates devised their figurational theory, which argues that aggression and violence have long been a part of the urban socialisation of young males. While other sections of society gradually phased violence and aggression out of their lives, this lowest section of society did not. Over time, the working class incorporated these young 'rough' groups, who go to football matches and see fighting as an acceptable form of self-expression. Thus for Dunning and associates, violence at football remains a part of the culture of this section of the working class as they have yet to be completely influenced by the civilising process (Dunning et al 1988), rather than it being a consequence of economic alienation, as Taylor sees it (Weed 2001: 416). For the 'Leicester School', violence has always been associated with football; it is just that the nature of it changed from reflecting events on the field to starting fights with each other irrespective of what was happening in the match. (Giulianotti 1999: 45). These researchers dominated the field of football research in the 1980s and into the 1990s and they have received substantial funding from the Football Trust and the old Social Science Research Council (Giulianotti 1999: 44). The primary focus in the work from Dunning and associates is the violence these 'rough' supporters demonstrate. The later ethnographic works I will discuss, however, show that the actual violence that occurs at football is rare, brief, and not really the centre of these men's lives. In addition, the entire logic behind the 'figurationalist' perspective has received much criticism (Armstrong 1998: 17–18). For example, some feel it is evolutionist and ethnocentric. Others have pointed out that the 'civilising process' can never be tested as the authors use the term 'decivilising spurts' to describe short periods of time where the civilising process was temporarily reversed and thus can quash any counter arguments (Giulianotti 1999: 46). Like Taylor, these writers tend to see football hooligans as one large homogenous male working class. In addition, Hobbs and Robins argue that the evidence the Leicester researchers use to validate the claim that hooligans groups are comprised of people from the lower working class is itself weak (1991: 557). Dunning et al admit that a large part of their data stems from an historical analysis of newspaper reports (1988: 8, 11), hardly an objective source. Armstrong (1993: 11) has slated the Leicester researchers for claiming to be 'experts' on football violence looking for a cure, and thus positioning themselves as government advisors. He feels it is not the role of sociologists to stop the phenomenon they study, but to better understand it. This criticism could also be laid on Taylor (above) and his discussion of a new moral education for disorderly football fans.

Morris (1981) offered a very different perspective on football supporters and hooligans in his attempt to better understand them. He believes that sports, primarily football, are developed from the instinctive human desire for the hunt. Football playing and football supporting are the modern equivalents of hunting and religion, complete with their own tribes, rituals and heroes. Sporting pastimes are 'primal' and provide a release for genetically encoded behaviours that are proscribed in civilised society. While this work has been very influential, especially in popular thinking, it has been strongly criticised by academics. Taylor (1983) has written a critical review of this book, suggesting that Morris has neglected the cultural origins of football. Its modern form could just as easily have been the product of 19th century industrialism, rather than biology. Morris also does not discuss contemporary and socially constructed aspects of the game, such as racism and nationalism, which he could have easily incorporated into his 'tribal' metaphor. Like the authors mentioned above, Morris is also seeing football supporters as a homogenous unit and ignoring the cultural and motivational differences between them. Football supporters in the

UK can be very different, let alone football supporters in other countries (see Giulianotti 1999: 54–61). I would also suggest that his discussion, while based on ideas of 'humanity', is actually male-centred and so needs to have a better account of the role of women in this discussion of sport.

The Scottish experience of football hooliganism and its attempts to stop it have also been analysed. Coalter (1985) observed and surveyed supporters at matches and interviewed police officers at three Scottish grounds. He suggests that the term football 'hooliganism' is used to cover a wide range of behaviours, not all of which are equally serious. This emotive label can refer to not only the minority of offences, which are truly dangerous, but also to the majority of offences committed in grounds (such as vocal aggression or provocative behaviour) that are largely innocuous. Armstrong and Young have also noted this tendency of the authorities at this time to see all fans who were vocal in their support as hooligans. 'In their deliberations they believed that the fans who fought were also those doing most of the singing and chanting; so that almost inevitably the "hooligan" label became related to words as well as actions' (2000: 176). Thus the hooligan 'problem' was seen to be larger than it probably was. The differences between fans and hooligans will be explored in more detail in the next section of this chapter.

Coalter (1985) found that the measures introduced to combat football disorder – segregation, all seated stadia and the ban on alcohol – had varying influence on supporter behaviour in isolation. They were most effective in combination with each other. However, they all have unintended consequences, one of the main ones being to displace football violence into the streets and the area surrounding the ground. Coalter also used five years of police records on football arrests and ejections for his data, but acknowledges that officers have a large degree of discretion in whether or not to arrest a troublesome fan. Thus police records could actually be better indicators of police behaviour than supporters' behaviour. This discussion is the first I have considered so far that takes into account the differences between the various acts labelled as 'hooliganism'. While it does not get into the differences between the supporters themselves and their motivations (and thus misses the usual themes of masculinity and class), at least it acknowledges that not all football spectating activity is worth worrying about. However, Coalter is also out to end hooliganism rather than to gain a deeper understanding of it and so misses a good sociological opportunity.

Anthropologists have also entered the debate on the nature of hooliganism. Marsh (1982) and his associates took a unique view of activity on the terraces and suggested that it is not a scene of uninhibited violence or mayhem, but an ordered system with established roles for the members and ritual expressions of masculinity and violence; no real harm is intended. 'Social exchanges between rival fans were typically limited to exaggerated threats, ritualised insults, and the denial of the opponent's masculinity' (Giulianotti 1999: 42). The researchers found that despite all the threats to the contrary, actual violence rarely occurred. They also discovered a hierarchy within the hooligan group that helped to maintain its order, with the respected older members at the top who leave the 'aggro' to the younger members at the bottom. Thus Marsh was one of the first writers on this topic to see the heterogeneity of hooligans and used actual fieldwork on them to gain a better understanding of who they are. The influence of this work can still be felt today. Weed (2001) has used this perspective to analyse the events of the European Football Championships in 2000. Despite the views of the media, he found that what really happened between the England fans and opposing supporters was largely innocuous masculine posturing. He does acknowledge that real violence does occur (as does Marsh) but that only a small minority do so and this is what encourages the posturing in the others. Marsh's work, while approaching the technique advocated by the ethnographers below, has received some criticism. Hobbs and Robins feel that Marsh was too optimistic about the ability of hooligans to self-police through their 'ritual' violence, as football-related deaths are not unknown (1991: 553). Giulianotti (1999: 43–4) points out that Marsh and his colleagues missed some of the cultural specificity of much hooligan conflict. Local rivalries and the specific histories of each club can have a large impact on the nature of the violence that occurs. It cannot be seen as a general phenomenon (see also Redhead 1991: 481). In addition, while their work was much more ethnographic than what had gone on before, it largely concerned the fans of Oxford United who have yet to be a major force in the hooligan scene.

In the 1990s, anthropologists Armstrong and Harris condemned earlier work on hooliganism for its lack of actual contact with hooligan groups. They write that, 'the evidence provided by participant observation shows clearly that the basic data regarding football hooliganism is significantly different from that previously assumed and, therefore, that much theorising on the subject has been misapplied effort' (1991: 432). Armstrong and Harris studied hooligans at Sheffield, and while they did not develop a specific theory, they urged more direct contact through ethnographic research with the groups in question and less distant theorising. Marsh was on the right track, but had not taken it to the extent they advocate. The work that did answer this call will be described next.

Post-Taylor: ethnography and identity formation in hooligans

The research I will consider next also looks at issues of masculinity, class and violence in relation to football fans and hooligans, like the previous research did. However, the impetus of the following work is to find a deeper understanding of the cultural *identity* of these people and their motivations than what those three topics allow. I feel this should be a key theme for work on football supporters/hooligans, as it will further illuminate their relationships with the police at matches. By focusing on an ethnographic study of identity new issues emerge, such as a hooligan sub-culture that crosses class lines, passion about their activity, seeking excitement, constructing a common history, the role of space and the political context in which the research is based. These topics demonstrate that there is much more going on at football than the cries of an alienated or uncivilised male working class looking to express themselves through violence. Primarily, this work studies those directly involved in football violence, which points out that while some supporters are very passionate about their team, not all become football hooligans.

Hobbs and Robins (1991) echo the sentiments of Armstrong and Harris. They feel that a true understanding of football hooliganism can only be gained from contact with the hooligans themselves. They conducted research like this and stress that not all football hooligans are the same and should not be seen as such. They found no leaders among the hooligan groups, but a 'hard core' of men who were adept at following fashion trends and techniques of violence, but they are a small and floating population. It is this 'nutter' minority, from whom violent behaviour is expected within the hooligan subculture, who conducts the majority of football violence. The rest of the group, who may not be as committed or competent at these skills, see the hooligan group as almost a second family (1991: 576) and are thus involved in a sub-culture, not a random collection of nameless 'hooligans'. They also argue that not all football hooligans are working class, uneducated, or unemployed, as some researchers would suggest, as shown above.

The work Armstrong (1998) takes this a step further by following one group of football hooligans for an extended period of time. These were the 'Blades' of Sheffield United, a team Armstrong supported from his childhood. As he knew the Sheffield men involved in hooliganism to some extent and was similar to them in background and age, he was able to gain entry to their group as a long-term observer. He shows that far from being a mindless group of thugs, football hooligans have a very intricate culture that has developed over many years. Fights with rival hooligan groups are often planned in advance and attacks on innocent bystanders are not only rare, but bring condemnation from other hooligans. '...Blades violence was not random, but was very discriminatory. Within this contest the aim of humiliating rivals played a larger part then injuring them...' (Armstrong 1998: 234). The biggest victory comes when one group forces the others to run away, rather than through any physical conflict. While the hooligans Armstrong met were not generally middle-class or highly educated, they were by no means from the bottom of the social pile. Most were in highly skilled manual work and could have a lot to lose if they found themselves subject to bad publicity after a court hearing. They were also not all from the same areas in Sheffield. They tended to congregate in the city centre to strike up friendships and develop networks (Armstrong 1998: 150–1, 265). For Armstrong, the Blade identity is not about having a good 'punch-up' once a week. It is 'bound up in the common activities of male leisure, drinking and football enthusiasm, and that has these simple elements surrounded by symbolic, semiotic and cultural forms that give them meaning and resonance' (1998: 169). Thus a football hooligan's identity is far more complex than the early research allowed.

However, Armstrong is also not without his own critics. Dunning has argued that this research, while based on actual field experiences, cannot be generalised as it only concerned 40–50 men in one northern English city (Weed 2001: 416, Dunning et al 2002: 14). Horne (1998) wrote a review of Armstrong's book and felt that he ignores more structural factors of hooliganism to the detriment of his argument by focusing on agency (see also Moorhouse 2000). Armstrong has written that '(f)ootball hooliganism cannot really be "explained". It can only be described and evaluated' (1998: 21). As such, Horne feels Armstrong is overly critical and dismissive when it comes to other writers of the sociology of hooliganism and as such prefers hooligan memoirs. He also suspects that Armstrong was not taking a neutral stance in his discussions of police officers in that the tone he uses is one of 'all coppers are bastards' (Horne 1998: 881). Armstrong himself admits that he became friends with the men he was researching, but far from this being a problem it is what allowed the research to continue for so long and gain the depth that it did (1993: 25).

Giulianotti (1996) conducted similar work in Scotland on the football casuals. The term 'casuals' refers to organised hooligan groups who do not generally wear club colours and whose main goal is to fight with other casual groups. The name, still common in Scotland at the time of my research, comes from the designer casual clothing that the members wear.[6] Giulianotti's work highlights the organised, deliberate, and rule-bounded behaviour of these types of football fans (1999: 51). Football casuals who attend matches do not tend to engage in any disruptive or violent activity within the grounds, but wait until the match is over to find the rival casual groups. Giulianotti followed two groups of casuals, those from Aberdeen and those who support Edinburgh Hibernian. Like Armstrong, his was an ethnographic study that developed a close relationship with the casuals and could accurately and completely discuss who they were and what motivates them to do what they do. He found that hooligans are far more incorporated into UK society than the Leicester researchers suggested. 'Money is important for socialising in pubs, clubs, football grounds and so on; for travelling to matches in the UK or abroad; for purchasing menswear or other commodities' (1999: 51). Hooligans have a particular 'taste' and have even become a trendy sub-culture with which to be associated if one is a young male. Giulianotti notes, however, that while masculinity is a key part of the football identity (as the early writers found), its expression is culturally specific. Some groups even adopt a deviant sexual identity in order to ward off further insults from opposing groups or are self-effacing for fun (for example, during my fieldwork I heard some football supporters refer to themselves in chants as 'sheep-shaggers' in order to prevent the other supporters from saying it first). Outside of football, many of these men are active and sensitive parents and partners (1999:155–6). Both of these studies stress, however, that being a hooligan is a key part to that person's identity; hooliganism is not something they do lightly or without passion (see Hughson 1998a, 2002). However, Giulianotti has also not escaped criticism for his work. Dunning et al (2002: 14) argue that it suffers from many of the same weaknesses of Armstrong's work in that the ethnographic method is too subjective and there is no engagement with the work of other authors to confirm or refute pervious findings.

While Giulianotti and Armstrong look at the meaning behind football violence, Gerry Finn (1994) examines differences within football violence itself. His work on Glasgow Rangers football hooligans suggest that there are different types of aggression and violence that are displayed at a football match and this needs to be considered. Both players and supporters seek out peak or 'flow' experiences (excitement, euphoric feeling) through the game (Csikszentmihalyi 1975). Players are allowed a certain amount of legitimate violence ('quasi-violence') and aggression to be effective sportsmen. Supporters identify with their team and its players and so exhibit some aggression themselves through shouting and chanting, but not actual violence. It is the game and their role as a supporter or player that gives them their excitement. Thus while they may be aggressive in their support of their team, they are *not* hooligans. This is an important distinction. Football hooligans, however, use violence and not the game itself to find their peak experiences. For all people involved, supporters, hooligans, and players, aggression and/or violence are a part of the football experience and thus a part of their football-related identity. This work is significant in that it brings us back to the wider picture of a football match and to all forms of aggression shown there, not just that exhibited by hooligans. It also demonstrates that far from being an immoral activity, football hooliganism can be viewed as just another aspect of the 'voluntary risk-taking leisure pursuits, such as scuba-diving, hang-gliding, and bungee-jumping' (Giulianotti 1999: 53). It is the pursuit of an intense emotional state, not the pursuit of destruction or mayhem. This links in with Redhead's (1991: 482) argument about the increasing ineffectiveness of the term 'hooliganism' to relate to any one object. He feels that not only are the activities defined as 'hooliganism' diverse, they are rapidly changing and enigmatic (see also Hughson 2002 for how this is expressed in Australia). However, the literature on the subject does not recognise this and thus creates the contours of an activity that may not actually exist. Using Baudrillard's concept of 'hyperreality', Redhead warns that what we are discussing and regulating and fearing is the created image of hooliganism, rather than any actual referent. We tend to focus on the signs of hooliganism, rather than any actual 'reality' of it, and thus need to learn instead what forms it is actually taking.

This focus on the flexible identity of football hooligans continues with the work of King (1995). He feels that any analysis of a football-related confrontation cannot be considered through objective factors, but needs to take into account the situation in which the encounter occurs and the specific people involved. Groups of football fans or hooligans bring to any situation their personal history, current identity and, in the case of international matches, their nationality. Their

'imagined communities', to use Anderson's (1990) term, can incorporate ideas of masculinity, militarism, and pride in the club. However,
these communities are not static, as any encounter with another football group will modify their history and thus their identity. Football
supporters and hooligans must then be considered in light of this
negotiable factor, and recognised as unique and constantly changing
entities. King (2001a) continues this discussion of identity formation
in hooligans by examining the role of violence more closely. He notes
that although it is 'the highpoint of the hooligan's existence, fighting
itself constitutes a negligible length of time in the lives of these fans'
(2001a: 570). He found that football hooligans spend far longer
discussing violence than they actually spend engaged in it. As such,
King argues that the focus of research should not be so much on why
violence occurs, but 'how the violence in which these groups engage
sustains group solidarity since the discussion of violence is the pre-
dominant social practice' (King 2001a: 570). According to King, it is
through the constant negotiation of shared memories of violence that
common values are established and the future of the gang is determined. For hooligans groups, ideas of violence are a key part of their
ever-evolving identities.[7]

Another aspect of the football experience that can be used in creating identity is space, both real and imagined. Hughson (1998b) discusses the idea of a 'thirdspace' (as introduced by Soja in 1996) created
by the supporters of Sydney United. This team was formerly known as
Sydney Croatia and some of its supporters have used the game and its
ground as a space to create a unique and stylised identity as Croatian,
despite the 'de-ethnicising' of the Australian game. Through his ethnographic research, Hughson found that they wear various colours and
symbols that reflect their origins, though not always in an extremely
obvious way as some symbols are traditional and some modern. Thus,
only they are aware of all the meanings implied and have created an
effective method of avoiding official control of their fandom and identity in the football ground. This is a 'thirdspace' in that it is both an
imagined (their subculture) and a real space (the football stadium).

For many football supporters, footballing spaces have a deep power
and significance. Bale has studied this phenomenon in great detail,
from the economic and geographical effect of a football ground on the
surrounding urban area to the meaning that football supporters attach
to specific spaces. Bale (1994) uses the term 'topophilia' to refer to the
love a person can develop for a specific place. Supporters often exhibit
this in relation to the home ground of their favourite football team.

For them, the football ground is not just the place where their team plays and practices; it is part of the team's history and is almost sacred in its significance. To take away the ground is to take away a part of what the team is and thus of what they as supporters are.

Space also has great significance in the management of football supporters and hooligans on game days. Giulianotti and Armstrong (2002) have examined the use of space by both the football hooligans and the police. Traditionally, violence inside the football stadium would occur in certain sections of the ground, mainly the area where the opposing sides encountered each other as one tried to take the other's 'end'. This no longer occurs with all-seated and segregated stadiums, but football hooligans intent on violent encounters have found ways to meet in the city centres instead. As Giulianotti and Armstrong point out, this means that what was once the 'front stage' for violent encounters (the stadium) is now the 'back stage' (Goffman 1959) where a supporter can relax with friends and plan their post-match activities. Thus football violence has been displaced into the city streets, pubs, and public transport stations. The police try to control football hooligans' movements outside the ground, but with varying degrees of success. They have succeeded, however, in making themselves one of the contenders in any attempt to organise football hooligan encounters.

It is important, however, to consider all of the above research in its cultural context. The political mood and agenda in the UK over the years has had some influence on the routes academics have pursued. Research has often presented the hooligan groups in a way complimentary to the dangers politicians suggested that they posed at the time (Giulianotti 1994: 30).[8] Giulianotti gives a detailed summary of academic work on football violence up to that point and the corresponding actions of the government, which are often correlated. More recent government legislation would suggest that football fans, especially those who travel abroad, are social deviants and need to be controlled. There is academic work to support this by Williams and Taylor (1994). They feel that despite different international trends, football in England is 'heavily and prohibitively masculinised, chauvinistic and aggressive' (1994: 215–16). When fans go abroad they see it as metaphorically enacting a military campaign against the foreign competitors, and the tabloids encourage this. Fans recognise that the game and stadiums are changing and they lament the loss of the overly masculine game, but actually draw on a mythologised past when doing so (Williams and Taylor 1994: 231, 233). Brick (2000) believes that this assumption of the xenophobic and violent English fan is based on an outdated knowledge of football supporters. According to Brick, many supporters are now trying to return to the idea of 'real' supporting, which is anti-hooligan and anti-consumerist. They reject the violent and aggressive supporter mentality as well as the softer comforts of a 'middle class' game. Thus the idea seems to be to re-connect with an idyllic and nostalgic past when football was terrace-based and attended by 'civilised' working-class men. Football is the focus, nothing else. However, Brick feels that in doing so these supporters are in fact buying into the definition of morality that modern consumerism suggests.

Giulianotti (2002) develops this relationship between contemporary football commodification processes and the supporter identity further. We have seen in the work mentioned previously that not all football hooligans are the same due to their unique historical identities and their internal hierarchies (e.g. the work of Marsh, Hobbs & Robins, Armstrong, and Giulianotti). Giulianotti (2002) demonstrates that not all football supporters are the same either. He argues that a process of 'hypercommodification' has been taking place within football since the 1980s. This has involved 'satellite and pay-per-view television networks, Internet and telecommunications corporations, transnational sports equipment manufacturers, public relations companies, and the major stock markets through the sale of club equity' (2002: 29). All these forces have contributed to a more financially and corporately driven game to a degree as yet unknown, which has had a noticeable impact on the identities of its supporters (see also Redhead 1997). Giulianotti identifies four types of football spectators based on two sets of binary oppositions: traditional-consumer and hot-cool. He sees 'supporters' as the traditional/hot spectators. These are the people for whom the club is a key part of their identity and has been for most of their lives. They feel obligated to support it in whatever guise it takes and it creates for them a social solidarity with other supporters. The traditional/cool spectators are the 'followers'. They do not engage with their favoured football club as deeply as the supporters do, although they are aware of the traditional forms of identity and community that each club brings. Followers tend to watch their preferred teams on television and do not have the emotional attachment to the football ground that supporters express. They also tend to follow favoured football people (players and managers) and not just clubs. 'Fans' are the hot/consumer spectators, according to Giulianotti. They have strong identification with a particular team or players, but this is expressed more distantly than that of the supporter. Fans focus their efforts economically by buying merchandise, football magazines or club shares to demonstrate their loyalty and tend to be geographically removed from the club's home. They tend to be wooed by the celebrity of individual players and develop non-reciprocal intimate relations with them. The final spectator category is the cool/consumer 'flâneurs'. These spectators tend to be wealthier than the others and are very detached from their favoured clubs. They are in the market for football experiences and thus wear club shirts more for their own aesthetics than for what they signify. They get their football experiences entirely through the media: television and the Internet. These four categories are ideal-types and so no one category may fit a particular football spectator perfectly. But they suggest that like with football hooligans, to see football spectators as being all the same is inaccurate. The market-driven nature of football is influencing its audience in various and significant ways and as such levels of consumerism may be a new addition to the hitherto prominent categories of masculinity, class and violence for studying football supporter identities.

This raises another important issue: while the identities of football spectators may have changed, what about their demographics? Are they all becoming more middle class and family centred as many believe (Gilman 1996), or is it more the flâneur who is bourgeois as Giulianotti suggests (2002: 39)? Malcolm et al (2000) have reviewed previous questionnaire studies concerned with these questions. They compiled research data from 1984 to 1997 and analysed it for signs of change in football supporter demographics. They acknowledge that is it difficult to draw definite conclusions from these works as many of the questionnaires had problems in their methodologies. For example, some had very low response rates and others over-represented specific groups. Despite this however, they feel the picture that emerged was one of stability rather than change. The supporter bases of the clubs did not appear to have altered dramatically over the years and this suggests (albeit tentatively) that the more cosmetic changes to football grounds did not have a noticeable impact on those who attend the games. This would support Giulianotti's categories as the middle-class 'flâneurs' tend not to go to the games but enjoy watching from their homes the traditional spectacle of the 'supporters'. However, this is a controversial finding, as many people, especially fans, feel that the game is becoming too expensive for the working-class supporter (Strachan 1999). Malcolm et al also suggest that survey research of this type needs to be executed with better methodological practice so that future longitudinal studies can reach more concrete conclusions. As far as the hooligans go, Giulianotti (1999: 52) finds more continuity than change. His work in Scotland suggests that while the overall numbers of hooligans have declined, there have not been many new generations of 'lads'. Thus the majority of those who make up the hooligan groups now have been active since the early 1980s or before, and are well into their 30s or 40s. With this maturity comes a well-developed yet informal hooligan information network across Scotland, England and Europe. Despite all the new communication technology however, organised battles are relatively rare in the UK now. So as this and the previous research in this section demonstrates, it is important to continue ethnographic research on football supporters and hooligans. Their football-related actives are a key part of how they form their identities, but none of these processes are static. Thus the original themes of class, masculinity and violence can no longer be sufficient to gain an understanding of these dynamic groups.

Policing football

Until now, this chapter has been concerned with research on football supporters and football hooligans to gain a greater understanding of whom it is the police are policing at football matches, what motivates them and how they view their football experiences. The relationship the police have with these groups was mentioned occasionally, but will now form the focus of this section. While football is only one aspect of police work, studying it can shed new light on the police as a whole and bring out some nuances of the occupational culture as officers who usually work alone or in pairs are now forced to all work together. The following is an examination of the few studies that have specifically examined the role of the police in football crowd control and football culture. As will be shown, few academic researchers have considered football policing in any detail. Some authors, like Hobbs and Young, research both football and policing issues, but not *football policing*. Even fewer use the method I advocate, which is the ethnographic study of police and supporter interaction. The research can be grouped into roughly seven categories: work by Eugene Trivizas; Leicester University studies; psychological studies; work by Stott, Reicher and King; research from Garland and Rowe; papers by Gary Armstrong and associates; and the few ethnographic studies that exist. There are also a few isolated papers that do not fit into any of these broad categories that will be mentioned as well, one of which is the first paper I will discuss.

In their study of interaction between spectators and athletes, Ingham and Smith (1974) also comment upon increasing social control in many aspects of sport. This includes restrictions on the behaviour of people involved (players, coaches, supporters, etc.), the increasing presence of riot-trained police and changes occurring to the grounds themselves (high walls, moats). While this study is a rather old one, it shows that even in the 1970s some academics were concerned that these increased control measures were actually contributing to the problem, rather than solving it. For instance, more arrests occur because more police officers are present at the games to make the arrests. With the obvious readiness of magistrates to sentence hooligans, the police know they will get convictions for sport-related offences. This high arrest and conviction rate in turn suggests that there is an increasing problem with violence at the games, which may not actually be the case (Ingham and Smith 1974). Trivizas in his work with police arrest records confirms this suggestion (1980, 1981). According to the data he studied, football hooligans are treated more harshly than people who commit similar offences in non-football related situations. He feels that magistrates see hooliganism as senseless or meaningless, and treat offenders accordingly. One of Trivizas' students, Ellis (1984), conducted a survey of attitudes among police officers and law students on five incidents of violence at football matches. She found that law students are more likely to suggest that a serious law had been broken but that punishment should be soft (such as a warning). However, the police are more likely to say that a less serious law had been broken ('Breach of the Peace', which is easier to prove) but that punishment should be harsh (arrest). Thus all these early studies suggest that the police could be treating football hooligans more harshly than other members of the public, simply because of their pre-conceived notions about football hooliganism. Similarly, part two of this book will discuss the typologies police have developed about hooligans that often guide their actions.

Research from the University of Leicester, while primarily focusing on football supporters, has also considered police officers on occasion. For instance, Williams (1980) echoes Ellis' findings in that while the police are hesitant to arrest hooligans for causing an affray, a very serious charge that is difficult to prove, it does not mean that the hooligans are any less violent. He feels that while the media tends to amplify occurrences of violence at matches, academics are just as guilty of minimising the violence that takes place. Ethnographic academics mentioned earlier, like Giulianotti or Armstrong, would probably

LIVERPOOL JOHN MOORES UNIVERSITY
LEARNING SERVICES

disagree and argue that they are not minimising football violence but making it more understandable. Dunning et al (1988: 5), also Leicester researchers, feel that police actions can have a direct impact on supporter behaviour. For example, they argue that more intensive policing inside the ground has probably displaced football violence outside the ground, and that the more sophisticated the police become in their methods the more sophisticated the hooligans become to evade them. Surprisingly, both of these points are similar to those raised by Giulianotti and Armstrong (2002) discussed previously and Armstrong and Giulianotti (1998), to be discussed below.

The field of psychology has also had a few contributions to make to the study of football policing. Canter et al (1989) look at football violence from an environmental psychology perspective. They feel that the environment in which a sport is played has a big impact on its supporters. In the case of football in Britain, legislation to control supporters has been implemented after crisis situations only (see later discussion). At the time of their writing, there had been no widespread attempt to analyse football crowd movement from a theoretically informed social science perspective, especially one that considered the environment in which football takes place. Instead, ground rules and legislation had built up over the years that encouraged more and more technologically based means of control. Canter et al feel this is a mistake as no long-term solutions are being considered. This mirrors police tactics in other areas in that they appear to be effective but only in the short-term (Bittner 1967, Reiner 1997, Loader 1997a). Canter et al suggest the ultimate solution to violence at football will not be simple and will not be the same for all clubs, but it will involve changes to the football spectating environment. Lord Justice Taylor seems to have confirmed this to some extent with his drastic changes to stadium structures. More recently, Kerr (1994) has conducted a psychological analysis of police officers and football hooligans. He suggests that the police are a part of the means the hooligans employ to achieve psychological arousal through violence at football. There are unwritten rules that guide action in the football context that are not present in other settings. So for hooligans, arrest and jail are not threatening but part of the excitement. The more the authorities try to clamp down on hooligans and control them, the more determined they are to be disruptive, and the more rules they have to break to do so. This is similar to how the police respond to new formal rules as well (see Reiner 2000a for a discussion on how the police have reacted to the Police and Criminal Evidence Act 1984). So from the psychological point of view, violence at football does not just originate in the supporters themselves but also from the environment in which it occurs and from police involvement. Armstrong (1998: 25) is highly critical of this work, however. He feels that Kerr proposes many interesting states of mind that hooligans can have, but does not clearly define these nor does he show examples from actual football matches to support his theories. Dunning et al (2002: 14–15) argue that much of what Kerr does is dress up simple sociological concepts in complex psychological jargon. In addition, most of Kerr's work came from studying newspaper clippings, rather than from fieldwork at the matches.

Social psychologists Stott and Reicher (1998a, 1998b, Stott et al 2001, Stott 2003) have also made contributions to the study of football policing, although some of their work involved crowds that are not related to football. In their social identity model, they suggest that football fans do not have a predetermined identity based on violence but develop their activities based on interaction with the police. Fans do not see themselves as a homogeneous unit, so when the police treat them as such they feel justified in retaliating. For Stott and Reicher, the police create a self-fulfilling prophecy in football fan behaviour. King (1999), a sociologist of football, suggests his work and that of Stott and Reicher have converging ideas. He feels that they are both suggesting that football violence is the result of an interaction between supporters and other agencies like police officers. It is not a predetermined process. Interaction is informed by prior occurrences, but not determined by them. Thus if football violence occurs it is because of the prior interaction and negotiation of officers and hooligans, not necessarily because the fans had planned it in advance. While I would agree with King on the importance of investigating interaction between police officers and supporters, the method I suggest is a long-term ethnography of all interaction (both peaceful and otherwise), not just the sporadic occurrences of football violence. I also feel that Stott and Reicher are viewing the *police* as a homogenous unit, and not taking into account the different operational tasks the officers are assigned and their positions in the internal hierarchy as I do in my fieldwork.

Garland and Rowe (1999) have written a great deal on policing racism at football grounds. They feel the main problem here rests not with the legislation but with the police and the stewards. These groups are unclear as to what the current legislation is regarding racism and how exactly they can act on it. They also suggest that lack of communication between police and stewards about the boundaries of each other's responsibilities exacerbates the problem, and urge more training on the issue for each. Issues about the boundaries between police work and steward work also emerged in my own research. Garland and Rowe (2000) feel that football violence itself has been changing. While organised football violence is largely under control, it is unorganised violence that is causing the biggest problem for football authorities. All the measures that are in place to combat football hooliganism (such as intelligence sharing, CCTV, stewards) are geared towards the organised offenders. The underlying causes of spontaneous violence, however, are not addressed.

The biggest single contributor to the study of policing football is probably the anthropologist Gary Armstrong. Although his PhD thesis and subsequent monograph (1998) deal primarily with his ethnographic study of one group of football hooligans, he makes many observations of police actions within these works and has co-authored several articles on the subject (which will be discussed next). In his book, Armstrong suggests that the police at football matches are aware that, to an extent, they are actors in a performance, participants in a ritual that occurs at every game. By the attention they pay to football hooligans, the police give those fans the drama they like to recount to others later. The hooligans in turn provide the police with an opportunity to practice tactics and train police dogs in methods that they will use in more serious public order incidents (1998: 38, 107). While it appeared to me in my own research that the police did feel they were giving hooligans an added element of excitement, they did not seem to see football as a practicing opportunity for more serious incidents. These officers treated football as a potentially serious incident in its own right, but did use it to publicly improve their image, as I will discuss further in part two of the book. Dick Hobbs echoes this suggestion in a video on football violence called *Trouble on the Terraces* (Castle Communications 1994). In it he states that the police use football as a technique to appear in control of social disorder, as a way of boosting their own image. With its high media presence, the police use this planned and regular event to appear effective because outside of football they are actually largely ineffective at crime control.

Armstrong and Hobbs (1994) also discuss the extreme covert means of control that the police have employed in the recent past to arrest football hooligans. They analyse the work of undercover police officers who attempted to infiltrate, gather intelligence on, and eventually – with the back-up of uniformed officers – arrest major hooligan groups in the 1980s and early 1990s. Most of these operations failed as charges were dropped due to a lack of evidence. However, some of

these 'dawn raids' have lead to convictions and in general 'the policing of football supporters is a political issue which has seen the nor-
malisation of surveillance and control without a political protest.
When applied to other citizens, voices are raised' (1994: 215). Thus,
the police and other authorities see football hooligans in a special
light and reserve treatment for them not given to others, as Trivizas'
work suggested earlier.

As Armstrong and Young (1997) point out, it is not just the police
who view football hooliganism as a threat to society. The many Acts of
Parliament that condemn this type of supporter have solidified the
public's and politician's view that nothing other than unbridled violence is in the hooligan's nature. Armstrong and Young argue that
what constitutes 'hooliganism' in the legal sense is mostly ritualistic
behaviour and harmless shows of male bravado. The violence that does
occasionally occur involves only those who wish to participate in it
(the hooligans) and takes place in the city centres and surrounding
areas (which makes it easier for the police to detect it). As soon as the
authorities established these actions as illegal, the image of hooliganism as a moral threat becomes extremely persuasive with the
public. The police then can enjoy both public and legal support in
exerting control over these groups. Armstrong and Hobbs (1995:
190–1) argue that by presenting football hooligans as a disease that
needed a cure, extreme surveillance techniques and the collation of
sketchy intelligence was normalised for this group. Also, the recent
Football Supporters Acts were actually redundant measures, but symbolically demonstrated the power of the government to isolate a societal group it doesn't like and gave them the chance to 'talk tough on
crime'. I will discuss this legislation further in the following chapter.

Armstrong and Giulianotti (1998) have studied the effects of the
police's surveillance techniques on football hooligans. This includes
undercover work, but also methods such as CCTV, intelligence networks, and photos. Their main argument is that while the police tactics
have become more and more technically advanced, so have the
methods of the hooligans to avoid them. For instance, many hooligans
own mobile phones (and did so before their use was pervasive among
the general public) and as such can communicate with each other
in ways the police cannot trace. They may also arrange for fights to
occur in areas where there are no surveillance cameras so as to avoid
detection. Actions of the police and other control agencies are in
fact helping to change the nature of hooliganism itself, rather than
discouraging it from occurring in the first place.

The last category of academic study into football policing that I will discuss is the one that most closely resembles the approach I advocate. This is the long-term ethnographic study of police officers and football supporters, through observation and interviews. The work of Lewis (1982) is most similar to the approach I take in my own research. He conducted a participant observation study of football policing in England. He describes the tactics used to police crowds and the styles the officers adopt when interacting with fans. He acknowledges that this interaction between police officers and supporters is important to consider as the subtle relationships the officers and the fans develop can be used to help crowd control. However, he also found inconsistencies between some police forces in the tactics they use at football games, as did I in my research. Unfortunately, Lewis' work does not go beyond this detailed description of interaction into a sociological analysis of the phenomenon itself, as I will do in later chapters.

White (1984) also conducted an ethnographic study of football that included an analysis of the interaction between police officers and supporters. He examined the football hooliganism debate from a 'socio-legal' perspective by including the views of fans, police, the law, and his own observations. He writes that, 'research should be focused upon the agents of social control as much as upon those stigmatised as criminals. Above all, it should be concerned with interaction between the two' (1984: xxvi). In his studies of the police, White found that the amount of discretion allowed to them is a source of conflict. The degree of deference a person shows a police officer will often determine whether the spectator is arrested, ejected or neither, except in the case of big games where police are told to arrest no matter what. Thus, there is no great continuity to police actions, especially when behaviour that is not tolerated inside the ground *is* tolerated outside the ground. White believes that because the situation (the football match) influences whether or not an act is seen as deviant, there is no need to criminalise (what he sees as) situationally non-deviant behaviour (e.g. swearing, flag waving, insulting others). This argument illustrates the importance of examining the interaction between police and fans, as White has demonstrated that it can have an obvious influence on the oft-quoted arrest statistics for games. My own research has revealed similar tendencies towards situationally specific arrests in contemporary Scottish football policing, as I will discuss in later chapters.

The final study I will mention that is an ethnographic investigation of football policing is by Hughson (1999) in Australia. In his work with football supporters of Croatian background (known as the Bad Blue

Boys, or BBB), he considers their relationships with police officers and stewards. He found that in general the BBB and the police have a very amicable relationship. The police do not seem to discriminate against the BBB because of their ethnic origins, but see them more as a youth subculture. The stewards, however, seem to have an aggressive manner when encountering these supporters. While this research occurs in a very unique context, it is important to mention here to demonstrate that football supporting and football policing are not the same the world over, as the perspectives seemed to be the exact opposite in the games I attended. Academic ethnographic research with these groups reveals this.

Studies by police officers

Police officers themselves have made no small contribution to discussions on football policing. Some of these papers are mainly devoted to analysing police tactics at football matches and give suggestions for how they can be improved. Many take a more academic approach and discuss possible causes of hooliganism, the culture of football hooligans themselves, and suggestions for legislation as well as police tactics.

Students at Bramshill Police Staff College in England are required to write papers as part of their training. The following is a discussion of two such papers on the subject of football hooliganism and the police response. Chief Superintendent Metcalfe (1984) analyses the current policing situation at football games during his Senior Command Course and makes nine recommendations for how it can be improved. Many of his suggestions have since been implemented (although probably not as a result of his paper as these suggestions had already been proposed by politicians; see discussion on p. 45 on government reports), such as all seated stadia and a complete ban on alcohol consumption on the way to and during football matches[9]. He also suggests that police regulate the ejection procedure by arresting offenders when possible and formally cautioning others. The charge given at arrest should be the most severe possible and not the charge of 'Breach of the Peace', which is most frequently used and carries a lesser sentence. His final suggestion is that members of sociology and psychology departments should be invited to study behaviour at football to give the police the best information possible on which to base their strategies. A group of superintendents have also conducted an investigation into football hooliganism (Bramshill Police Staff College 1985) for their

Intermediate Command Course. Their main focus is the monitoring of supporters, the tactics used by the police and current legislation. It suggests that a national intelligence network be established to collate information on football hooligans (which is now in place with NCIS). Their discussion of police tactics seems to view football supporters as a potentially riotous mob that must be strictly controlled at all times. They do not feel that segregation is a good idea as it creates an 'us' and 'them' mentality, nor do they like perimeter fencing as it poses a safety risk. They do like the proposed Public Order Bill as it will allow the police to 'reduce fear among ordinary supporters and ensure a return of family orientated support' (1985: 56).

These papers above did not really investigate the nature or causes of football hooliganism, just police tactics and possible legislation. Other police officers have considered hooliganism itself, and some of these papers will be considered next. The West Yorkshire Metropolitan Police Authority (1977) produced the earliest paper I have found on this topic. They have a very low opinion of football hooligans, as was openly expressed in their report. These immature 'vandals' use the football crowd to blend in and alcohol to feel liberated. The combination of these factors leads to trouble at games. While their opinion of football hooligans may be somewhat dated, their suggestions for addressing the situation are not as many of their recommendations were eventually implemented after the Taylor Report (but again, it is doubtful that there is a direct connection). A few years later, Chief Inspector Howard (1979) produced a paper on the same subject. He feels that even 'normal' people can be influenced by 'the crowd' and can fall into a trance-like state (similar to LeBon 1895). Other fans use football as merely an excuse to be disorderly. However, he does not advocate new legislation to address the issue, merely changes to the grounds themselves, especially the removal of perimeter fencing. The debate on policing football has also reached the highest levels of the police hierarchy. Chief Constable Sloan (1989) discusses the difference between Scots Law and English Law in this matter. He feels that the Scots have a better system to deal with problems at football as they can act to prevent serious incidents under common law. Supporters accept the exchange of some personal freedom for greater safety at games. Sloan advocates the eventual elimination of segregation at games.

In addition to these purely police-generated discussions of tactics, legislation and the nature of hooligans, the police have also become involved in academic debates on football violence and football policing. Philips (1988) presented at a University of Leicester conference on the issue. He states that so far academic research has not been doing the police service much good. In contrast to their beliefs, police control at football matches *is* a good thing and needs to develop even more intelligence practices to be wholly effective. He has a low regard for football hooligans and feels that a change in the atmosphere at football games would contribute to a decrease in disorder. The Leicester influence can also be detected in two other police papers on football hooliganism. Harper (1990) researched football violence and policing to find long-term solutions to the problem. He conducted several surveys of police officers and shopkeepers, and he interviewed a few football hooligans. He frequently cites Dunning et al (1988) as one of the academic authorities on the issue. Harper's recommendations for football policing include gradually eliminating segregation from the football grounds, police being friendlier with the fans, and encouraging the fans to be self regulating so that the police can reduce their manpower at football games. He feels that football hooligans are not the same as youth gangs, but that some criminals use football as a cover for other illicit activities.

Middleham (1993) is an inspector who worked closely with the Sir Norman Chester Centre for Football Research (University of Leicester) to produce his report on football policing. His purpose is to analyse the views of police officers and supporters on football hooliganism and make recommendations on how the police can improve their procedures. He surveyed supporters, supporters' organisations and police commanders for the bulk of his data. He makes 43 recommendations including improved communication/rapport between the fans and police, clearer division of responsibilities between police and stewards, more responsibility for stewards, how to move supporters safely, using the same officers at all football games, and maintaining segregation policies. This is in great contrast to the study mentioned earlier from the West Yorkshire Metropolitan Police Authority in 1977 which suggests that a change in society as a whole to promote better behaviour in people and more power to the police are the only ways to address disorder at football. Middleham's study finds that current police methods could actually be making the situation worse by polarising groups of fans and need to be modified. A Swedish police chief, Nylen (1994), also suggests that more collaboration is needed between police officers and football fans. Not all football hooligans are the same and each needs to be treated differently. However, he disagrees with Middleham and urges the desegregation of football grounds.

These papers from senior officers suggest a change in their attitude towards football hooliganism over the years. In the early reports the focus is on tighter control of one of society's social demons. The later papers, however, feel that the police could get farther by changing their methods to emphasise communication with supporters, greater power to the stewards and possibly even desegregation. They feel that greater control is not necessarily beneficial. It is mostly the later papers that also welcome the input of academics, although it appears that the University of Leicester is their main source of information. As was discussed earlier in this chapter, ethnographers feel that football violence is not mindless nor really all that threatening to the general public. Football hooligans are not 'thugs' but members of a unique subculture. Considering that the later senior police officers mentioned here are urging a focus on police and supporter interaction, ethnographers would be better placed to advise them.

Summary

Before beginning my analysis of police and football supporter interaction, it is important to consider who these supporters and 'hooligans' are. Just who is it the police are policing at these matches and what motivates them? To that end, this chapter has considered previous academic research on football supporters and hooligans and on football policing specifically. It also looked at research and publications by those in the policing profession on this issue. The first section addressed how the identity of football fans has been constructed in academic research. These people have been viewed as working class thugs, as an intricate subculture, and just as normal people. The methods employed to study them have ranged from archival research of old newspaper reports from over one hundred years to face-to-face ethnographic study of the people in question before, during and after their violent encounters. Various types of supporters have been identified through their motivations, club affiliation, use of space, specific histories and the influence of the football market. This wide group of people have generated many different impressions and debates over time in this and other countries. I feel that the work of the ethnographers (such as Armstrong, Giulianotti and King) presents the most accurate picture of these groups. While I recognise the ethnographic method has its own shortcomings, I feel that it is only by prolonged exposure to the groups themselves that any true understanding of them can be gleaned, and this work must be continued to keep up with their changing trends. Otherwise, discourses (be they academic or political) on football followers will be based on constructed images, rather than on any actual 'reality' (Redhead 1991). It is through ethnographic work that it was made clear that not all football supporters are 'hooligans' and that not all hooligans are the same as each other. As I will show in section two of the book, ethnographic work on the police is also vital in understanding their different identity-forming processes and how these influence their relations with the public. Not all police are the same, and this is expressed in the interactions I observed between them and the football supporters/hooligans.

While these academic perspectives described above vary quite widely and some directly contradict each other, few mention the role of the police in forming a football supporter's identity. Thus the second section of the chapter considered academic writing directly on football policing. This work has come from several different disciplines and has employed varied research techniques (statistical, archival, observational, and ethnographic). A common observation among these writers is that the police role at football is more than to be neutral observers who are only called upon when needed. They are a part of the events, and the process by which they identify who needs to be arrested/ejected/talked down is an inter-subjective one. Their perceptions of the events at hand and the people involved are formed by things such as personal interaction with those people, current policy initiatives and the pervasive stereotypes police officers hold of football supporters. In addition, two authors suggested that the police can inadvertently provide the excitement that many supporters crave, and the increasing powers given to police at football are only adding to this effect. They are far from neutral observers, as my own work will also show.

Writings by police officers, discussed in the third section of the chapter, focus mainly on the tactics police employ or current legislation to deal with hooliganism. However, some papers have openly mentioned their opinions of football supporters and hooligans, and they are not usually complementary. These documents are important to consider as they reflect some of the attitudes police officers bring when working at football games, and these may influence the interaction they have with the supporters.

My own discussion of interaction between the police and the fans will in effect be a new way to understand how these supporter teams are constructed. Football supporters are argued to have their own culture, as the police are seen to have, and their own internal rules of interaction. My research will analyse the rules of interaction *between* the police and the supporters, rather than discussing them in isolation. This has not been considered before, especially not with non-hooligan fans and the football stewards. Up until now, football supporters' identities have largely been understood through ideas of masculinity, violence and class. These broad themes are often used in understanding the police culture and its internal rules and boundaries as well (Smith and Gray 1985, Reiner 2000a, Muir 1977, Heidensohn 1992, Fielding 1994, Hunt 1990). My work will show that a deeper understanding of the construction of these groups' identities can be gained from looking at how they all interact with each other. The broad themes are important and this is why I have discussed them, but a consideration of interaction can bring further insights.

However this literature review was deliberately brief. The study of football is a growing field and one too broad to be covered in great depth here.[10] Regardless of the academic or political position employed, football supporters are without a doubt a changing entity due to their own experiences and outside influences from the authorities. One of the main turning points in this field for all concerned was the disaster at Hillsborough and the resulting Taylor Report. The next chapter will consider in depth the government's view of football disorder by examining this and other official reports it has produced on the matter and relevant legislation.

2
Government Reports and Football Legislation

This chapter will consider what the government has published on the topic of football policing and supporters through their reports and legislation. It is important to know what the government has written about football supporters, the legal powers the police have at their disposal and the corresponding rights of the supporters before analysing my own research on interaction in football policing. When considering the interaction that actually takes place, it is interesting to note whether or not these statutes are employed, or if more informal rules come into play. As such, I will discuss the *Green Guide* (1997), the handbook published to guide the analysis of stadium safety, and the current football legislation for England and Wales and the legislation for Scotland. While much of the legislation for these areas is similar, there are important differences to keep in mind. Primarily, laws for the English game do not usually apply north of the border.

Government reports

This first section will discuss inquiries and other reports by the UK government on the policing, control and safety of football supporters. Many of these reports lead to the introduction of new legislation, some of which is still in place today. The focus here is what the government has published over the years about the causes of and solutions to football disorder and its recommendations for ensuring supporters' safety at football events. Current legislation will be discussed at the end of the chapter.

The earliest government investigation into football safety and control happened after the first Wembley Cup final in 1923. The disorder that occurred at that game resulted in the Shortt Report of 1924.

Its primary focus was crowd control and it recommended that the police should only concern themselves with preserving law and order. The football ground authority should hire and properly train stewards to assist the public and ensure their safety. It did not feel that legislation was necessary to ensure that these things happened. However, it seems as though little changed after the report (McArdle 2000).

Overcrowding in Burnden Park, which resulted in 33 deaths in 1946, was the subject of the Hughes Inquiry. During a FA Cup tie at the home ground of Bolton Wanderers a man who wanted to leave the park picked a lock on an exit gate. Once that was opened, supporters outside gained entry and overfilled the terraces 30 minutes before kick-off. More supporters were allowed in at the turnstiles and the barrier behind the goal collapsed from the weight. Like most other football grounds at the time, this stadium's capacity had never been properly assessed. The report recommended that capacities be scientifically calculated in all grounds and that a mechanised counting system be installed to monitor the turnstiles. It went a step further however, and urged that legislation be introduced to allow the Home Secretary to establish regulations for stadium safety that would be enforced by a license from the local authority. As with the previous report, these recommendations were ignored (McArdle 2000).

A series of reports were then conducted in the late 1960s. Sir Norman Chester chaired the first, which was commissioned in 1966. The main focus of his report was status and conduct of players, organisation and government of the game and the financing of football. He noted that crowd behaviour had been deteriorating in recent years and that representatives from police forces and the football authorities had met to discuss it. However, Chester's committee did not have the time nor the resources to fully investigate football crowd safety and control. They did suggest that improved stadium facilities, better refereeing and more action from club management would help the situation (The Department of Education and Science: Report of the Committee on Football 1968). In that same year, Denis Howell, the minister of sport, commissioned a private research group lead by Dr. J. A. Harrington to investigate football hooliganism. As with the Chester report, this was not prompted by a disaster at a football ground. Regardless, they seemed to expect the worst from fans and were surprised that the situation was not more dire. They made many generalisations about how hooligans feel, the effects of alcohol and the effects of being in a crowd. They urged more police control of fans and increased use of technology to monitor them. However, ultimate responsibility for order at games was laid at the feet of the clubs themselves. The report recommended stadium improvements and the increased use of stewards. It did not feel new legislation was necessary to control what it perceives to be a psychological problem among some football fans. What was needed was more 'scientific' research of them (Harrington 1968). The final report of this kind appeared the following year by Sir John Lang. Its purpose was to further examine the issues raised by the Harrington report. It recommended the use of CCTV in grounds that could afford it and cited alcohol as a contributing factor in football violence (The Home Office: The Popplewell Report 1986).

All of the above inquiries and reports were conducted at English grounds. However, Scotland has also produced its own football disasters and thus its own inquiries. The first is the Wheatley Report in 1972, after a stairway crush at Ibrox in 1971 when 66 fans were killed. The focus of his inquiry was the procedure by which sports grounds in the UK are deemed to be safe. He found that existing legal statutes did not completely apply to sports grounds and that the recent certification system introduced by the Football Association was inadequate and vague. Wheatley recommended a new certification system that would be implemented by the local authority, rather than the Football Association. He recognised that there might be some resistance to this as it would mean clubs would have to improve grounds with funds that they would rather spend elsewhere. However, he and the evidence he received suggested that these changes were long overdue (The Home Office: The Wheatley Report 1972). The result was the Safety of Sports Grounds Act 1975, a new licensing system and the development of the *Guide to Safety at Sports Grounds*, also known as *The Green Guide*, which will be discussed later (The Home Office: The Popplewell Report 1986).

In 1977 The McElhone Report was produced to investigate crowd violence in Scotland. Unlike the Wheatley inquiry this investigation considered crowd behaviour, rather than crowd safety, in sports grounds. McElhone wrote that 'a hooligan is a hooligan no matter where he operates' (Paragraph 4) and so the best way to deal with him is to contain incidents of hooliganism as best as possible (cited in the Popplewell Report, The Home Office 1986). His recommendation was to make it illegal to be in possession of alcohol inside a football ground or to try to enter a football ground drunk. He felt it also should be illegal for anyone to possess alcohol or be drunk in a vehicle hired for transportation to a football match. The report urged the segregation of supporters at turnstiles, fencing around the perimeter of the pitch, all-seated stadiums and harsher punishments for convicted football hooligans (The Home Office: The Popplewell Report 1986). The result for Scotland from this report was the implementation of the Criminal Justice (Scotland) Act 1980, which banned alcohol consumption and possession on the way to (via hired or public vehicles) and inside football grounds (McArdle 2000). The Department of the Environment in London set up the Working Group on Spectator Violence in 1984. The group said that more action needed to be taken by clubs to prevent football violence (The Home Office: The Popplewell Report 1986). However, it did not feel that a complete ban on alcohol in English grounds and on trains and coaches was needed. Despite this recommendation, The Sporting Events (Control of Alcohol, etc) Act 1985 was passed in England and Wales and is very similar to the Scotland act (McArdle 2000).

The Popplewell Inquiry began in 1985 after the Bradford fire and the Birmingham death and included the terracing crush in Brussels. These football disasters all happened that May, the first two on the same day. In Bradford, a discarded cigarette set alight a pile of rubbish that had been allowed to accumulate over the years under the wooden terracing at Valley Parade and 57 people were killed. In Birmingham, disorder broke out between Birmingham City and Leeds United fans. One supporter was killed when a wall collapsed. Two weeks later, after the Popplewell Inquiry had already began, a wall collapsed from a crush in Brussels' Heysel Stadium after Liverpool fans charged Juventus supporters and 39 people died. Popplewell's remit was to investigate both stadium safety and hooliganism; a pairing that caused some resentment in Bradford (Giulianotti 1994). Popplewell made many recommendations including improvements for stadium safety, better police training and equipment, better fire training for stewards, amendments to the *Green Guide*, changes to fire regulations including requiring smaller grounds to abide by them, widening police powers of search and arrest, and the implementation of a football club membership scheme (The Home Office: The Popplewell Report 1986). The resulting legislation was the Fire Safety and Safety of Places of Sport Act 1987 and the Football Spectators Act 1989. The *Green Guide* was also updated. The 1989 Act caused a great deal of controversy, however. Part I proposed issuing all football club supporters with membership cards. This would allow fans to be easily identified and banned if they caused any disorder. The cards could also be used to prevent away fans from entering the grounds if so desired. This part of the act was never fully implemented and has since been abandoned. Part II has been

implemented and provides that those who have been convict\
'football related offences' can be banned from leaving the UK w
the national side is playing abroad (now called a football bann ₋ₒ
order). According to the 1989 Act, 'football related' meant that the
offences had to occur no more than two hours before the kick-off of a
designated game (McArdle 2000).

Probably the most famous and by far the most influential government report into football safety was by Lord Justice Taylor in 1990,
following the disaster at Hillsborough. In April of 1989, 96 people died
from overcrowding at Sheffield Wednesday's ground. Taylor condemned not only the clubs for the neglect of their stadiums and lack of
attention to their supporters' needs, but also the police for their inadequate response to the situation as it unfolded and the government
for prioritising hooliganism over safety. Over sixty years of inquiries
and reports had gone largely unheeded (McArdle 2000). He recommended that all designated sports grounds become completely seated,
that perimeter fencing be removed or at least reduced, and that
all perimeter fencing be equipped with exit gates. He also suggested
many changes to safety certificates and police planning, increased co-
ordination with emergency services, new offences and penalties for
football disorder, and improvements to the *Green Guide*. He reviewed
Part I of the Football Spectators Act 1989 and urged that it not be
implemented. He felt that there were too many logistical problems
in setting it up and also questioned its overall ability to reduce disorder
and increase safety (The Home Office: The Taylor Report 1990). What
did result from his report besides widespread stadium reconstruction
(although not to the extent that Taylor suggested) and improvements
was a fourth edition of the *Green Guide* and the Football Offences Act
1991, a controversial anti-hooligan measure. This Act made it an offence to throw any object inside a football stadium, to shout or chant
with one or more others in a way that is racist or 'indecent' and to
invade the pitch without a lawful reason. It is the second provision
that has caused the most difficulty, as 'indecent' was never clearly
defined. As such, just about any derogatory outburst by a supporter
could fall under this remit (McArdle 2000) and this gives the police a
great deal of discretion. Both the 1989 and 1991 Acts have since been
amended, but this will be considered in the next chapter section.

Recently, a government working group chaired by Lord Bassam published a report on football disorder. The group was formed as a response
to disturbances by English fans during the European Championships in
2000. This disorder in Charleroi and Brussels appeared to be motivated

in part by English nationalism. The government had introduced new legislation (as will be described in the next section) to tackle the problem of English hooliganism abroad but also wanted to study the dynamics of the disorder itself. The report makes many suggestions in this regard and stresses that football violence needs to be considered in its wider social context. It includes recommendations for tackling racism in professional domestic football, grassroots clubs and throughout the local community. It also suggests that the government and football authorities work together to improve the image of English football fans overseas; that fans be more included in governmental discussion about football disorder; that a new English Membership Club (EMC) be established that is more representative of society in general; that the EMC, the government, the police and the Football Association work together to plan the safety of supporters at tournaments; and that the government considers sending English stewards to overseas games (The Home Office: The Bassam Report 2001).

Some of these kinds of recommendations are echoed in the Council of Europe publication, *Prevention of Violence in Sport* (Comeron 2002). This document charts good practice already in use around Europe to stem football violence and makes suggestions for how international matches should be policed and organised. It stresses that all prevention policies should be used in the context of hospitality so that supporters do not feel targeted or defensive. It discusses the use of supporter 'coaches'; these are people who work with the most disruptive of supporters year-round in organised social and educational activities. The idea is to help these individuals find other outlets for their energies and to encourage a good rapport between the coaches and the supporters. If incidents then happen on match days, the coaches can act as intermediaries between the supporters and the police, but not as sources of police intelligence as that would ruin the trust that had been established. It also urges for fan 'escorts' to move with the supporters and assist them as needed as well as stationery 'fan embassies'. All this and well co-ordinated policing with local and national agencies is seen to go a long way in preventing football violence from ever occurring. The task now is to encourage all European countries to adopt these measures.

Currently in its fourth edition (1997), the *Green Guide* is a Home Office document that makes recommendations for ensuring safety at football grounds and other venues. It is not a legally binding document as it is designed to provide guidance for safety in all types of entertainment facilities in the UK. However, any ground that fails to

standards will probably not be issued with a safety certificate
will not be able to hold public events. The *Green Guide* was
oped after the Wheatley report and subsequent editions were
d by football disasters. The current edition is the first one not
to be so motivated and as such focuses more on supporter service and
comfort than on crowd control (McArdle 2000). The police are listed
among several other groups (such as the local authority, ambulance
service and the fire service) as safety advisors to the stadium management. The implication being that while these services have key roles to
play in ensuring ground safety, ultimate responsibility lies with the
ground management, be that the owner or tenant of the football
ground (The Home Office: Guide to Safety at Sports Grounds 1997).
This chapter will now turn to an examination of the current legislation
in place related to football disorder.

Football legislation in England and Wales

This section will be devoted to a brief overview of the football-related
legislation that remains in force in England and Wales,[11] some of
which was mentioned previously. The two most important Acts to consider here are the last two. Not only are these the most recent, but they
also include several amendments to the others. They will be discussed
last. The oldest statute still in force is The Sporting Events (Control of
Alcohol etc) Act 1985, as was discussed above. Next comes The Public
Order Act 1986. This created the new offence of disorderly conduct.
This is defined as behaviour that is not actually violent but 'which is
likely to distress, harass, or alarm' another person, and so could be
employed to arrest unruly football supporters.

The next two pieces of legislation have also been discussed previously. These are The Football Spectators Act 1989, the result of Popplewell's Inquiry; and The Football Offences Act 1991, a response to
Taylor's report of the Hillsborough disaster. While the 1989 Act applies
only to England and Wales, it does allow that if residents of England or
Wales commit a football-related offence in another nation (such as
Scotland) they can still be subject to a banning order. The Criminal
Justice and Public Order Act 1994 made it illegal for an unauthorised
person to sell a ticket for a designated football match to members of
the public. The Crime and Disorder Act 1998 amended the 1989 Act to
increase the penalty for failing to report to an authority when under a
football banning order and to make such a violation an arrestable
offence.

The Football (Offences and Disorder) Act 1999 is the first of the two new football-related statutes that amends the others. It was designed to 'tighten up' the previous legislation to compensate for their loopholes and vague terms and in general to provide the police and courts with greater powers in dealing with football offenders (McArdle 2000). It amended the 1989 Act so that a 'football related offence' includes actions that happen up to 24 hours before a domestic game begins and even longer for an international game. These offences do not necessarily have to be committed on the journey to the event nor does the person have to intend to go to the match. It changed the 1991 Act to say that racist chanting could be conducted by a lone person as well as by two or more persons chanting together (the Act previously only provided for the latter definition). It also amends the 1994 Act to prohibit unauthorised persons in England and Wales selling tickets for English and Welsh games whether or not the games actually take place in England and Wales. In addition to these amendments, the Act also provides a few new laws. Courts are now required, not just allowed, to make a football banning order when the appropriate circumstances are present. People subject to football banning orders may be required to surrender their passports during the game in question, and up to five days in advance.

The Football (Disorder) Act 2000 is the most recent football-related legislation. It has four main provisions. The first abolishes the distinction between domestic and international football banning orders. Now the consequences of a football banning order on a resident of England and Wales are the same no matter where the offence took place. The second change is that the courts are now required to have the subjects of football banning orders surrender their passports. This is no longer a matter of the court's discretion. The last two changes are temporary unless renewed by an Act of Parliament.[12] One states that a person may be given a football banning order after a complaint from a police officer, even if that person has never been convicted of a football-related offence. The other allows police officers to require people they suspect of being involved in football violence to surrender their passports to the officers and to report to a magistrate for banning orders. Again, the persons in question do not have to be previously convicted of football-related offences.

Football-related legislation in Scotland

While the legislation above does not directly apply to residents of Scotland, residents of England and Wales can be guilty of certain offences mentioned above even if the offences occur in Scotland. Football-related legislation for Scottish residents can be found in three main Acts. The oldest of these is the Safety of Sports Grounds Act 1975, which was enacted after the disaster at Ibrox in 1971. Its primary provision is to require local authorities to issue stadiums with safety certificates, what those certificates should contain, and how to appeal a decision about a safety certificate. The Public Order Act 1986 is the next applicable piece of Scottish legislation. This defines 'racial hatred' and provides that a person who intends to 'stir up' racial hatred is guilty of an offence, whether the act occurs in a football ground or any other public or private place. Police officers are allowed to arrest a person without a warrant for such an offence if they have reasonable grounds to believe the offence occurred.

The third act concerns alcohol at football matches. The Criminal Law (Consolidation) (Scotland) Act 1995 brings together many different offences that were previously covered in separate pieces of legislation. Part III of this act supersedes The Criminal Justice (Scotland) Act 1980, mentioned previously. It states that to have alcohol in a football ground, to be drunk in a football ground or to have alcohol in hired or public transport to a football game is an offence. It also prohibits bringing explosives or flares into football grounds. General football violence is handled in Scotland by Common Law, namely the offence of 'Breach of the Peace'. There is no Scottish legislation that specifically addresses behaviour at football matches, other than that mentioned above.[13]

Summary

Government investigations and reports have considered both football violence and general stadium safety over the past 75 years. What is most surprising though is that no major changes to policing policy or ground safety were implemented until the mid-1980s. Since then, the emphasis has started to shift from seeing fans as cultural demons to focusing on safety, comfort, and understanding the social roots of xenophobic nationalism. Thus the government can have a large impact on police and supporter interaction at football by deciding (or declining) to give new powers to the police and determining how the ground is to be structured. It can also support or condemn stereotypes of supporters, and this may also have a role to play in later interaction.

As the last two sections revealed, football legislation in Scotland is rather different from that in England and Wales. The English courts have felt that the best way to deal with football disorder is increased police powers, strict controls and tougher sanctions on those who are convicted of offences. The courts have even tentatively extended their controls to people who have not yet been convicted of football violence. Stott (2003: 640–1) has argued that this kind of policing and legislation is ineffective as the police do not already know most people arrested for football violence and the mere presence of hooligans does not necessarily mean that violence will occur. In contrast, the Scottish courts are content with laws about alcohol use and flares in sports grounds and leave the rest of the behaviour sanctioning to the 'Breach of the Peace' or other existing legislation. While some may argue that this is because Scottish and English supporters are different, especially when travelling abroad (Giulianotti 1991), it nevertheless shows the importance of studying football supporter and police interaction in Scotland as a separate case. The powers the police have at their disposal are different north of the border and so may have a different effect on the interaction that occurs there. My research to follow will discuss what exactly is involved in that interaction. The police were one of the groups Lord Justice Taylor blamed for the Hillsborough tragedy and until now have been almost invisible in football disorder studies.

It is also important to consider the effect of these reports and legislation on police action in light of the more recent pressure the police face to appear efficient in their work. From 1979, the Conservative government initiated a system of reform whereby the public sector began to purchase services from private companies, rather than provide them itself. This was seen as a more cost effective and efficient approach. This management-focused reform reached the police as well (McLaughlin and Murji 1997). A 1983 report by the Policy Studies Institute (PSI) showed that very little of what police officers do is visible to their supervisors and that the management style is overly hierarchical, inflexible and actually encourages malpractice. After several Home Office circulars and Audit Commission reports, police forces became compelled to account for the use of their funding and resources and restructure their management practice into one that is more flexible and goal-driven. McLaughlin and Murji (1997) discuss these events in great detail so I will not repeat them all here. The main thing to mention is that while the upper ranks of the police eventually admitted that reform was needed, they only agreed to some of it and refused to turn the police force into a business.[14] Nevertheless, a severe blow was given to the 'sacred' status of the police officer. Even they have to bend to the forces of new managerialism.

Despite their best efforts, some aspects of consumer culture have infiltrated the public police force. As Loader (1999) demonstrates, not only have issues of new management come into play, but also consumerism and promotionalism. The police are no longer presented to the public as a *force*, but as a public *service* provider (although some believe the police have yet to achieve this, such as Walklate 1996). The Metropolitan Police have even enlisted the help of a private company to improve their corporate identity. With the rise of private security firms, the once authoritative police now have competition for their services. Loader argues however, that despite all these efforts to the contrary, the public police do still maintain to some extent their '"sacred" status as symbols of law, order and nation' (Loader 1999: 387). This can be evidenced by the disappointment felt by members of the public when the police fail to meet the still unrealistic expectations set upon them.

While the police have experienced dramatic changes in their management and organisation due to doubts over their effectiveness and impartiality during the past forty years, the public still hold them to be the main defence against disorder and crime (Loader 1997a). The strong police presence during any British football match also suggests as much. This is no accident however, as police forces have many techniques to encourage this view, which will be discussed in the next chapter. In a political atmosphere of pressure to appear cost-effective, opportunities to demonstrate efficiency through competent policing are welcomed. Public events such as football matches present such an opportunity, especially when the police have such great legislative powers at their disposal in these events (in England these are officially and specifically mandated whereas in Scotland the police have the ultimate power of discretion under 'Breach of the Peace'). The chapters to follow will examine to what extent these formal rules and guidelines are actually used in football policing or if more symbolic action and informal rules prove to be better at demonstrating the power and efficiency of the police to their audiences.

Part II

3
Uniformed Police Constables

This chapter is an analysis of the kinds of interaction that occurred at both calm and more eventful matches between the uniformed police constables (PCs) and football supporters during my fieldwork and the informal rules that guide it. This, and Chapters 4 and 5, will use concepts derived from the work of Erving Goffman to provide the analytical framework. However, Goffman states in both *The Presentation of Self in Everyday Life* (1959: 236) and *Behavior in Public Places* (1963a: 5) that his analysis of interaction is mostly based in a middle-class American context and so cannot necessarily be generalised to all social groups. He urges undertaking other empirical work to explore these different social settings. This chapter will do just that.

To fully understand the interaction and behaviour rules of the police and supporters at football, I must examine each type of officer separately. The term 'rules' will refer to understood, though not formally established, proscriptions of behaviour for both groups when they encounter each other in the football context. Thus its meaning here is slightly different from its traditional one. As will be demonstrated at the end of this chapter, each type of police officer interacts with the supporters in a different way and thus the rules of one cannot be generalised to the other. I will only consider the uniformed police constables in this chapter. Subsequent chapters will discuss the uniformed mobile officers, the plain clothes detectives or football spotters, the senior officers (into which I have included sergeants), female officers, CCTV operators and the stewards. As Fielding (1988: 88) has noted, 'the police organization does not encourage inter-rank dependence' and this is reflected in the way the various police groups operate at football matches, as the following chapters will demonstrate. As such, it is necessary to consider the constables separately from the other ranks. However, not even the uniformed constables are a united force. At times in this chapter it will be necessary to demarcate between those officers who work in the football stadium and those who work in the city centre. Officers employed during football matches often come from different sub-divisions of the police force and each patrols a different geographic area. This has implications for the way they interact with supporters.

The starting point of any encounter is the outward appearance each participant projects so this chapter begins with a look at Goffman's concept of 'performance' and how it is enacted between uniformed police constables and supporters at the matches. This not only includes the physical appearance of the actors, but also that of the surroundings and the way each actor manages the information that is given off in an encounter. The next section of the chapter will establish the basic rules from which each actor orientates his or her behaviour in this particular context. To do this I will describe the supporter typologies that guide police action and the unspoken 'rules of engagement' that both the police and the supporters observe during any match day. These are not concepts that Goffman used in his work, but are inspired by him and his methods to illustrate the informal rules at work. All these informal guidelines (including 'performance'), in conjunction with an awareness of the formal, legal ones discussed in the previous chapter, inform police action at football matches.

The latter sections of the chapter continue from this basis to examine what actually happens when the uniformed constables and supporters encounter each other, or, how these guidelines and rules are enacted. This will utilise Goffman's work more directly to examine the interaction 'teams' I noticed during the football games. I will discuss how the uniformed police officers present themselves and the situation to their audience at various points during a football match with a special consideration given to the use of space and time. I will also analyse how the various interaction teams in question can be identified and what the audience is for each team. Thus by establishing throughout this chapter the informal rules of interaction, presentation and interaction teamwork I will demonstrate the nature of social interaction between police constables and supporters at football matches.

While Goffman is the main inspiration for this analysis, there are similarities to be drawn here with Bourdieu's 'habitus' and 'field', which Chan (1996) has also used in relation to the police. The police field involves 'the historical relations between certain social groups and the police, anchored in the legal powers and discretion police are authorised to exercise and the distribution of power and material resources within the community' (Chan 1996: 115). For her, police habitus is comprised of what the officers refer to as 'commonsense', 'policing skills' and a 'feel for the game'. This habitus includes those resources upon which officers draw to deal with and guide them through unexpected situations (Chan 1996: 115). So we can see how football supporters and police officers could have developed a common field (in the way they enact their informal rules, the latter sections of the chapter) in their relations with each other over the years. This will influence how the police utilise their informally developed understandings of football policing (their habitus or informal rules of interaction, the initial chapter sections) when interacting with the supporters.

Sociologists, like Goffman, influenced Bourdieu in that they 'have paid attention to the ways in which social action shapes social structures, and stressed the ways in which *inter*action even shapes who the actors are and what strategies they pursue' (Calhoun 2000: 710). But Jenkins feels that Bourdieu does not discuss the importance of the actor as much as he claims to do. Jenkins' reading of Bourdieu sees power flowing from the top down and that Bourdieu's 'social universe ultimately remains one in which things happen to people, rather than a world in which they can intervene in their individual and collective destinies' (1992: 90–1). Bourdieu's theories will thus fall short in the focus I wish to bring to football policing. As this and other chapters will show, I will place a great emphasis not only on personal interaction and choice, but also on subtle forms of resistance to outside influence. Other writers have also influenced this analysis, but they will be discussed throughout this and the remaining chapters.

Performance: front

In order to discuss performance, I will use Goffman's (1959) concepts of front, dramatic realisation, idealisation, and maintenance of expressive control. This section will just be concerned with 'front', with latter sections addressing the other three concepts. Goffman describes a person's front as 'that part of the individual's performance which regularly functions in general and fixed fashion to define the situation for those who observe the performance' (1959: 32). This same front will be employed each time the particular performance is given. He then subdivides front into 'setting' and 'personal front'. Personal front is also sub-divided into 'appearance' and 'manner'. I will analyse each of these aspects of football policing for the uniformed PCs in turn.

Setting

Goffman used setting to include all the background aspects of an inter-action. Furniture, layout, decoration and other aspects of the scenery are involved in this (1959: 32). In football policing, the main aspect of the setting is the football ground. It is inside and around the exterior of the stadium where much of the interaction between police and foot-ball supporters occurs. Some interaction also occurs outside in the city centre on the pavement and inside pubs. If a supporter is arrested in the ground, the setting changes to the police room in the stadium, the back of the police van, and then the holding cells at the police station. Arrest in the city centre would take a supporter from there to a police van and then to the holding cells in the police station. Thus the setting for any police and supporter interaction in football is not static during the match, but the same settings are encountered at each football game.

Personal front

The personal front of the uniformed police officers at a football game is also a mixture of consistency and change. Goffman (1959) divided this aspect of interaction into 'appearance' and 'manner'. Appearance is the stimulus that tells us a performer's status and ritual state (i.e. what social position he or she holds and whether he or she is at work, relax-ing, socialising, etc.). For the PCs, these stimuli include their uniforms, equipment belts, florescent jackets, knife-proof vests, notebooks, hair-styles, and gender. Generally, their ritual state is one of being at work, specifically, working a football match. The equipment (props) the police use is very important to them. They complain if the florescent jackets are not available in the appropriate sizes; that the knife-proof vests do not fit under the florescent jackets; and, at one point, that not all the officers had ear-pieces for their radios or any radios at all during the football match. More officers work during a football game than do for the rest of the week and for a while there were not enough radios to go around (this situation has since been remedied). One PC said he felt 'funny' without a radio. As will be discussed in more detail later, the appearance of a uniformed police officer carries certain connotations with it. As Goffman notes (1959: 41), the police are one of the groups in society whose visible activities vividly communicate the attributes claimed by the performer.

The subject of manner is less clear-cut with the police. According to Goffman, manner is the stimulus that informs us of the role the per-former expects to play in the ensuing interaction (1959: 35). For example, an authoritative and superior manner suggests the performer will take a leading role, while a more meek and submissive manner suggests the performer will follow the lead of another. As will be discussed in more detail later, the PCs before, during and after a football match can present a variety of attitudes towards their task. Differences also exist when one considers where the officers are positioned, either in the stadium or in the city centre. Generally speaking, the manner of the city centre officers is distant but calm and controlled. Manning (1997: 201) found this in his own work in that police try to convert emergencies into routines and to show themselves to be fair and open-minded when with the public. In my research, supporters in the city centre are not really approached unless need be and usually the encounter is an amiable, or at least civil, one.

Around the football ground before a game, however, more of an effort is made by the uniformed stadium officers there to be overtly friendly to the supporters. The idea is to create as non-hostile an environment as possible and a smile at the turnstiles is one way they see of doing that. If children are encountered, they always receive a joking and friendly manner from the officer in question. The police have also developed an informal ticket distribution service with the supporters outside the turnstiles. If someone has extra tickets and does not care about getting any money for them they often give them to a uniformed police officer. The officer then holds on to the tickets until someone comes along who is looking for extra ones. The police never ask for money, but give the tickets away to those who need them.

Inside the ground though, the stadium police may take a more stern approach to the supporters and tend to resent any requests for assistance other than responding to troublesome supporters. The PCs want to make it clear that misbehaviour will not be tolerated and that it is the job of the stewards to be helpful. However, in other areas of the ground that are not expected to become hostile, the PCs may maintain the friendly and jovial manner they donned before the game. After the game, everyone is intent on getting home, so efforts to initiate interaction with the supporters are rare and thus the PCs' manner is a distant one. If the PCs are dealing with a more violent supporter, their manner is usually one of calm firmness. However, if the officer is pushed too far, he or she may start to get agitated and shout or swear at the supporter. This will be discussed on p. 70.

So while the appearance of the stadium PCs and the city centre PCs does not vary, the manner any particular PC may adopt can vary throughout the football match day. Goffman (1959) suggests that we tend to seek a consistency between appearance and manner and sometimes even setting, appearance, and manner. For the police, this consistency cannot be found by looking at them as a whole, but by considering them in small units. For my purposes in this chapter, I will concern myself with only uniformed police at a football match and have taken into account where they are posted (stadium or city centre) and at what point in the game they are encountered (before, during or after). Only then can a consistent police front be found, for even within the broad category of uniformed police constables great variety exists.

Performance: dramatic realisation and idealisation

The next aspects of performance to be considered are dramatic realisation and idealisation. While these factors are important to consider in general daily interaction, they have a special significance when it comes to the police, especially the police at football.

Dramatic realisation

Dramatic realisation refers to the way a performer indicates to others important facts about the performance that might otherwise be hidden from view. It is necessary for the audience to know these facts if the performance is to have the needed impact and convey the desired definition of the situation (Goffman 1959: 40). For the police, this is usually rather easy to do. The act of being a police officer in itself is dramatic and does not really need additional work on the part of the PC to convey its importance (Goffman 1959: 41). The appearance and manner of police officers as described above also aids this dramatic quality. Seeing an officer in uniform, hearing the squawk of the radio, watching the lights of the police van flash, one is easily convinced that a PC's job is important and powerful. These images act as outward symbols of the state-authorised use of force the police can wield (Westmarland 2001: 1–6). Manning (1997) found many examples of symbolism and metaphor within the police forces he studied. He argues that the main reason the police must use these dramaturgic devices is that there is a discrepancy between what the police can do and what they claim, or are expected, to do. Police officers can only control the arrest rate, not crime itself even though the public expect them to do so through a popular misunderstanding of police work. As Reiner (2000a: 170) notes, '(t)he historical and sociological evidence should have made clear that crime-fighting has never been, is not, and cannot be the prime activity of the police, although it is part of the mythology of media images, cop culture, and, in recent years, government policy'. Reuss-Ianni (1983: 19–20) also discusses this common myth, pervasive among the police themselves, which brings them additional stress because they feel they are not living up to the (impossible) ideal they were taught in the academy about being crime-fighters. Most of police time with the public actually involves peacekeeping, or social service work.

Thus the police end up using dramaturgic techniques to present themselves as being in control and a unified force committed to the eradication of crime (Reiner 2000a: 138). As Manning (1980: 253, 1997: 120) noted, the police can have an influence on the external world (by employing dramatic devices like technology, statistics and secrecy) as well as being subject to pressures from it. Heidensohn (1992: 77) would agree with this in that she feels the police have a hand in how the public view them. Loader (1997a) has observed how the right of the police to speak publicly on issues they feel are important is rarely challenged. What they say might be, but their entitlement to this position is taken for granted due to their symbolic power. In the public mind, the link between the police and public order/crime control is an automatic one and the police encourage this through things such as community policing initiatives and hiring professional image advisors (Loader 1997a: 3–4). Even just a police 'presence' is seen as being enough to bring about public order due to the authority they project (Heidensohn 1992: 299). This image of authority and control is especially important to maintain during large public events, such as football matches, when their actions can be immediately scrutinised by the ever-present media should something go wrong. Football hooligans are thus a good opportunity to reinforce the symbolic fight against evil, as there is no question among the police and the public that that is their nature and the media is more than happy to present them this way. Thus we live in a culture where any reference to the emotive topics of crime or safety necessarily involves a consideration of the police.

Loader warns against seeing the police symbolic power as perpetually static, however. It may vary over time and certainly does vary within certain sections of the community. Those who are socially excluded or young may not see the police as agents of security but as something to be feared (1997a: 8–9). Holdaway (1989: 69–70) has critiqued Manning for separating the symbolic and instrumental aspects of policing so much. He agrees that police tactics and procedures have very strong symbolic effects. He also feels, however, that they are instrumentally effective as well and that these two aspects should not be separated to such an extent. In addition, he argues that the symbols in question can be denotative as well as connotative. For example, an arrest suggests that the police have a ubiquitous authority and are the protectors of the moral order (connotative). It also represents the punishment and re-education of a prisoner (denotative). Holdaway urges police researchers to take all these aspects into account.

During a football match, the police feel they can make use of their dramatic power to influence the behaviour of the crowd (Lewis 1982). I was told on several occasions that the main reason the police are at the football is to act as a 'presence' (Hale 1996: 127). In their view, just the fact that they are there and visible goes a long way to ensure a peaceful football game. This relates to Foucault's (1977: 201) discussion of the ideal Panopticon situation, where individuals police themselves and the actual use of disciplinary power is not necessary due to constant and ubiquitous surveillance. Heidensohn (1992: 299) has also noted the emphasis the police place on their effectiveness through presence by the authority they project and how they can use their physical presence as a type of interaction in itself. The police feel that supporters who might cause trouble see the police presence and are dissuaded and nervous supporters will feel safer knowing the police are there. Thus the PCs I spoke to felt that the police will always be present at football if only for these reasons. However, whether or not this is true is difficult to prove. As was mentioned in Chapter 1, disorder in the ground has dropped in recent years, as has the number of police officers due to the increase in stewards. One wonders then if the police can really link their presence to a lack of disorder.

However, the dramatic aspect of uniformed police officers is realised by more than their physical presence. Action PCs take in the ground against violent supporters is used as a demonstration of their ability and they believe that it serves as a warning to other would-be violent fans. For instance, match commanders instruct their PCs to only arrest one or two members of a disruptive group to give a warning to the rest. Again, just by being visible and demonstrating their powers they feel they are influential. Once a person in custody is taken to the police station the booking procedure itself has its own dramatic quality to it. I found it to be almost ceremonial. Forms are filled in, statements are read out, procedures are followed, and everything is caught and recorded on internal cameras. This will be discussed more fully in the next chapter.

Idealisation

We can see how police easily make their roles at football matches seem important and meaningful through dramatic realisation. The police also need their performance at football to seem acceptable and necessary. As was mentioned earlier, more clubs are using fewer officers in the grounds due to financial constraints (Loader 1999). Stewards do the majority of the work now in stadiums that are relatively tranquil compared to those of the 1970s and 1980s. Thus the presence of police at football is no longer a certainty. However, the police have a vested interest in remaining in the grounds. While some games may be very slow and boring to police, others keep the PCs busy the entire time. Stories of chases in the streets and scuffles with the fans at the dividing wall are regaled in the coffee room or canteen afterwards, often with glee if there was a successful capture at the end (Westley 1970, Manning 1980, Smith and Gray 1985, Westmarland 2001). Football can make for excitement in an afternoon that might have otherwise been spent on paperwork or other routine duties. There is occasionally a financial incentive for the police to work at matches as well. If an officer loses a day off to work the football, that person is paid overtime. Many officers, especially just before Christmas, have told me that the money was the main reason they agreed to work that day. And lest we forget that football is one of the main sporting passions in the UK, some officers certainly like to work the matches in order to watch the play on the pitch. A football team from England came to play a testimonial match at the ground I was studying on one occasion. A police sergeant said there were so many officers there to watch the match they were 'tripping over themselves'.

In addition to the above motives for the police to work at football matches, there is one other, more symbolic one that can be identified. The police have come to expect and even rely on football supporters to be disorderly and exhibit behaviours that violate society's norms. The police can then demonstrate their unique ability to quell this disorder, as was discussed earlier. Football is the ideal situation for the police: games happen on a regular basis and at pre-determined times. The size of the crowds and a tradition of hostility between some teams make for predictable aggressive responses from the supporters. For example, supporters from Aberdeen Football Club and Glasgow Rangers Football Club have a well-known and established rivalry[15], as do supporters from Rangers and Glasgow Celtic Football Clubs[16] (Giulianotti and Gerrard 2001). Hostilities between these supporters will rarely fail to materialise. As football violence has become hated in wider society

(Armstrong and Hobbs 1994), it is easy for the police to find a reason and opportunity to arrest and convict those deemed to be hooligans without a public backlash. Even ejecting a supporter from the ground can be useful as it appears to onlookers to be an arrest but carries none of the paperwork and time constraints of an arrest.

This is where Goffman's notion of idealisation comes in. Goffman suggests that 'when the individual presents himself before others, *his performance will tend to incorporate and exemplify the officially accredited values of the society*, more so, in fact, than does his behaviour as a whole' (1959: 45, emphasis added). The police are no exception to this observation, and football presents a regular opportunity for them to demonstrate their roles as society's moral guardians (Skolnick 1966: 56–7) and reconfirm the importance of their existence at football.

This may seem to contradict Goffman's (1959) assertion above that performances between actors are attempts to conform to moral standards, since football hooligans intentionally break social norms. I suggest, however, it is not that police and supporter interaction conforms to or violates the standards of *society*, but the standards of the *situation*. Thus even in breaking some of 'society's' laws, football hooligans are in fact still conforming to the laws of *football policing* and so conforming to the behaviour standards of the situation. Becker has noted that rules 'may be formally enacted into law, and in this case the police power of the state may be used in enforcing them. In other cases, they represent informal agreements, newly arrived at or encrusted with the sanction of age and tradition; rules of this kind are enforced by informal sanctions of various kinds' (1963: 2). As will be demonstrated later in this chapter in the section on 'rules of engagement', police and supporters at football have their own unique rules of interaction. Some behaviour that is allowed in the football setting would not be permitted in wider society so it is useless to talk about 'accredited values of the society', as they do not actually dictate interaction here. Box (1971) has suggested that we should not view society as a consensus as there are many definitions of what is 'normal' behaviour. One of these definitions has become dominant, but it is not the only one that exists. Manning (1980: 248–9) has noted that the police organisation develops its own rules based on situated interaction and shared understandings. I would take this a step further to suggest that the fans outside the organisation can also take part in the creation of its rules. In football, what is normal behaviour between the police and the supporters is not the same as that dictated by the dominant definition in our society. Thus I suggest that Goffman's work needs to be developed to allow for performances that exemplify the values of the specific interaction situation, even if they simultaneously break the values of 'society'.

However, these situationally specific values are not generally apparent. When the police decide to arrest or eject a supporter who has broken their football specific interaction rules, this then allows the police to appear to be safeguarding dominant social values and ensures the continuation of these values' existence. The general public is not aware of the disruptive actions that the police have ignored which did not violate *football* interaction rules. It could be suggested that the police actually use the routine disorder in football to present an idealised image of 'a police officer at a football match', rather than an ideal police officer. By routine disorder, I am referring to overly aggressive shouting, chanting, or taunting of the opposition. It is behaviour such as this that exceeds what the police say is 'normal' for football or that which allows people to just 'blow off steam' that will lead them in invoke their formal control powers. However, the general public is more likely to perceive this police action as the 'ideal police officer' persona. Goffman's discussion of 'frames' also applies here. We use frames to comprehend the activity in any event, based on definitions of the situation and the event's principles of organisation (1974: 1–14). In this case, the general public views football disorder through one frame while the police and the supporters use an entirely different one. Each frame though helps its viewer to make sense of the action that goes on within it.

Performance: maintenance of expressive control

Until now I have considered what should happen during a performance and examples of this within football policing. However, I have not directly assessed what happens when something in the performance goes wrong. This section will deal with what happened when the performance the police were trying to give at football fell short or failed entirely; when they failed to maintain expressive control. Goffman (1959: 60) refers to these incidents as 'unmeant gestures' and suggests that even though we do our best to avoid them, even the smallest infraction can ruin a performance or the delivery of a desired impression. These accidents present a different definition of the situation than that which the actor is trying to portray.

Football policing is not always very exciting. If the game is going slowly or the visiting supporters are small in number, there may not be a lot for the police in the football ground to do. The PCs often talk about how bored they are or how they wish something would happen to make the day pass more quickly. Cain (1971) has described several different techniques the police employ to make life more interesting, such as 'easing behaviour' where they find illicit means and places to relax, or they go out looking for arrests, such as with the drunk or homeless. Many other writers have also noted the amount of boredom prevalent in police work and their various coping mechanisms (Smith and Grey 1985: 339, Manning 1980: 228, Heidensohn 1992: 74, Reiner 2000a: 89). Police at football, however, do not have many opportunities for easing behaviour other than through chatting to each other, but this can work against them. Towards the end of a very slow game with a smaller team, two sudden surprise goals caused the supporters in the area to become very exuberant and caught the police off guard. The police snapped to attention and a few had to run down the aisles and stand in front of the gates to the pitch to prevent supporters running onto it. The uniformed officers had not been paying enough attention to their role because they were chatting and lost control of the situation for a moment. In the other extreme, younger officers who are new to football policing have a tendency to pay too much attention to the movements of supporters, according to the older officers. For example, I saw a PC who was instructed to organise the queue at the concession counter spend much more attention and far longer with that task than an older officer would have, and thus it was apparent he was new to football policing and did not know the informal rules yet. Both of these examples support Goffman's suggestion that over or under attention to one's performance can damage one's expressive control (1959: 60–1).

The most common unmeant gesture I noticed was what Goffman calls 'insufficient dramaturgical direction' (1959: 60–1). Although at times football supporting can be a very emotional and animated experience, the police are supposed to maintain a calm and controlled demeanour while on duty at the matches (Westmarland 2001: 171). Whether angry or happy, football supporters do not hide their emotions and this proved consistently to be very challenging for the police. On a few occasions I witnessed police officers shout back at supporters who had been arguing with them about a barrier the officer would not let them cross or a special consideration the officer refused to give them. The officer had been patient as long as he or she could and then just let his or her expressive control slip. Sometimes the uniformed officer would just be in the way of two opposing supporters who were trying to get at each other or shout at each other. In an effort to restore calm, the officer would sometimes lose his or her own calm and swear at one or both of the supporters when ordering them to sit back down. When pushed too far, many officers lose the expressive control they had been maintaining over their manner by giving the wrong performance, as Goffman suggests. All these unmeant gestures described above ruin the calm and controlled demeanour the police try to present. To rectify this, officers usually return to their posts, smooth out their uniforms and try to appear calm and controlled again. However, the damage may have been done for that day.

Typologies the police employ

During their football duties, uniformed PCs see or encounter thousands of football supporters. Consequently, many officers have devised a system of typologies into which they mentally place these fans to make coping with them easier and they often employ these typologies when speaking about the supporters to each other. Manning (1997) and other authors to be discussed in the next chapter (e.g. Reiner 2000a and Smith and Gray 1985) identify similar methods of police stereotyping to order what could otherwise be an overwhelming public. However, the typologies they mention concern the general population while the ones below only refer to people involved with football. The following is a discussion of the most common ones I encountered when speaking to the uniformed PCs about their duties at the matches. The typologies employed can be divided into discussions about football supporters vs. the general public, football supporters vs. other sport supporters, and differences between types of football supporters. Hunt (1990) has also noted the tendency of the police to use binary typology systems (although in her analysis they revolved around genderised themes of 'dirty' and 'clean'). Manning suggests that the police are cynical about the general public and have no name for 'respectables' (1997: 203). However, my work will show that when compared to football supporters, the police consider most people to be decent and non-violent.

Football supporters vs. the public

The first thing that becomes apparent when a police officer speaks about football supporters in relation to the general public is that football supporters are not 'normal' people. They are often described as being 'tribal' or 'animal'. A few times I heard police officers say that football supporters are normal people outside the ground, but once they enter a 'red haze' comes over their eyes and they become a different person. This new person seems to act more on the basis of territorial instinct than reason. This is reminiscent of LeBon's (1895) view of the crowd. He argues that when people become involved in a crowd, they lose their own individuality and are enveloped by the 'collective mind'. Normally rational and civilised persons can succumb to the primitive instincts suppressed deep within them and take part in the crowd's irrational and destructive acts. During pre-match briefings, the senior officers would urge the police to make sure the supporters walking around town do not disturb the 'normal' people doing their shopping. This suggests that football supporters are regarded as outside normality, even though they are present (as supporters) in the city at least twice a month (on average) for the majority of the year.[17] Foucault (1977: 19) has suggested that the focus of the criminal justice system has shifted from judging crimes to judging persons and their souls.[18] That thought is reflected in the comments above, as it is not behaviour being described as abnormal but people.

Football supporters vs. rugby supporters

Another common distinction made about football supporters is how they are categorically different from supporters of other sports. The main comparison drawn here is with rugby supporters, and this often involves a class distinction. I was told on several occasions that rugby supporters can sit next to members of the opposition and watch their favourite sport without any violence. The reason for this, suggested by many PCs, is that rugby supporters traditionally come from a public schooling and/or a middle class background. Football supporters are said to come from working class backgrounds and state schools. The implication is that they are a different class of people who are more prone to violent outbursts. These comments from the police mirror the figurational arguments of the Leicester researchers. Dunning et al (1988) suggest that the lower working classes experienced the civilising process differently from the other classes and as such use violence as a legitimate means of self-expression. The police also feel that the football supporters do not like having police at the match because they may know each other from previous legal encounters.

Football supporters vs. themselves

The more detailed typologies come from comparisons between football supporters. There are three main distinctions that the police make.

First, PCs often hold predetermined ideas of what each visiting team's supporters will be like. Supporters of Glasgow Rangers Football Club are generally held to be the worst behaved. Glasgow Celtic brings many supporters with them, but the police give divided answers as to the potential trouble with these supporters. In general, they are seen to be friendly to the officers, but many Scottish hooligans are said to be willing to fight with *any* supporter from a Glasgow club, whether or not that person is a football hooligan. This is the one exception to the usual hooligan codes where only fights with other hooligans can bring acclaim (Armstrong 1998). The police regard the rest of the teams in the league as mostly harmless, especially the smaller ones. PCs often speak of how much they wish their local team would get relegated to the First Division because there would be fewer visiting supporters and their job at a match would be much easier.

However, all these distinctions fall by the wayside when the national football team is concerned. Supporters of Scotland's team are generally seen as fun loving, friendly, and family oriented. During one international game, I saw officers lifting children 'over the fence' to get them into the ground for free. In general the PCs seemed to take a much more relaxed attitude towards this kind of match. Granted, many of the people there were probably supporters of teams within the league, but the police drop all previously held league stereotypes when Scotland's national supporters are concerned, as the 'Tartan Army' stereotype prevails[19].

The second type of distinction the police make about football supporters concerns where the supporters sit in the ground. During normal league play, each section of the stadium is seen to have its own type of supporters and is policed accordingly. The family section and the season ticket holder section have a very minimal police presence. Families are not regarded as a serious threat to public order (Murphy et al 1990) and season ticket holders are easily identifiable and have too much to lose if they cause trouble. The visiting supporters, however, have a very heavy police presence around them. They are physically segregated from the rest of the home supporters, and the area they occupy has many officers around it. Any anger or jubilation the home supporters feel is always directed in some capacity towards the visiting support who respond just as aggressively. The police feel their presence in such an atmosphere is essential (Loader 1997a).

The areas of home supporters on either side of the visiting supporters are also heavily policed. The stewards in the main ground I studied refer to the section at right angles to the visiting supporters as 'cosy corner'. The home supporters here are generally vocal young men who employ a wide variety of gestures to express their feelings towards the visiting supporters. Coins are often thrown between the two groups, and I once collected over a pound in change by standing in the open ground between and below them for about twenty minutes. The home supporters parallel to the visiting fans but on the other side of the hard segregation wall are also vocal and aggressive at times. Any officer standing next to that wall can expect to dodge many different kinds of debris as they are hurled between the opposing fans. A further discussion of the use and management of space in the football ground will appear later in this chapter. These home supporters described above are known as the 'troublemakers' and the police pay special attention to them.

The police make one final distinction between types of football supporters. This is between football hooligans and 'real' supporters. The PCs often speak of the hooligans as being different from other football supporters. I was told frequently that the majority of the people who come to games are not there to cause trouble. Only a minority tries to spoil it for the rest. So it appears that by being involved in this orchestrated violence, hooligans relinquish any claim to being a 'true' football supporter (See Giulianotti 1996 and Armstrong 1998 for counter arguments).

It is apparent from the above discussion of the typologies the police employed when speaking about football fans that they have many ways of thinking about them. This varies between considering them in relation to the wider public, to other sport supporters, and in relation to each other. The ones described above were the most reoccurring ones. Despite all these commonly used typologies, however, the type of person who could fall into each varied with the type of police officer encountered. This will be discussed in more detail at the end of the chapter.

Rules of engagement

Now that I have examined police officers' performances during a football match day and the typologies the police hold of football supporters, I will consider the underlying rules of engagement of football policing. These three analyses together (performance, typologies and rules of engagement) form the informal guidelines for interaction the police and the supporters use. How the police enacted these rules will be discussed in the next section on 'teams'. I will use the term 'rules of engagement' in this section to refer to the explicit and implicit guide-lines, structures, and boundaries football supporters and police officers observe (or violate) during their interaction. These rules dictate when interaction may be initiated and what can happen during it. Goffman (1959: 27) refers to this as a 'part' and describes it as 'the pre-estab-lished pattern of action which is unfolded during a performance'. I felt, however, that 'rules of engagement' was more descriptive of what actu-ally happens. This analysis of rules is also slightly different from that of other writers on the police (such as Chatterton 1976 and Smith and Gray 1985, see Holdaway 1989 for a critique of 'rules'), who found broad types of rules that can be applied by different kinds of officers in a variety of situations. Examples include 'working rules', 'inhibitory/ formal rules', 'presentation rules', and 'accounting rules'. These all serve to guide police action in the field and help keep them out of trouble with senior management. The rules of engagement I found are more subtle than that and vary depending on where the interaction occurs, when it occurs, the type of supporter and football match in question, and the type of officer in question. As this chapter is con-cerned with the actions of uniformed foot patrols, interaction with only this type of police officer will be considered here. I will begin this discussion of the rules of engagement by examining interaction outside the football ground with the city centre patrols.

Engagement in the city centre

Usually when police constables outside the ground encounter support-ers, the resulting interaction is friendly and light. In fact, having such a large police presence in the city seemed to be helpful for the general public in that officers were on hand to give directions, provide a quick chat or assist with non-football medical emergencies. Very little of the officers' time was actually spent dealing with football disorder (O'Neill 2004: 98). It usually just involved approaching and directing visiting supporters along the appropriate route to the ground. Otherwise, the rules of engagement dictate that 'normal' football supporters are mostly left alone.

If the city centre PCs spot people that they deem to be 'hooligans', however, these supporters are watched very carefully (see the summary of this chapter for a discussion of how this distinction is made). Uniformed Mobile Support Unit officers, who are either in their van or walking alongside it, frequently escort hooligans (see the next chapter for more on this). Segregation is a priority with these fans and if the opposing groups are anywhere near each other, the PCs and Mobile

Support Units quickly get in between them and force the hooligans to opposite sides of the street, if possible. This is not a common occurrence however, and so any PC in the city centre before the game is likely to just chat with colleagues and members of the public while watching hundreds of supporters walk by.

The rules of engagement with the city centre PCs after the game are somewhat different. Most of the visiting supporters will be on their buses and on their way out of the city and so are no longer a concern. The home supporters that are walking around could be very happy or very agitated, depending on the outcome of the game. The central station radios the police the match result, not only for their own interest, but so they have an idea of the kind of behaviour to expect from the fans. For example, more disorder is expected if the home team wins and this has a significant impact in their position in the league tables than if the result was a draw and the tables were largely decided already. If the visiting supporters' coaches go past a group of home supporters in the first scenario, the home fans may shout and gesture at the people in the vehicles. The PCs I was with when this happened once took a very calm approach to it and just made their presence and attention known to the home supporters in question. The supporters stopped what they were doing for a while, but continued again a bit later. A pair of home supporters walked past the PCs at a different point and asked the time. The PCs took this to be asked in sarcasm, so one said he did not have a watch and the other gave the supporter the wrong time intentionally. The first then gave him the right time, but the supporters had never stopped walking during this entire interaction. It would appear that even though the visiting supporters are mostly away and thus not a factor for PCs in the city centre after a game, interaction with the home fans can be a bit more edgy than it was before the game as emotions are more volatile.

The football hooligans are not as much of a concern for the PCs after the match. The plain clothes detectives or football spotters and the Mobile Support Units closely monitor their movements. Uniformed PCs really only encounter the hooligans if called to an event in progress, and this is rare. Otherwise the PCs watch the 'normal' supporters disperse and are called down relatively soon after the match ends.

Engagement at the ground

The rules of engagement between PCs and supporters in and around the stadium are quite different from those applying in the city centre, although this too can vary depending on where the interaction occurs and at what point in the game. Before the game starts, there will be a few PCs inside the ground, but many will be just outside the ground standing by the turnstiles. These officers check for people who may be bringing in 'controlled containers' (a term used in the relevant legislation to refer to alcoholic drinks or anything that alcohol could have been put into) or objects that could be used as weapons. Fans with bags or bulging pockets are frequent targets. They also check for people who may be under the influence of alcohol.

While the fans queue at the turnstiles to get in, they often speak to the police standing nearby. Engagement here is usually friendly, often with a few jokes exchanged. Some people with bags not only do not seem to mind them being searched, they often walk right up to the officer without being asked and offer their bags to him or her. Fans sometimes ask the officers for directions to the appropriate section of the ground or if the officer would take a photo of them in front of the stadium. Children or disabled supporters who wave to the police at the turnstiles always receive a wave in return. A superintendent told me that it is important to have friendly banter with the fans outside the ground to gain familiarity with them in case this can carry over inside the ground and help behaviour there.

However, it appears to me that sometimes the banter between the police and the fans takes a sarcastic edge and it appears that the supporters try to make fun of the police in a subtle way. They seem to be testing the limits of what the police will tolerate. For instance, a few visiting supporters deliberately went in a turnstile that the officer had just told them was for juveniles only. The police in turn would sometimes speak about the supporters in non-complimentary ways to each other or me, but without really trying to prevent those supporters from hearing. They comment on the supporters' appearance or behaviour while those supporters in question are still outside the turnstiles and probably within earshot. Thus the friendly exterior each group adopts is a fragile one that can easily be dropped and replaced with sarcasm or one-upping. This is still relatively civil interaction though. The actions that break police tolerance will be described later.

Soon after the game begins and the turnstiles have been closed, the stadium PCs immediately outside the ground move to new positions inside and join their colleagues there. Again, the rules of engagement here are different from those I have discussed so far. One of the reasons for this is the presence of stewards. Most professional football grounds now employ stewards to provide general assistance to the supporters in the ground, ensure supporter safety and conduct some amount of security and supporter behaviour control. Stewarding was introduced in part to help with the cost of policing the matches, as professional officers inside the ground charge the club to be there (Loader 1999: 375) and cost considerably more than stewards. However, there is a larger social consequence from the stewards' presence (Wakefield 2003: 62). The police inside the ground now only have one job – law enforcement. They are not required to help supporters find their seats or direct them to the toilets. Their remit is only to react to those who are suspected of breaking the law (mainly through the Scottish criminal offence of 'Breach of the Peace'). Thus the police presence in the ground can reduce itself to that of confrontation only. This is in contrast to the PCs in the city centre and outside the ground who spend most of their time being friendly and supportive of the public (O'Neill 2004: 99).

However, getting the PCs in the stadium to the stage where they will arrest a supporter is not always as easy as it may seem. First of all, an arrest at a game takes the officer out of the stand for long periods while he or she processes the person. It might be more productive in the long run to just control the situation and remain in the stadium rather than take one supporter out and reduce the overall number of police present. Secondly, as was discussed in the previous section on a performance's 'idealisation', much behaviour that would justify arrests in the general public (outside a football game) or even within a football game and its specific legislation is allowed. Football supporters stand (in seated stadia), shout, swear, throw debris, and sing abusive songs. Legally, the police are able to arrest for behaviour like this if they feel it breaches the peace. However, as one stadium PC pointed out, if they did that all the time it would just make matters worse. Once a PC takes one person out the officer returns to the supporter's 'four angry mates' and the process starts all over. This PC feels that shouting and swearing is what football is all about (Hobbs et al 2002: 354). He lets it happen because it allows people to give off steam (O'Neill 2004: 101). This explanation of aggression in football supporters is similar to that proposed by Marsh (1982), in that it is mostly ritualistic. So another rule of engagement would be that as long as a fan's behaviour does not exceed what is 'normal' for football, it is allowed.

While this hesitance to arrest on the part of the police may not be obvious, the supporters seem to sense it. As both police and stewards have told me, the fans know what the unwritten limits are to the behaviour that will be tolerated. They will try to push those limits, but will stop if the police tell them they have gone too far. If a supporter does push the limits too far and gets arrested, the police like to escort him or her out of the ground along the pitch, if possible. The idea is that the arrested supporter will serve as a warning to the other support-ers. This seems to contradict Foucault's (1977: 9) belief that the public spectacle is no longer used to deter crime. While a police escort is not the same as the public floggings to which Foucault referred, the police believe it does serve as a deterrent and use it. This also seems to provide a source of great amusement for the opposing supporters, who make a lot of noise when a fan is being escorted out of the ground. Once the person is brought to the police room, he or she is not neces-sarily taken to the central station for processing. A senior officer may decide to just give the fan a lecture and warning and let him or her go home (but not back to the game). The likelihood of this happening depends on if the police actually saw the person commit the alleged offence and how contrite and respectful he or she is to the officers speaking to him or her (Skolnick 1966: 233). This is similar to Chambliss' discussion of the 'Saints' and the 'Roughnecks' (1976). Both groups of youths engaged in delinquent behaviour, but the former was penitent and apologetic when confronted by the police while the latter was more hostile. Chambliss identifies this as one of the reasons the Saints were never arrested while the Roughnecks frequently were. This issue of respect for police also seemed to be a deciding factor in whether or not the fan was taken out of the ground in the first place. PCs would sometimes suggest that because the fan had been 'annoy-ing' them or would not do what they said, that was the final straw that led to the arrest or ejection. For instance, a police officer who was getting a lot of abuse for not letting an aggressive supporter into the ground grabbed the man and shouted 'Dinnae swear at me!' It would appear that another rule of engagement is that supporter misbehaviour is not to be directed at the police or in obvious contradiction to a request from a police officer.

Interaction inside the ground during the game between supporters and stadium PCs is not always as tense and aggressive as described above. Most of the time the supporters and the police either do not directly interact at all, or if they do, the encounter is usually amiable. Even though it is mainly the job of the stewards to direct people to their seats, the police are often approached for this reason. They do the best they can, and I even saw one officer hold a young boy up so his head was over the crowd to find his seat. The PCs pass the time at the game chatting to each other, the stewards, or the supporters nearby. However the newer officers do not often demonstrate this ease at football. PCs who are at a game for the first few times appear to be more tense and very attentive to the movements and actions of the supporters. Police constables receive no specific training for football duty (at the time of my research only the Match Commander had specific football training). The new PCs learn as they go and so do not have as much time to chat. The more experienced officers are able to relax and allow themselves to be social.

The above discussion about the rules of engagement between football supporters and uniformed police officers at the ground did not include a mention of football hooligans. As was described earlier in the chapter, these supporters are seen as different from 'normal' football supporters. They do attend the football matches and so they are a concern for the stadium police. However, severe football violence inside a football ground is a relatively rare occurrence in recent years.[20] Football hooligans confine their violent encounters with each other to the city streets, and go to the football ground mainly to watch the match (Giulianotti and Armstrong 2002). As such, there is little direct interaction between the uniformed police officers and the football hooligans. But the uniformed PCs often apply this term 'hooligan' to the more boisterous and vocal home supporters who like to direct their aggression towards the visiting fans. Their interaction with police thus follows that which I have outlined above. The plain clothes police detectives (football spotters) do not agree that these supporters are 'hooligans' in the sense of being involved in organised violence outside the ground. This definitional incongruity will be discussed further in the summary of this chapter.

The final aspect of uniformed police and supporter interaction at the ground that I will discuss is that which occurs after the game. Uniformed foot patrols escort the visiting supporters to their coaches. The buses are then escorted by police officers on motorcycles, cars and/or vans to the main road out of the city. If the number of visiting supporters is small enough, their buses will be brought right up to the gates of the stadium so that the supporters do not have to walk any great distance to get to them. Otherwise, it can take about 15 minutes to get the fans to their coaches. Many of the older football grounds do not have a space big enough near them for the buses to park. The police follow the visiting supporters as they make their way to the coaches to ensure that they do not encounter any trouble with home supporters. The visiting supporters do not always seem to be appreciative of this police presence. Moreover I have heard a few make passing insulting comments to police officers as they were being escorted.

Again, the police did not do much about it but just made sure the fans got on their buses and out of town. They are so keen for this to happen that sometimes traffic is stopped to allow the buses to get through. These are unique rules of engagement for the visiting supporters.

Interaction with the exiting home supporters is somewhat different. They are also escorted, but not as carefully. As the fans leave the ground, the police follow them in pairs, but leave the stadium gradually so that they are dispersed among the supporters. The interaction the supporters and the stadium police have exiting the ground is rather minimal. Once though, a young supporter was kicking over traffic cones as he walked along. The officer I was with grabbed him by the shirt and made him right all the cones before he could continue on his way. When the officer came back to us, he called the kid an unflattering name, but only so we could hear. Other than that, I did not see much engagement between the fans and police at the end of a game. The fans tend to leave the ground as fast as possible and the police are only too happy to see them go.

The above discussion on the rules of engagement between uniformed stadium police officers and football supporters mainly concerns the regular league football fixtures of the Scottish Premier Division. However, these rules change if the game in question is an international fixture or a friendly. During these matches, the behaviour the police expect from the supporters is very different and they change their policing strategy accordingly. Primarily, the aggression and violence associated with league games is not expected at these matches. The crowds may be larger than those expected at most league games, but this time the fans are presumed to be there for the football only (not to start fights) and quite often come as families. The police seem to relax their approach to the game and relax their enforcement of ground rules and football legislation. As was mentioned in the section on typologies, the police allowed a few young boys into the ground who did not have tickets during an international game. On another occasion, a supporter approaching the gates was confused about which one to enter. He explained his confusion to the stadium PC nearby as due to being intoxicated. The officer did not stop him entering the ground, although legislation allows him to do so. I noticed at one of these matches that the area behind the last row of seats in a particular stand (a concourse) had quite a few people standing in it for the entire game. The police did not seem to be asking anyone to find their seats (as they would at a league match). Also, fans are assumed to be unfamiliar with the football ground for these non-league games whereas during regular league games they are assumed to have this familiarity (even the visiting supporters). In general, during these special games the engagement rules are that the police are friendly with children, chatty to adults and more relaxed about the event. Friendly banter instead of boundary pushing seems to be the order of the day.

Teams

Now that I have discussed the performance, typologies and rules of engagement between uniformed police constables and supporters on a football match day, I will consider exactly how interaction within all these informal rules is executed. This next section of the chapter is concerned with the various police interaction 'teams' at football matches. The term 'team' refers to a group of people who work together to stage a single routine and definition of the situation (Goffman 1959: 85). Thus it is a different entity than a football or other sports team, and is not the same as discussing the police in relation to their formal ranks. To analyse how this works in football policing, I will discuss the various teams that can be identified there and how each relates to the situation at hand. The implication is that the police at football do not operate as one team, but as several (O'Neill 2004). Cain has written that 'The critical question of the nature of the policeman's relationships with the people he polices is so inextricably linked with the previous question, about the characteristics of his work situation, that any attempt to disentangle them must be artificial' (1971: 77). Thus we need to pick apart the nature of each police group to ascertain how it relates to the public, as each will do it differently. To demonstrate this, I will present the membership criteria of the various police teams, the audience for the action of each police team and the definitions of the situation each audience receives.

Membership criteria

As with the rest of this chapter, my main concern here is the uniformed foot patrol officers involved with the policing of a football match. In fact, this is representative of the first membership criterion. Uniformed officers on foot define the football policing situation differently than do uniformed officers in vans, detectives/spotters, CCTV operators, etc. Each policing specialty or duty assignment within the ranks is one of the interaction team membership criterions. Another membership criterion is rank itself. PCs do not belong to the same team as more senior officers and senior officers (even sergeants) are excluded from team membership with constables. This will be demonstrated below during the discussion on 'audience'. However, it is important to point out that while rank is a factor in deciding team membership it is not the only one, and teams cannot be demarcated on rank alone. Interaction teams transcend the formal ranking system. These suggestions cannot be supported here, but will become clear as each of those groups of officers is discussed in subsequent chapters.

Thus the main group of officers I will analyse here are uniformed PCs on foot at a football match. However, I suggest that there are still several separate police teams within this larger group. The uniformed police at a match often come from separate subdivisions within the local police force. As I have shown for the main police force I studied, one subdivision deals with policing in the city centre during the game and one subdivision deals with policing immediately outside and inside the football ground. These teams have separate briefings, supervisors, and commanders and as such this marks the third membership criterion as they operate entirely separately from each other. Again, this will be supported in greater detail in the following section on the audience for each PC interaction team.

Audiences and definitions of the situation

Two teams must be present in order for interaction to take place. Goffman (1959: 97) wrote that it is necessary 'to call one team the performers and to call the other team the audience or observers'. Each performance team needs to present a consistent definition of the situation to its audience. However, it is unlikely that the football hooligans are the main audience for the uniformed police constables. PCs have a general idea of the dress and manner of troublemakers at football, but do not have much experience in identifying established football hooligans. They have a certain type of person in mind (in the way police in general use 'reasonable suspicion' to implement their stop and search powers, see Jefferson and Grimshaw 1982: 84) but this not a perfect system as some non-hooligans may intentionally adopt that kind of dress and manner (see the next chapter for more on this). A much more consistent, reliable and important audience for the PCs is the senior officers. Even if the PCs are unsure of what exactly they are supposed to be doing during their football duties, they always ensure that they present themselves as confident and in control of their area when a senior officer is encountered. For example, on one occasion when I was observing a group of officers chatting to each other in the city centre, they quickly ended their conversation, broke up into their pairs and walked off in different directions because an inspector was fast approaching. They needed to present a different definition of the situation to the senior officer than had been the case with the many football supporters who passed by. These same officers had only just previously been asking each other how exactly they were supposed to be shepherding groups of visiting supporters. This suggests that the uniformed PCs are in their front stage of interaction when senior officers are encountered, during which time they present a calm and controlled definition of the situation (O'Neill 2004: 99–100).

The stadium PCs who work outside the football ground before the game have a different audience for their actions. This team tends to perform more for the benefit of each other (Manning 1980: 227) than for the supporters. As was mentioned earlier in the chapter, many football supporters approach the turnstiles only in the last few minutes before kick-off. As such, the police spend a lot of time before then chatting to each other, as there is nothing else for them to do. When supporters do start to approach, the PCs will occasionally speak about them and their appearance to each other, such as about their questionable fashion sense. This was occasionally done within earshot of the supporters. It seemed to me then that if the PCs were not concerned about hiding these derogatory comments, then they were not very concerned with the definition of the situation they were giving to the supporters. Additionally, if a supporter does manage to get the better of a PC before disappearing through the gates, the PC would try to rectify the encounter to the other PCs by making fun of the supporter. For example, a supporter once shouted at a WPC about the organisation of the turnstiles and she said she agreed; it was a disgrace. When she came back to her police colleagues, however, she said sarcastically, 'I know what the problem is. He was special and I didn't realise it'. This face-saving technique (Goffman 1967: 9) suggests that the PCs were more concerned about the impression they were giving to each other rather than to the supporters.

However, there are occasions when the stadium PCs immediately outside the ground do perform for the supporters. The ticket distribution service that was mentioned before is an example of this. The PCs in this case present themselves as friendly, helpful, and the situation as one of informality and fun. If children are encountered, especially ones that are asking for spare tickets, they are teased a bit in an amiable way before the ticket is handed over. Some officers share in the despair the home fans feel about their team's chances of winning. So in this case, the audience for the PCs actions outside the ground and the definition of the situation that is fostered varies.

Segregation of the supporter sides is the largest influence on interaction between police and supporters inside British football grounds. Each football team's set of fans is separated from the other by either a hard physical barrier or by a large cloth tarpaulin that runs down a column of empty seats, next to which sit a column of stewards and police officers. Senior officers claim that the soft cloth tarpaulin method not only keeps supporters from fighting, but because they do not feel safe from retaliation the supporters on either side usually ignore each other as well. However, in the grounds where the hard barrier is used, supporters apparently know they are safe from actual harm and hurl insults and coins or other small missiles at each other throughout the match. The police officers assigned to these barriers are often the unintended targets of this abuse. Thus for uniformed officers in the stadium, football supporters are the main audience for their performances. The thousands of emotional supporters that surround them command much more of their attention and effort than the handful of senior officers in the stands or in the CCTV room do (O'Neill 2004: 100).

However, there is great variety in the police performances the supporters see and the restrictions placed on their behaviour, both between football grounds and between sections of the same ground (see the earlier sections on typologies, stewards and also Lewis 1982: 419). There has yet to be a uniform policy on football supporter segregation in Scotland, so supporters may at times be unsure of the definition of the situation with which they will be faced in any particular football ground or section of it (Armstrong and Giulianotti 1998: 123). The police do recognise this variability as one officer with whom I spoke said that visiting supporters might get reprimanded for behaviour in this stand that was acceptable at their home ground. Because the police operate as separate teams both between and within the various football grounds, there is no one set of rules of interaction for the supporters to follow. Behaviour violations may occur which were actually unintentional (O'Neill 2004: 100–101).

The main problem with these preventative arrangements inside the ground is that they cannot be used outside the ground after the game. The police have less control over this open area and often resort to the old segregation and reactionary tactics to control the flow of the exiting supporters. In one city I visited, the opposing supporters are kept separate by a line of police officers and dogs as they pass within four metres of each other on their way home. This technique escalates tension while they are held back during the organisation of the police line, and much verbal aggression ensues as the rival fans pass. The police are often the focus of the aggression as the supporters resent this restriction on their movements. Yet again the supporters are faced with a new definition of the situation. The uniformed PCs outside the stadium after the match are presenting a different performance from the PCs who worked there before the match. This time instead of the atmosphere being one of fun and familiarity, the supporters are herded into predetermined areas and moved along quickly.

As the above evidence shows, it is not the case that the uniformed police constables at a football match are just separate parts of a larger whole. Goffman suggests that members of a team may stage different performances, but an overall unified impression is given (1959: 85). That is not the case if one considers the uniformed police constables as a unit. Each police interaction team I identified among the uniformed constables has separate membership criteria, different audiences, and presents a different definition of the situation to those audiences. Thus several impressions of the situation are given, not one (O'Neill 2004). As Goffman said himself, just because people may all come from the same organisation does not mean they are teammates. They must also co-operate to stage the same definition of the situation (1959: 108), which the uniformed police constables clearly are not doing here.

Regions

The final aspect of my analysis of police and football supporter interaction concerns the existence and use of regions. A region can be identified as any place that has barriers to perception as its boundaries. Goffman (1959: 109) says that 'when a performance is given it is usually given in a highly bounded region, to which boundaries with respect to time are added'. The definition of the situation conveyed in a region must conform to these spatial and temporal boundaries. In addition to this, I suggest that these boundaries can be flexible. During interaction, I found that one or more performance teams may attempt to manipulate time and/or space for the benefit of their performance. This will be demonstrated below by an analysis of the use of regions in football by both the uniformed PCs and the supporters. In this chapter, I will focus on activity in the 'front' region. This is what Goffman identified as the place where a team's performance is executed (1959: 110). No contradictory or discrediting information should be revealed there, as the audience would see it and the definition of the situation would be ruined. The 'back' region is the area where a team's performance is rehearsed, constructed or knowingly contradicted (1959:

114), as the audience is absent. However, this region mainly involves police interaction with each other, so will only be briefly analysed here as it did not play a large part in my study of constable and supporter encounters. However, the back region does feature more prominently in the next chapter so a fuller discussion will be found there. As Goffman suggested, time as well as space should be a consideration when discussing regions so I shall look at each in turn and how the PCs and supporters use them in the front region. I will also discuss the use of a second type of space I have identified in my research, symbolic space. This type of space is more personal than physical and is also used in interaction at football between the PCs and the supporters.

Time

The most effective control the police have over the temporal boundary of the front region is directly before the ground opens and directly after the game ends. It is the Match Commander of a football match (usually a chief inspector or a superintendent) who decides if the ground is safe enough for people to enter. If there is a problem, the Match Commander can postpone or even cancel a match. The fans cannot get into the ground unless the Match Commander says it is safe, and the uniformed PCs must make sure the supporters remain orderly during this time. After the match, certain groups of fans can be held back from leaving the ground or from walking down certain streets until the supporters from the other team have left or are far enough away. This technique is used in many grounds and continues the segregation tactics after the game by carefully timing the movement of the supporters. If a supporter has been arrested, the police decide how long that person will be held. Sometimes it will be until the next working day (when the person will then go to court), other times they may let the person go after a few minutes because the main objective of stopping a disruption or violent incident by removing the person from it has been achieved.

Supporters, too, have many ways of manipulating time to the advantage of their performance. Zerubavel (1979: 51) has said that 'one can exercise social control by dictating the timing of others' activities'. Football hooligans and supporters [21] do this to the police every match day. Generally, most supporters and even the football hooligans have a routine to their behaviour before, during and after a football match. Usually the games go smoothly and there is no serious violence or disruptions. However, any change in this routine can be very difficult for the police. For the hooligans, the element of surprise is their advantage. Despite their best efforts at intelligence, the police can never really know for certain when a hooligan encounter may occur. There have been occasions when the PCs were still in pre-match briefings or had already been called down from football duty when violent hooligan encounters occurred. These events happened outwith the usual time frame and caught the PCs off guard. Similarly, if the home team is doing exceptionally badly, the supporters may start to leave early en masse. This will also catch the police out as the patrols outside the ground come back to headquarters during the game. They will not be fully present and ready if a sudden exodus occurs and the supporters will have the advantage. Thus supporters can bring police out of their back regions and force them into front region interaction. This link between the front and back region will be discussed further in the next chapter.

The PCs cannot control exactly when supporters will arrive and leave the city for a match. Many visiting fans come with their families and make a day out of the event. They can be in the city for several hours in large groups, swelling the numbers in the already full shopping areas and pubs. The PCs have said that this causes problems in the city centres as the football supporters shout and sing and generally disturb 'normal' people. Visiting hooligans who arrived by train have been known to dawdle when in the station before returning home, as the police are so anxious to be rid of them that they are unlikely to arrest them and may even hold the train to ensure all of the hooligans leave. In all these cases, the police can only react to the schedule that the fans set themselves. They are not in total control of the situation.

Both groups, however, have little or no say in the basic temporal structure of a match day. The league decides the fixtures for the season and more recently, television companies can determine when a specific game happens to suit their programme schedules (Armstrong 1998: 179). In the 1998–99 season this was done without consulting the police, which resulted in several Sunday evening games. The police find these undesirable as fans have access to alcohol all day (which police identify as a direct cause of disorder) and public transport after the game is very limited, making it difficult to get the fans home again. A further aspect outwith police or supporters' control is any event on the pitch. Surprise occurrences on the field can cause a sudden change in the behaviour and mood of the fans, which may affect their behaviour later. For example, the two sudden late winning goals I mentioned earlier in the chapter did this, as can violent tackles between players or controversial referee decisions. Neither group can predict nor control these events.

Space

The other important boundary to perception in interaction for Goffman (1959: 109) is space. The police have a great deal of control over spatial boundaries to interaction regions inside a football ground, segregation of the support sides being the main example. In addition to this, the PCs may treat each section of the ground differently, depending on which kinds of PCs are assigned where. Officers are assigned to certain sections of the ground depending on their compatibility with the resident supporters and so different performances are given in different sections, suggesting that there are many front regions within one football ground. Rubinstein notes how the police come to be aware of what is 'normal' for each area in his or her sector (1973: 151), but my work here takes this further to argue that the police help to construct that normality by the way officers are assigned. Thus the police have a degree of control over the affective environment the fans find themselves in. The police also restrict the access supporters have to certain sections of the ground, while they are free to go wherever they wish.

Outside the ground, the PCs will direct the movement of supporters and hooligans in order to preserve segregation as long as possible. As was mentioned before, some PCs erect barriers or hold back one group of supporters at the end of the game in order to let the other group pass. This creates a buffer of space that is hoped to prevent violent encounters between opposing fans. PCs may also move visiting supporters' buses to the back of the stadium to restrict supporter movement after the game. The PCs carefully choreograph the movement of the fans in all the front regions before, during, and after a game (Armstrong 1998: 179).

However, no performance is flawless. Supporters have found many ways to get around the controls the PCs impose on their space. Coaches with visiting supporters are supposed to take their passengers to designated areas close to the ground. Sometimes though, the driver can be convinced to let the fans off in the city centre where they are much more likely to encounter opposing fans (Armstrong and Giulianotti 1998: 120, Armstrong 1998: 189). Generally, the movement of the supporters and the places they choose to park in the city centre are completely outside the police's control. Inside the ground, all supporters have a specific seat in which they are supposed to remain for the duration of the game. However, they will often stand behind the last row of seats (if there is a concourse) to watch the game. PCs can tell them to go back to their seats, but the officers do not always do so, especially if the game is almost over. Similarly, if a supporter in a stand is on his or her way out to the toilet, he or she will often stop and look back if something is happening on the field. Thus a gathering of supporters in the concourses of the ground is common and the police and stewards' efforts to remove them are not completely successful or enforced.

The contestation of space inside the ground can become violent. One visiting crowd of Glasgow Rangers supporters was angered when 'Flower of Scotland' was played over stadium loudspeakers.[22] They tore up the seats around them (several hundred) and threw them at the home supporters. While they only had access to a limited space in that front region, they can still manipulate the space to express their identity. Outside the ground, the police view certain areas of the city centre as flashpoints: these are areas where the paths of the opposing supporters to and from the ground are close and attempts to police them insufficient. Hooligans are aware of these places and can use them to start fights with visiting fans. As noted in the discussion of time, the hooligans have the element of surprise over the police in the areas they choose to stage their violent encounters. They have a general routine to their day in the places they frequent, but the police cannot anticipate all deviations from this routine. They can only react to the event after it happens.

Certain spatial features of a football match day are beyond the control of both the police and the fans, however. The layout of the city centre in which the stand is located and the structure of the ground are two of these. Each group must use the leeway it can find within these structures to assert its will.

Symbolic space

The second type of space supporters and uniformed PCs use in their interactions in the front region is symbolic space. By this I mean the area immediately around a person's body, the body itself, personal possessions, personal information, and a person's appearance. This term encompasses several categories that Goffman (1971) uses, such as 'the sheath' (skin and clothes), 'personal territory' (personal effects, objects), and 'information preserve' (personal information that one guards). Rather than looking at each in turn, I have combined them into the one concept of symbolic space. These areas may not be important in quantifiable terms, but for the person in question they have much qualitative significance. Encroachments on these spaces can be personally insulting and damaging, even if no physical space has been breached.

The police occasionally exert their powers in the realm of the supporters' symbolic space. At the turnstiles, if an officer suspects that a supporter is trying to enter the ground with alcohol or other forbidden items, the PC has the legal right to search the person. Officers are also supposed to ask supporters to let them look into any bags they are carrying to check for dangerous items. This shows how the PCs have some legitimate control over supporters' personal property and body. Inside the ground the police in certain sections can only watch the crowd if they stand below it and look up. This seems to be difficult to do as not only is the officer invading the supporters' personal space again by staring at them and blocking their view, the PC is also running the risk of being watched in return. As a result, the police tend to watch the game and look up at the crowd occasionally.

I observed many occasions where supporters used the symbolic space of the officer to contest the treatment that they were receiving in both their physical and symbolic space. This often involved speaking to the officer in an informal way. For example, a supporter at a turnstile was asked to leave his Union Jack flag at the gates and not take it into the ground. He tried to resist this by telling the PC in question that the flag represented the officer's country and he should be proud of it and respect it. In this way, the supporter was trying to level the field between himself and the officer by presenting them both as patriots. The officer would no longer be a person in authority performing the objective duties of his occupation, but a fellow Briton and thus an equal in his subjective loyalties to the same country. This attempt was not successful however, and the flag was removed.

The football hooligans are particularly adept at entering the personal space of the officers they encounter in order to gain some level of control in the front region of interaction. This will be described in more detail in the following chapter on the plain clothes detectives and spotters. Hooligans more than any other type of supporter have a need to balance the infringement of symbolic space with the police. The police feel that they know a great deal about the hooligans' identity and movements (although Armstrong [1998: 264, 312–14] might disagree), as it is the sole remit of the football spotters or detectives to seek out and collate this information on match days. The hooligans and a few other supporters I saw use the techniques mentioned above (and those to follow) to enter the symbolic space of the officers they encounter and even annoy them if they can. In this way, they can regain some control of the interaction in the front region.

I will briefly mention the back region of interaction here, as it does not involve police interaction with supporters but does lend insight to the regions police use. This is the area where 'suppressed' facts of a performance make an appearance so that they are hidden from the audience (Goffman 1959: 114). On the whole, supporters do not get a chance to enter the police back regions. Even the police room where the PCs go for a break and a chat in the stadium becomes a front region when a supporter who has been arrested is brought there for booking. This accords with Goffman's (1959: 127) finding that some regions can serve as either a front or back region, depending on the situation. It seems, however, that the police at football do not need to worry about their main back region being invaded, as that is the police station where access to police back regions can be strictly controlled. One PC did mention though that he tends to keep secret the football team he supports. This kind of personal information is often kept for back region discussion only. However, he said that if a supporter asks, he would tell the fan the truth. It has never been a problem for him except if he then has to eject or arrest the person. The fan may accuse the PC of doing it only because the officer supports the team that he does. In this way, the definition of the situation the PC is trying to foster is tainted by this back region information. I did not ever see this happen though.

As can be seen from the above discussion on regions, they are not background factors to interaction like 'setting' is. Rather, regions are a part of the interaction itself. Police and supporters use and manipulate the temporal and spatial boundaries of the front region to increase the influence their team has over the definition of the situation, as I have just shown. This is not something that Goffman (1959) considered, as he tended to describe time and space as markers to indicate the boundaries of a performance. In football, we can see that these are flexible boundaries that can be used to alter the performance and the definition of the situation at hand, sometimes maliciously. However, I have not yet discussed the issue of arrest here. This is one aspect of interaction where the supporters cannot meet the police on equal terms. The police have the ultimate control over one's time and space through their ability to place someone under arrest. In such a situation dramaturgical co-operation ceases (Goffman 1959: 90) as the police are now using force to meet their ends. The supporter can only hope to resist in subtle ways such as calling for the sergeant in charge of the cells and asking for anything that might be available: cigarettes, toilet paper, the doctor, etc. I have also seen many people in custody complain that the handcuffs are too tight. Loosening them not only gives them more physical space but has made the police once again respond to their wishes and stop whatever they were doing before. However, until an arrest has occurred, football supporters will continue to negotiate interaction with the PCs in the front region through dramatic use of time and space.

Summary

This chapter has examined the interaction between Scottish football supporters and the uniformed foot patrol police officers who encounter them. I have discussed two main areas of this: the informal rules of interaction (performance, typologies and rules of engagement) and the enactment of those rules (in teams and regions). These revealed that not only do the uniformed police constables and the supporters act as separate interaction teams, but also the police themselves are several separate interaction teams (O'Neill 2004). Muir (1977: 15) suggests that on the surface, the police are seen as all the same, but I have revealed that in practice at football they operate as several autonomous units, even within the one rank of constable. Thus, discussing police groups in terms of rank alone is not an accurate reflection of how they actually operate. We have seen here though how each of these units actually has its own rules of interaction that it follows. In addition, I have also demonstrated that the typologies that the police use to categorise football supporters are much different from those they use with the general public (e.g. Manning 1997, Reiner 2000a). Thus this group of people show that the previous categorisations were incomplete.

In light of the discussion in this chapter, the question of *normalcy* arises. What is 'normal' behaviour at football? Do the police see it as such? From the evidence given in this chapter, I would suggest that each police team has its own definition of 'normal' behaviour for football fans and at times it is the same as that which they expect from members of the general public. The PCs outside the ground expect the supporters to be seen and not heard. It is acceptable for them to look like football supporters, but they are not allowed to sing and shout and act like supporters until they are in the ground. So even though the supporters behave like this every time a game is on, the police still treat it as 'abnormal' behaviour because it disturbs the 'normal' public. The PCs inside the ground, however, allow the supporters to go beyond the limits of what is 'normal' behaviour outside the ground, as that is what football supporting is all about. Normal behaviour inside the ground is much more boisterous and aggressive (Armstrong and Young 2000). However, even this joyous and emotive occasion has its limits, and breaking those is what will get a supporter arrested or ejected (Chatterton 1976: 117). Thus there is an expectation of order within this chaos. Fielding (1988: 193) has noted that officers need to learn what is 'normal' for each area they police, as it can vary. However, I do not think he meant that it could vary so strongly for the same people in the course of a few minutes, as is the case in football.

These police teams also differ on their approach to the football hooligans. There is no unified police opinion on what the normal dress is for the hooligans, their normal movements, where they normally sit in the ground, and the normal amount of disorder in which they engage. Police in the city centre look for large groups of young men, predominately wearing baseball caps. Police inside the ground look for the loudest young men sitting close to the visiting supporters. The plain clothes detectives/spotters have yet another perspective on all this as will be discussed in more detail later in the next chapter. This is different to what Hester and Eglin (1992) suggest when they say the police operate with their own theories about the nature of crime and criminals. It would be more accurate to say that the different police *teams* have their own theories of crime and criminals, not the police as a whole.

As I mentioned at the start of the chapter, this has connections to Bourdieu's concepts of 'field' and 'habitus', in that the police and supporters at football could be seen to have developed their own field of interaction with each other, as Chan (1996) suggests the police do with certain social groups. But what my use of Goffman's 'team' concept has done is take this a step further to show that the police as whole do not have a common field with the supporters, but rather that each police interaction team does with its own rules to follow and rewards to achieve. The officers and the fans are active co-creators in these fields as well, something for which Jenkins (1992: 90–1) says Bourdieu does not allow. This will become even more evident in the next two chapters as I demonstrate how the team divisions continue with the other police groups at football.

From this chapter we can see that there is not a unilateral social order dictating the actions of police and football supporters, even though the police may act like there is (Manning 1997). As football is an important, routine, and predictable event, it is an ideal situation for an often controversial organisation to improve its image of control and effectiveness in reference to this presumed social and moral order.

However, this is not to say that there is no social order at all, just one specific to football policing and the various teams within it. Thus Goffman's interaction rules do not conform to 'society's' norms (as he suggests), but to those of the interaction situation. Football is far from being a chaotic event, but one that is carefully controlled and ordered by both the police and the supporters in their own unique ways. It is only when this unique social order is violated (which does occasionally happen) that police officers bring in their legal sanctions and thus dramatically demonstrate their effectiveness to a wider audience via the media. The following chapter will continue this discussion with an analysis of the Mobile Support Unit officers and the plain clothes detectives and football spotters at matches.

4
Mobile Constables, Detectives and Football Spotters

This chapter will continue from the same basis and follow the same structure of Chapter 3. But while that chapter was concerned with interaction between uniformed police constables and supporters, this chapter will discuss supporter interaction with the next two key police groups at football: Mobile Support Units (MSUs) and the plain clothes detectives or football spotters. I will be discussing these two police groups together as they both focus their work on the football hooligans and rely on each other for support during the football match day. However, their approach to these fans differs dramatically, as this chapter will discuss.

At the main police force I studied, each of the two subdivisions with responsibility for football policing has its own set of MSUs. Each set has its own routines and geographic area of responsibility. Both are there to prevent disorder if possible (by their highly visible presence) and arrest those causing disturbances if need be. The MSUs from the stadium sub-division are responsible for patrolling the public streets around the stadium itself and the city areas north of the city centre. It is also their duty to transport people who have been arrested or detained at the football ground to the police station for processing. The city centre sub-division MSUs are mainly concerned with patrolling areas in the city centre, especially those associated with the city's many pubs and clubs, although they occasionally patrol around the football ground, too. So while they may be doing a similar job, these two sets of MSUs operate relatively independently from each other although there is some degree of cross-communication, especially if it concerns the stadium. Each MSU van consists of a driver and two to four other officers, often one of which is a sergeant.

The plain clothes detectives or football spotters have a much different remit and have the most autonomy of all police staff in a football match. They decide where and when they are going to go largely on their own by considering the intelligence (i.e. information that has been gathered about the hooligans and their planned activities) at hand. During the time of my research at the main force I studied, these officers were detectives, although this is not the case in all police forces. Some forces use constables in plain clothes as spotters on the match days, but the intelligence will be centrally collated and processed by detectives during the week. These detectives then pass back the relevant information to the spotters to direct them in their actions on match days.[23] If the detectives or spotters identify a group of football hooligans on a match day, they radio the information to the Mobile Support Units or other officers who will then respond to the situation. Although they are not in uniform, the detectives do not try to maintain a covert presence among the hooligans, as each knows who the other is. However, the detectives or spotters are not to become involved in altercations with or arrest football hooligans unless absolutely necessary. Usually two detectives are on duty for a football match. Occasionally officers from the opposing city's police force will join those from the home city to work together in spotting all hooligans present.

Before continuing, it is important to emphasise again that the exact policing methods used in the main police force I studied as described in this chapter may not be the same as those used elsewhere. For example, elsewhere in the country MSUs may carry riot gear with them which they don should the need arise. The main force I studied did employ specialist units with riot gear for the larger football matches (called Police Support Units, or PSUs), but they were only deployed if absolutely necessary and did not participate in the routine patrols that I observed with the MSU officers (who do not carry riot gear) and which I will describe here. Unlike in England, Scottish police forces do not have a uniform approach to football intelligence gathering processes and football spotting. Some will use detectives on match days and others will use plain clothes constables. Their work is not centrally co-ordinated through the National Criminal Intelligence Service (unlike the way football intelligence in England is[24]) so this variability is understandable. While the methods I saw in this particular force at that particular time may not be the norm for other parts of the UK, this does not diminish the analysis to follow (Roman 1993). It is not the exact nature of the policing methods at football that interest me,

LIVERPOOL JOHN MOORES UNIVERSITY
LEARNING SERVICES

but the human interaction that occurs within them. To that end, the policing techniques employed are rather immaterial and this discussion will still have relevance to other police and supporter encounters around the country.

As in the previous chapter, I will employ several areas of analysis in order to fully explore the interaction between the MSU officers, detectives/spotters and the football supporters. The first of these is Goffman's (1959) idea of 'performance'. This will discuss how the various groups in question visually present themselves to each other. Performances help set the scene for the interaction to follow and so are important to consider. I will then turn to look at the typologies each police team has developed to mentally categorise the people they encounter at a football match. Typologies help illustrate the main groups of concern for each police team and thus where they will focus their interaction. The next topic of analysis is what I have called the 'rules of engagement'. These are the more general, yet unspoken, rules that guide the MSUs' and detectives'/spotters' behaviour with football supporters. The following section on 'teams' (another of Goffman's concepts) takes this analysis into greater detail by showing how it is illustrated by, and thus helps to delineate, each of the small, independent police teams present among the MSUs and detectives/spotters. The last section looks at Goffman's 'regions of interaction' – those temporal and special boundaries to interaction that each team employs to control the situation at hand. The chapter will close with the main conclusions to be drawn from these analyses, one of which is that even clearly unique police groups have separate interaction teams within them and thus there is no such thing as a unified police force.

Performance: Mobile Support Units

The first part of understanding interaction through Goffman's dramaturgical perspective is to analyse how each group in question presents itself visually to the others. In keeping with the stage metaphor that Goffman employs, this is referred to as the 'performance', and will be discussed here for both the MSU officers and the detectives/spotters. We need to have a clear understanding of a group's appearance, the first impression it makes, before we can go on to explore their interaction with others.

Goffman analyses an individual's performance by examining his or her 'front' (1959: 32). This refers to that 'expressive equipment' a person employs to convey a desired impression. When considering the performance front of the MSUs, we must look at the setting in which the interaction takes place and the appearance and manner of the officers (Goffman 1959: 32–4). These are aspects of the performance that help define the situation for the audience at hand, and provide the context for the resulting interaction. For this police group, there were three main settings during football: outside the ground and on the city streets, inside the van, and in the charge room of the station. Most supporters were only encountered in the first setting. They only made it to the second and third if they had been arrested or detained. The police are able to manipulate the first setting to their performance's advantage somewhat through the use of roadblocks and CCTV, for example. The back of a police van, the second setting, is very small, cramped and a temporary setting, but the police do have complete control over this area unlike on the city streets. The charge room and other police manipulation of space will be discussed in more detail later in the section on regions of interaction.

The appearance and manner (also known as personal front, see Goffman 1959: 34) of the MSUs include their uniforms, reflective yellow jackets, handcuffs, radio, and baton. If they must intercept an event in progress or deal with potentially violent hooligans, the MSU officers' manner tends to be forceful, formal, and commanding. Once a custody (someone who has been arrested or detained) is in the van, however, things can lighten up a bit and the officers may be friendlier, or at least less forceful. On one occasion, an MSU officer sat in the back with the custody. There are benches on either side of the van walls. The officer sat on one and put his feet up on another. In order to keep his hat on he had to tip it forward a bit. He ended up looking like he was relaxing in the sun and catching a quick snooze. The custody thanked the police for saving him from the other hooligans. Despite this easy atmosphere, the custody was still processed for engaging in football violence.

A second aspect of performance is dramatic realisation. This is the term Goffman (1959: 40) uses to describe how an actor can highlight important aspects of his or her performance to ensure the audience is aware of them. Although the formality of the uniforms and the officers' general appearance and manner as described above go a long way in demonstrating the significance of the police officer's role (Goffman 1959: 41), there are other techniques they employ to enhance this. A prime example comes from the apprehension of a coach full of hooligans, which happened during my study. A call came through to the MSU I was in to meet this coach and its police escort at a certain location. Just about every MSU on duty that day turned up to see it, and police cars and vans with lights flashing and sirens blaring surrounded it. Apparently, the lead car had been running red lights to get the bus to the location as fast as possible. The officers I was with felt this attention was not necessary and was just giving the hooligans the attention and importance that they wanted. It would have been hard to miss the dramatic significance of this event.

The third and final aspect of MSU performance I will consider here is the maintenance of expressive control. This term refers to the actions one takes to prevent or rectify any flaws in one's performance (Goffman 1959: 59). There is one main incident that comes to mind that demonstrates this with the MSU officers. After a particularly bad game for the local club early in the season, the supporters held a demonstration outside the ground. The police allowed it to continue for a while and then announced that it was time to go home. The MSU officers got out of their van at this point and helped press the supporters back and onto the pavement. Some supporters did not appreciate this and were shouting at the police. The driver of the van I was in noticed that this treatment was angering one of his colleagues and shouted at him, '(name)! Cameras!' Officers are often reminded in briefings that football matches are riddled with television and newspaper camera crews and they need to watch their language and their actions during these events. Otherwise the image of calm and controlled policing that they wish to present to the public audience via the cameras will be found lacking.

Performance: detectives

The football detectives (or spotters) have a unique performance front (Goffman 1959: 32) among the police involved with football. The main setting for their actions is the city centre, and occasionally inside the football ground. The detectives/spotters may also encounter the football hooligans in pubs in the city or around the ground before or after a football match. Their personal front of appearance and manner (Goffman 1959: 34) is always more casual and relaxed than that of the other officers at a football match. They wear plain clothes and usually carry only radios or mobile phones. As their job is to act largely as observers, they do not bring along the usual police equipment for arrest. They tend to keep their manner informal and friendly if possible. They will become serious and forceful if necessary, but resume the friendly approach with the hooligans as soon as possible. All this acts to present the detectives or spotters as quite separate from the rest of the police presence at football matches (this will all be discussed more in the later section on 'rules of engagement'). Marx (1988: 61) notes that the detectives' goal is to observe and ask unobtrusive questions but not to direct the action at hand. The detectives at football follow this to some extent but without attempting to be covert, as the hooligans are well aware of who they are after many years of football-based encounters.

Due to the nature of their work, the plain clothes detectives and spotters at football cannot grasp many opportunities to demonstrate the significance of their role through dramatic realisation (Goffman 1959: 40). They are supposed to be inconspicuous observers, unlike the MSU officers. However, there were a few occasions I observed where this did happen. When driving by the visitors' entrance to the ground before a match, the detectives spotted a few local hooligans among those supporters. One detective jumped out of the car and chased a few of them while the second detective drove the car into the rest. This was done carefully and did not hurt anyone, but did demonstrate quite dramatically who was in charge of the situation. On other occasions, the local detectives would regale stories to visiting detectives/spotters or me about the successful and particularly violent encounters with the hooligans that they were able to stop. While the detectives' audience was small, this was successful in demonstrating to us how important their role is. Fielding (1994: 50) also notes the importance of story telling for dramatic realisation: 'Excitement and status attached to physical danger are crucial in policemen's self-image and lifestyle, fuelling occupational imageries featuring exaggerated stories of violence and sexual conquest amounting to a "cult of masculinity".' The hooligans themselves also engage in dramatic realisation with the police. For instance, they once told the police that they were planning on 'bashing' another group of hooligans later, but not to arrest them until then. By openly telling the detectives their plans, they are implying that the hooligans are powerful men who the police are unable to stop.

Despite their good rapport with the hooligans, mistakes did happen in football spotting. For instance, there were times the detectives expected more/less hooligans to appear than actually did or they would incorrectly guess to which pub the hooligans were going. There were two main ways I noticed that the detectives attempted to maintain expressive control (or 'save face', Goffman 1959: 59). The first was to blame other officers. While driving around the city, the detectives would complain aloud about the distribution of officers or the slow MSU response to their requests for back-up. Their dissatisfaction may simply be due to a lack of communication between the two groups. According to Marx (1988: 159) 'the need for secrecy accentuates problems of coordination, increases the potential for error, and lessens the probability that problems will be discovered', thus co-ordination between the detectives/spotters and the uniform officers is frequently difficult. These complaints did, however, provide a protective shield over the detectives from any blame that may have been directed at them if fights had occurred between hooligans who should have been segregated. The other technique was story telling. While this was used to demonstrate the dramatic importance of the detectives' work, it also helped change near-disasters into success stories. Manning (1980: 228) discusses how detectives tell stories to relieve boredom and to improve their image in the eyes of other detectives. He too, found (1980: 281n) that tales are mostly about how things went *wrong*. An event I witnessed earlier in the season between the detectives and a group of fighting hooligans was retold to a visiting detective a few months later. I was surprised at how the story was framed as a victory for the local detectives. My memory of it was that the detectives had nearly missed the fight in question altogether. The detectives had been following a group of visiting hooligans and knew which pub they had entered, although they were not watching the entrance. What they did not realise was that the local hooligans had also entered that pub from another direction and a fight started before the detectives discovered what was happening. The detective telling the story did acknowledge that they were late in arriving on the scene, but the focus of the story was that the detectives then did enter the pub and pull the combatants out before much damage was done. Thus this retelling was perhaps a way of restoring their shared sense of reality, a coping mechanism to deal with the ambiguities of the job (Westley 1970: 76). However, the element of contest in this story is interesting to note, as that is a trait usually attributed to the hooligans fighting each other. This affinity between the detectives and the hooligans will be developed later in the chapter on p. 118.

Typologies used by the Mobile Support Units

It is not uncommon for fairly closed occupations to develop common-sense typologies about the public, and the police are no exception. Many authors have used a study of police 'typologies' to better understand how these officers view and interact with the public. Typologies also help reveal who commands the bulk of police attention in those situations. Manning (1997: 203) shows that the police have many nick-names for members of the public (non-criminal), but none of them are complementary. His research suggests that the police often see people as at best inconvenient, at worst violent or threatening. Westley (1970: 145) found a similar attitude among the officers he studied in that 'the public is at worst evil and dangerous, at best misguided and ignorant'. According to Manning's research, criminals come in two main cate-gories, 'villains' and 'good villains' where the latter group are criminals that co-operate with the police, have a long record and will admit their crime. Villains have records (criminal or otherwise) but are not as willing to play by the police rules as the good villains are (1997: 203). Smith and Gray (1985: 347) also identified the category of a 'good villain', but for them the term was used more for those people who the police feel are worthy adversaries. These are offenders involved in a series of crimes and as such have been rather successful at their craft and are not one-time criminals.

Reiner (2000a: 93–5) also discusses police typologies of the public. His category of 'good-class villain' is a combination of Manning and Smith and Gray's 'good villain'. These are worthy adversaries who do not challenge the police authority. 'Police property' is a term used to refer to those sections of the public that are seen by the majority as distasteful and so the police are left to cope with them in whatever way they see fit. These are people like vagrants, the unemployed or deviant youth. 'Challengers' are those who have the power to invade the police realm and may try to change it. These are people like social workers, researchers or journalists. Women, children and the elderly can be seen as 'disarmers'. They can weaken police work as they are seen to be more vulnerable and so can receive real sympathy if they allege police misconduct. Police monitoring groups or civil liberty groups are 'do-gooders' who are trying to limit police autonomy, or, in police minds, stop them from doing their job. 'Politicians' are no better as they are remote idealists, susceptible to corruption but who have vast powers to make and change the law.

Typologies help order what could be a very chaotic working environ-ment. Police feel that they are 'getting it from all angles' (Reiner 2000a: 95) and so become a tight-knit community with their own conceptual categories to order a threatening world. It is clear from the above that there is a distinction in the police mind between the 'rough' and 'respectable' sections of the community, i.e., those who challenge and those who adopt middle-class values. But all these categories of people can pose a threat for the police and they are divided by what *kind* of power they hold to cause problems (Reiner 2000a: 93, 106). Westley (1970: 76) found that the police definition of the public becomes stronger through the stories they tell each other of their experiences. 'It is abstracted to a symbol of intolerance, hatred, and injustice. It becomes the lens of interpretation, and reality is shaped by it. The experiences then become ever more frequent and the exceptions more scarce. Memory selectively reinforces the conviction, and the tales passed from man to man constitute an expression of the feelings and a support against the hostile world'. Typologies not only order the outside world, but they can help to increase the solidarity of the officers across the subcultures they may form. Thus in this analysis of interaction at football it is important to consider the typologies the police have developed for that particular context as it not only gives insight into their views of football supporters, but shows how each police team has increased its own unity by clearly marking off what constitutes the 'other'. It also shows that the previous literature, as discussed above, does not cover all public encounters as football supporters have their own unique categories in police officers' minds.

Like the uniformed PCs in the previous chapter, the Mobile Support Units maintain typologies of the supporters and other people they encounter during a football match. The main distinctions they use are between 'hooligans', 'supporters', 'vandals', and 'regular people'. The MSU officers are primarily concerned with the actions of the football 'hooligans' and so have a more developed typology for them. This will be described below. 'Supporters' are just anyone else who is attending the game but is not a hooligan, such as families or young people wearing club shirts. They represent what hooligans are *not* in the minds of MSU officers: calm, orderly, out to just watch the game and wearing scarves or other club colours. Some supporters may be drunk and thus need to be prevented from entering the ground, but this was more a factor of being in the pub too long than a sign of malicious intent. 'Vandals' are a category mostly used by the MSU from the stadium sub-division, as that is more of an issue for their area. They patrol not only for football hooligans, but also for locals who take advantage of the influx of unattended cars during the match. Anyone else the MSUs encounter who is not associated with football or car vandalism is generally regarded as a 'normal person' and left alone. These are people out doing shopping or just walking from one place to another. These MSU typologies are no more sophisticated than this.

Their main duty is to help control the football hooligans, so they did not devote much attention to the other categories.

The 'hooligan' typology, as mentioned above, is more detailed than the other MSU typologies. To be considered a hooligan, or suspected of being a hooligan by an MSU officer, a person needs to fit a specific type. The person should be male, young (late teens through thirties), dressed in nice leisure clothes but with no club colours, wearing a baseball cap, and travelling in a large group with other similarly dressed men. The MSU officers I met all seemed to agree that hooligans are not all from the working class (in contrast to the views held by Dunning et al 1988). They feel that attending football games is expensive and so hooligans need a good income to participate in this activity. They also feel that hooligans are easy to spot as their overall style is unique to them (based on the descriptions above which may not be entirely accurate, see later discussion on detectives' typologies) and they want police attention as it adds to their excitement (Kerr 1994). If hooligans really wanted to hide, the MSUs feel they could do it easily, but they do not.

The MSU officers look down upon older hooligans. It seems that this kind of activity is understandable in younger people, but older hooligans according to one officer, 'should know better'. A final distinction is made with a group of hooligans from several cities in Scotland who frequently band together, known as the 'National Firm'. These people gather occasionally to challenge lone hooligan groups (according to the police). The National Firm hooligans are regarded as pretty tough, and any suggestion that they might be coming to the match puts all officers on full alert. Thus the MSU officers have a more developed typology system for the hooligans than the PCs do, as they have more direct interaction with them, but a less well developed typology system for other types of supporters with whom they have little interaction.

Typologies used by the detectives

When the detectives or spotters discuss football supporters, there are only two main types to which they refer: hooligans and 'scarvies'. This latter term is the nickname they use for any non-hooligan football supporter. These types of supporters tend to wear club colours often in the form of scarves (hence the name). This term is similar to one used by the hooligans themselves to describe the same group of people: 'Scarfers' are supporters who don the regalia of the team they support and who do not get involved in hooligan activity (Allan 1989). This suggests some degree of a common sub-cultural set of definitions between the hooligans and the detectives. The detectives' 'hooligan' typology, however, is far more detailed than that of the MSUs and includes a few sub-sections. Not only is the detectives' hooligan typology more developed than that of the MSUs, but at times the detectives' definition of a hooligan conflicted with that held by the MSUs. Manning (1980: 135) noticed the same definitional incongruity with the term 'major violator' in his work with vice squad officers. 'Axial terms meant to focus investigative activities, such as major violator, are actually like rotors, pointing first to one connotation of the words and then to another'. In Manning's research, these incongruities are perpetuated through the lack of communication between the organisational sections, just as I found in football policing in that police operate as several separate interaction teams (to be discussed more later in relation to detectives and MSUs).

Goffman (1969, cited in Manning 1980: 50) has argued that actors in a performance 'give off' (rather than give) messages during their performance, called 'expressive features'. These signs 'indicate the extent to which the person is linked to the socially defined role'. The detectives use these expressive features to identify a football hooligan. In general, the detectives say that hooligans come in a certain type and baseball caps are certainly one identifying feature. However, on one occasion when we were observing some young men horsing around as they came out of the train station (some with baseball caps) a new detective said that even he could tell those guys were not hooligans. He did not elaborate on how he could make this distinction, but it seems to me that the criteria the detectives use are more specific than that used by the MSUs. They feel they have a sense of how the hooligans walk, how they dress and the general attitude they exude (Norris and Armstrong 1999: 122, Giulianotti 1999: 53). Young men wearing baseball caps are not hooligans if the rest of these expressive features are absent (such a calm and cool demeanour). The detectives also feel that the hooligans keep a low profile. They have good jobs that they do not want to lose by getting arrested so they try not to stick out.[25] This again contrasts with the opinion of the MSUs who suggest that the hooligans want to be noticed by the police. According to the detectives, the main people the hooligans will fight with are hooligans from other cities. They do not attack civilians or regular supporters, unless those supporters come from their arch rival team. These fans are fair game because of the strong animosity between the support sides. Other fans however, are left alone.

One detective said that it is hard to trace hooligans outside of football, as they do not tend to be involved in other illegal activities. This touches on another area of disagreement among the various police groups as some feel that hooligans are definitely involved in other crimes. During my interview with detectives from the National Criminal Intelligence Service, they suggested that some hooligans even use the football as a front for engaging in illegal transactions. Armstrong (1998: 287) also suggests that some football hooligans engage in other crimes, but that these are not related to their actions at football. Thus it appears to be unclear as to whether or not the hooligans are members of the 'criminal class'. According to the detectives I studied, they are not.

The main division within the hooligan typology that the detectives use is between the 'hard core' and the 'periphery'. Hard core hooligans are the ones most likely to get involved in fights and have been with the hooligans for a long time. They are known to the detectives and are the ones the detectives look for first in a group. The detectives I studied never mentioned one leader among the hooligans, just a main group of men around which activity is focused (Armstrong [1998: 115] found a similar police theory). The periphery are the other hooligans who are either too new for the detectives to know or ones who do not come to all the matches. The detectives are less concerned about these men as they are not considered to be much of a threat on their own. Younger hooligans are also grouped into this category. Reiner (2000a) has noted that many writers have criticised the police for stereotyping likely offenders, and then seeking out only those people who fit the type, thus creating a self-fulfilling prophecy of deviance amplification. 'However, stereotyping is an inevitable tool of the suspiciousness endemic to police work' (2000a: 91), and so the question becomes not whether the police use stereotypes, but just how based in reality those stereotypes are. The detectives feel that they have a well-developed sense of who is a hooligan and who is not, based on years of experience and shared information with other forces and to some extent with the hooligans themselves. It has been argued, however, that this may not actually be the case (Armstrong 1998: 312–13). For instance, the police often look for 'ringleaders' in the hooligan hierarchy to arrest (Armstrong and Hobbs 1995: 176) while Armstrong has argued that there is no such hooligan organisation. Armstrong feels that the police, themselves agents in a hierarchy, cannot understand organised hooligan activity without reference to hierarchical structure (1998: 264). Reiner warns that the police thus could in fact be using stereotypes that reflect and reinforce wider social inequalities (2000a: 91) and so help glamorise police activity through the fight against this evident 'evil' (Armstrong and Hobbs 1995: 176).

The detectives I observed draw a further division between their local hooligans and those from other cities. According to the detectives I studied, their local hooligans are the worst behaved and have the worst reputation. These hooligans are also more organised than the hooligans from other cities, according to one visiting detective. The National Firm was another hooligan force of concern, although they never managed to mount an attack on the local hooligans during the time of my research.[26] Thus, according to the detectives, not all hooligans within the UK are the same and not all hooligans within their city are the same.

In general, the detectives seem to regard hooligans in the context of a football match as non-persons. They are normal people when not at the match and have good jobs. However, they too fall victim to the 'red haze' (mentioned in Chapter 3) of a match and become something different during that event. One detective told me that hooligans have a different mentality from other football supporters. When discussing the police method of following hooligans to the ground, one detective said that the hooligans deserve what they get. He feels that 'if they are going to act like children they can be treated like children'. So it would appear that by virtue of appearing to be a hooligan, one has already relinquished claim to full personhood and thus civil liberties.[27] This reflects one of the typologies the police have constructed for the public mentioned earlier, that of 'police property'. These are low-status persons and the majority of the population is content to let the police manage them as they see fit (Reiner 2000b: 93). Armstrong and Hobbs (1995: 183) discuss how the same covert tactics used against football hooligans without public protest caused great public concern when used against striking miners or drunk drivers, such as photographing suspected offenders and keeping the photos to develop dossiers even if no charges are brought.

Rules of engagement: Mobile Support Units

Now that we have considered MSU and detectives performances at football and explored their typology systems, we will turn to an examination of some of the general unspoken rules that guide their interaction with supporters. These rules will be developed in more detail in the next section to show how they are manifested by, and also help define, the distinct interaction 'teams' within the MSUs and detectives. This current section will thus set the scene for the next by giving an overview of MSU and detectives encounters with football supporters.

As with the uniformed officers on foot, the Mobile Support Units have basic rules of engagement (or 'parts' as Goffman describes them [1959: 27]) that they observe with the supporters at a football match. As before, these are not rules in the official sense, but working standards of behaviour that tend to be observed when the groups are in contact with each other. I will discuss the rules of engagement that I observed before, during and after a football match with the MSUs and detectives.

The initial aspect of MSU activity in the city that needs to be addressed is the officers' willingness to violate traffic rules. When the van is responding to an event in progress, this can involve not only flashing lights and great speed, but also driving on the wrong side of the road and running red lights (Holdaway 1983, Smith and Gray 1985: 340). Some of these techniques are also used if the van is escorting a visiting supporters' bus that has gone astray and needs to get out of the city or one that is suspected to be full of visiting hooligans. As was discussed in Chapter 3, this also suggests that the rules of behaviour for 'normal' citizens do not apply in the football context. It is a unique situation with its own code of conduct.

When dealing directly with people, the MSU officers usually interact with supporters who are doing something wrong or look like they are about to do something wrong. However, the stadium sub-division officers did occasionally speak to some supporters on a friendlier basis. For example, a supporter approached the van when it was parked by the visitor's entrance to ask how much it cost to get into that section. When he returned later with a few friends, the officers asked them which team they supported. They let them in even though the officers were suspicious when they answered the visiting team.[28] Waddington (1996: 126–7) argues that public order policing is now highly organised and controlled, so that a balance between coercion and accommodation can be met in police action with the public during pre-planned events (such as football matches).

The majority of the interaction I witnessed between the MSUs and the supporters occurred when trouble of some kind was involved. Thus, MSU relations with supporters are usually quite tense before and during an arrest. Even if the van is just following along next to a group of suspected hooligans (who are regarded as having a great potential for trouble), the young men will jeer and shout things at the officers in the van. This is tolerated as long as the supporters continue walking along towards the ground where they will soon be out of harm's way. The MSU officers frequently respond to events in progress. Hooligans involved in a fight are chased and either given a lecture and released or arrested and taken into custody. What seems to determine the end result is the behaviour of the supporters, not just the offence they (may) have committed. If they calm down and listen to what the police say, they are generally released. If they talk back or try to avoid the police, they are more likely to get arrested (as is the case with supporters and foot patrol officers). Once when I asked why a particular hooligan was arrested, the answer was 'He wouldn't take a talking to'. In practical terms, the police cannot arrest all hooligans involved in an incident, so they focus their efforts on the ones who are least receptive to police intervention (Cain 1971: 83), or who are known to the police previously for football violence.

However, once a custody is taken into the van, he or she is not brought to the station right away. Other incidents could still happen until the game starts or enough time has passed after the game ended so the custody is present in the back of the van while the officers continue with their duties. Interaction here is quite different from that in the streets. One particular custody was very talkative. At first the officers teased him by pretending to ignore him and saying to each other, 'Do you hear talking in this van? Is there a talking person here?' Later they did speak directly to him, but in a sarcastic kind of way. For instance, the custody complained that visiting supporters never get arrested, only ones from the home city. One of the officers said that they had no idea he was from the home city because he was not wearing any club colours. This was an obvious joke as no hooligan wears colours anyway and they knew where he was from because of his accent and the people in his group. The MSU officer thus drew on a common sub-cultural understanding of football hooliganism, which both the police and the hooligans share. One of the officers did get drawn into a serious discussion with him about how if the custody had wanted to see the game so badly then he should not have been 'jumping about on (the street)'. The custody kept talking and heightening the officer's annoyance. Eventually the conversation ended in a 'Fine!', 'Fine!' exchange with the officer clearly very worked up. These interactions are similar to the 'obedience tests' Goffman noted in total institutions (1961a: 26) where staff challenge the inmates' initial behaviour in an attempt to communicate to them that only by deferential action will they get by. The above examples suggest that the police are not always successful at this.

This battle of wits was displayed again with other officers and custodies in the charge room of the city centre police station. Interaction is very important here in that each group has something the other wants. After a person has been arrested the police need the custodies to speak about the incident and perhaps give them the names of the others involved. The custodies need to stay on the good side of the officers to get any special attention or favours (Goffman 1961a: 45, 51). For instance, they can request to see the doctor, but it is up to the sergeant on duty to decide if this is a genuine need and how urgent it is. While the custodies are waiting to be processed, there is a lot of civil banter between them and the police officers. However, as with supporter and police constable encounters in and around the stadium, it always seems to carry a sarcastic edge to it and that neither side is taking the other very seriously. The custodies claim they are not the guilty party and give all manner of explanations as to why they were there at the time, such as 'I was on my way to get my diabetes injection'. The police listen politely, acknowledge what the custodies have said, and continue to hold them in the van or the station. The officers feel that they know the real scenario and will not be persuaded by the hooligans' stories, no matter how amusing they find them. Like the example of the hooligan in the van above, the police have an advantage over the custodies if they can keep themselves calm and use the hooligans for their own amusement. Once a hooligan gets an officer worked up and annoyed though, he or she has demonstrated some degree of power over the officer. Though custodies may be in handcuffs or in cells, they are still able to influence the police if they can win the battle of wits that starts after the arrest. The action in the charge room will be discussed in more detail in the section to follow, including more similarities to the processes of a total institution (Goffman 1961a).

Rules of engagement: detectives

As was discussed in the section on detectives' 'typologies', the football hooligans are the detectives' main group of concern. They do not interact very much with non-hooligan supporters so all the rules of engagement to follow will focus on the former group.

The detectives use interaction with the hooligans to get to know them personally. To do this, they tend to violate the usual rules of civil inattention as described by Goffman (1963a: 84). He suggests that in most encounters between unacquainted people, a quick glance is allowed to demonstrate that the other person has been seen, but the gaze is to be dropped at that point so that the other person does not feel threatened. Goffman acknowledges that the police are sometimes an exception to this rule, although that was in the context of uniformed officers with specific reasons for approaching members of the public. In the case of football policing, we have plain clothes detectives approaching known or suspected hooligans and asking them for personal information. This ranges from their names to what their plans are for fights that day. The hooligans may indeed feel threatened by this attention from the detectives, but the encounters are usually civil, sometimes friendly, as the detectives only chat to them for a short while before letting the hooligans continue on their way.

This friendly, informal approach is very specific to the detectives when it comes to the football hooligans. They need to keep relations with them on good terms so that they can get as much information from them as possible. This is in stark contrast to the actions of the MSU officers (prior to arrests), who tend to be formal, short tempered, and not amused at the antics of the hooligans. It is only on the rare occasions when the detectives get involved in hooligans' fights that the friendly approach is dropped. However, as soon as the situation calms down, the detectives and the hooligans may re-enter their friendly banter and laugh together over what just happened.

Initially, the detectives at football were meant to be a covert presence. The idea was to get close to the hooligans or follow them secretly to find out what they were doing. However, this proved unmanageable and the detectives decided to adopt an overt presence instead. This way, the detectives can let the hooligans know that they are there and are watching. Hobbs (1988: 206–8) describes this as 'unarmed combat'. The groups get to know each other quite well and this has even extended into friendly teasing of each other. Sometimes when the detectives are in an unmarked car and pass a group of hooligans walking on the pavement, they flash their lights or sound the horn to get the hooligans' attention. Waving and shouting to each other usually follows this, sometimes with accompanying hand gestures from the hooligans. The detectives are able through overt interaction techniques and humour to keep relations with the hooligans informal and perhaps encourage a greater exchange of information. When the friendly approach is not successful, I was told that the detectives sometimes use 'legitimate persuasion' to elicit information from the hooligans. This does not refer to violence on the part of the detectives but perhaps some bartering techniques. However, the detective did not elaborate on the exact methods used.

Through their interaction with the hooligans and after considering the result of the football match and the reputation of the visiting team's supporters, the detectives say they 'get a feeling' about whether or not there will be violence. It is this feeling that dictates how long the detectives stay on duty after a football match. If the hooligans appear to be 'up for it' and there is another group of hooligans present, they will stay on longer and try to prevent any incidents occurring. However, once it reaches evening and the immediacy of the match has passed, the detectives can return to the station and let the MSU officers handle things.

The final rule the detectives use is that the hooligans want the police to be there. Although the hooligans may keep a low profile (as was suggested earlier) the detectives know who they are and feel that the hooligans like it that way. There is an added element of chase and escape with the detectives involved and, should a fight happen the police are always close by to make sure it does not get too serious (Armstrong's research [1998: 33, 240–1] suggests this as well). No hooligan has to lose face by backing down, but no one gets too badly hurt, either. The detectives believe that if they really wanted to elude the police, the hooligans could take different routes to the ground and go to different pubs. They like the police attention. Marsh et al's (1978) interviews with football hooligans even suggest that the police have a functional role to play in the resulting violence. Their informants said that hooligans would not be nearly as brave if the police were not there to stop things from getting out of hand.

However, there were some signs that this was starting to change towards the end of my research period. One detective said that the hooligans are starting to split up before the start of the game, making it more difficult for the police to follow them. In addition, this close police attention may make apprehending the National Firm more difficult. On the one occasion when they made an appearance during my fieldwork their bus was spotted on its way to the ground and detained for the duration of the game (discussed earlier in the section on performance). The detectives acknowledge that this was a significant event and a victory for football policing, but said that the National Firm may choose other forms of transport in the future. These may not be quite so easy to detect. Thus, the police must be prepared to continuously develop their rules of interaction with the supporters if they are to maintain some degree of control in the situation.

Teams: MSUs and detectives

I will now discuss teamwork in football policing with the MSU officers and the detectives. This will provide a more detailed analysis of police and supporter interaction than that in the previous section on 'rules of engagement'. Teamwork is important to consider, as this is the primary concept Goffman (1959: 83) used to analyse interaction. He found that an overall performance was often the product of a group of people working together, an interaction 'team' (Goffman 1959: 85). Both MSU officers and the detectives will be considered in this section, as it will be easier to demonstrate how they operate as separate teams by directly comparing them. They will be considered separately again in the following section on Regions.

I will break my discussion of teams into four parts. The first three will look at police teams in a Goffman-esque approach. Each police team has a different relationship and method of interaction with the supporters. To demonstrate this, I will discuss the membership criteria of each team, the audiences for each and the definition of the situation each audience receives. The four teams I have identified from my fieldwork are the stadium sub-division MSUs, the city centre sub-division MSUs, the home city detectives or spotters, and any visiting detectives or spotters. The last part of this section on teams will take a different look at the idea of teams, and present my own adaptation of Goffman's work. I will suggest that teams may be more interdependent than Goffman proposes.

Membership criteria

For the first part of this discussion of teams, I will review the membership criteria of each. The MSU officers and the detectives/spotters must be regarded as separate teams. Not only do they have drastically different appearances and manners from each other (as discussed in the 'performance' section), the definition of the situation that they each maintain is different. This will be developed later. Secondly, the MSU officers and the detectives/spotters must each be further divided into two more teams. As was mentioned before, the MSUs originate in two separate sub-divisions and have two different areas to patrol (although there is some overlap around the stadium). They attend separate briefings and are called down at different times. They may communicate with each other during the course of the game, but they largely operate as separate units. In addition, outside the football match day the stadium sub-division MSU officers are more involved in plain clothes detective work than mobile unit patrols. Thus their job as a whole is different from that of the city centre sub-division officers.

The detectives from the home city do indeed work as a unified force, separate from that of the MSUs and other officers. They know each other and their collective audience well and have many shared routines and procedures with each other that do not involve the other police teams. However, when detectives or spotters from other forces come to help spot visiting hooligans, two teams are now present among the detectives. The two groups of detectives/spotters work well together for the most part, but they are each more familiar with their home hooligans than they are with the other detective team. For example, the local detectives often know where the local hooligans live, where they work and who their best friends are, but they may have only just met the visiting football spotter sitting with them in the car. Visiting detectives/spotters often have slightly different tactics for dealing with the hooligans, such as having a large rotating team of about ten officers to do the spotting rather than the two or three officers the main force I studied use at every game. The visiting spotters are temporary allies, but not teammates. So, for all four teams in question here, *point of origin* is the main membership criterion as each has a different one that determines their actions for the day. These teams are thus constructed through their appearance, manner and point of origin, as further highlighted by the points below on audience and definition of the situation.

Audiences

There must be an audience in order to have a performance (Goffman 1959: 97), and the audience for the MSU officers from the city centre police station is usually the football hooligans. The MSU officers drive in a large van as a team of four or five, and so are called to the more aggressive incidents in order that their force is put to best use. I was told when I started my research to stick with the MSUs because they have the most contact with the 'rougher element'. As was suggested in the section on typologies, their definition of a football hooligan may not be the same as the detectives or spotters, but it is these people that they look for and with whom they interact. They do not concern themselves with other supporters or the general public unless absolutely necessary, but this never happened when I was with the city centre sub-division MSUs so they will not be discussed as audiences here.

The officers from stadium sub-division MSUs interact with the hooligans (for the above reasons), but also with people from the city who may be involved with vandalising cars and with the more rowdy regular supporters. If supporters are arrested at the match, it is usually the stadium sub-division MSUs who transport the custodies to the station for processing. Thus their audience base is a bit wider than that of the city centre sub-division MSUs. For this reason, their knowledge of football hooligans may not be as developed as that of the city centre sub-division MSUs. They have told me that they cannot put names to faces, but generally know what hooligans look like. I felt that they probably had a good idea of who are the more prominent hooligans (the ones who are frequently arrested or detained), but that they may not be as adept as the detectives or city centre sub-division MSUs in identifying more low-profile members. But this is due to their geographical remit rather than any lack of ability, as they are not patrolling the area where hooligans are deemed to be most active. In general, this shows that as the city centre and stadium MSUs have different audiences they cannot be members of the same team.

For the home detectives, their main audience is the suspected local football hooligans, whom they often know not just by appearance, but also by name, address, and other personal information. Their main audience is the 'heavy' or 'hard core' hooligans: people they feel are most likely to be involved in violence and have been doing it for a while (Hobbs and Robins [1991: 563] also identify a 'hard core' but see it as transient). The alleged 'periphery' hooligans are a concern, but only if there is a large number of them. If suspected visiting hooligans are also spotted, then they too are an interaction audience. That is not a usual occurrence, however. When visiting detectives or spotters are present to assist in football spotting, they focus their interaction on the hooligans from their own town or city. They do not know the local hooligans that well, but are on speaking terms with those from their own town. For the detectives any other audience is a distant second to the football hooligans.

Definitions of the situation

The definition of the situation is the overall mood or impression that the actors want to convey and maintain in any situation where they are performing for an audience. For the stadium sub-division MSU officers of all ages that I studied, violence at football is nothing like it was in the early 1980s. They do not feel there are many hooligans left and any fights that do happen are really quite minor. They also feel that the presence of an MSU van is enough to reduce the chance of violence happening around the ground. If they were not there the situation would be worse. When interacting with supporters, these officers tend to be abrupt. Their definition of the situation seems to be that they are there because they have to be and they are the ones in charge now, not the hooligans. They are often bored and wish the supporters would just go home. For example, during the demonstration that the supporters held after one match (see later section on 'regions' for more on this) the MSU officers were joking to each other how they wished they could just open the back of the van, scoop everyone in and get on their way.

The definition of the situation suggested by interaction between the city centre sub-division MSUs and the supporters is somewhat different. They too present themselves as in charge of the situation but in a less formal way. Once a supporter has been arrested and is in custody, the talk between him or her and the MSU officer seems to be a delicate game of who can withhold the most from the other and yet elicit the most from the other as well. This was discussed previously in the section on rules of engagement. Each has something the other wants but neither wants to give too much away. Hooligans give many reasons for being where they were, but never attribute it to wanting to fight. However, they will also never blame the other hooligans formally or press any charges against them, not something you would expect an 'innocent' person to do. The MSU officers expect this response, but always ask anyway and so the game continues (this will be explored further in the section on regions). This civil definition of the situation is not always the case between the MSU officers and the supporters, especially when a supporter is first getting arrested. Once an officer decides to apprehend a supporter, there is not much he or she can do to change the MSU officer's mind, especially if the supporter resists. The definition of the situation here suggests that the police are in charge and there is no negotiation about arrest. For example, a supporter who was arrested for ignoring police instructions to stop walking in the direction he was refused to give the police his name. The arresting officer just calmly asked him, again and again, until he finally relented and gave his name. Once the situation has calmed though, the interaction game described above begins.

The two detective/spotter teams have similar definitions of the situation that they present to the supporters. For both, the situation is relaxed and informal. This even extends to one detective allowing a self-confessed drunk hooligan into the football ground. The detectives are also willing to barter for information, such as when one hooligan agreed to tell a detective his name if the detective told him his own first. However, if the situation gets serious, the detectives do not hesitate to act to remind the hooligans that the friendly nature only goes so far. For example, the detectives were informally chatting to some hooligans outside a pub when they suddenly ran inside to stop a fight that was starting between the rival hooligans left there. However, the main difference between the local detectives and the visiting detectives/spotters at the football matches I attended is that the local detectives will never arrest a supporter at a game while visiting detectives/spotters may do so. Thus visiting detectives are willing to damage their rapport with the hooligans and leave the streets by executing their police power of arrest while local detectives will not. Visiting detectives/spotters may also carry small batons while local detectives do not. Thus their definitions of the situation are slightly different from each other and very different from that of the MSUs.

Alternative reading of teamwork

It might be tempting to see the two MSU teams and the two detective/spotter teams described above as two sets of 'colleagues' rather than four sets of teams. Goffman uses this term to describe people who put on the same kinds of performances to the same kinds of audiences, but who do not interact as teammates. Colleagues are not present in the same time and place as each other, but share similar difficulties, points of view and a common social language (1959: 158–9). An example might be people who meet for the first time but discover they are from the same small town. They will have common understandings and a sense of familiarity that other strangers meeting would not. But as the above discussion of membership criteria, audience and definition of the situation has demonstrated, these four groups cannot be considered as colleagues. They have different audiences to encounter and different definitions of the situation to present and enforce. Their circumstances are not similar enough to be considered as colleagues.

So as what can they be considered? This last part of the discussion on teams will look at an alternative reading of teamwork at football. To do this, Goffman's definition of 'team' will be modified to one that allows for more flexibility in team boundaries and more interdependence of the teams. There have been a few examples in this chapter already of shared meanings between the police groups and the football hooligans. One such example is the joke the MSU officers made about the hooligan in custody not wearing club colours and the way the detectives and the hooligans have a similar nickname for scarf-wearing supporters. These similarities above and the ones to follow suggest that the boundary between the hooligans and the MSU and detectives is not as strong as one might think.

When the MSU officers receive a call about an event in progress, they get visibly excited before they even arrive at the scene. Reiner (2000a: 89) says this is not only because the chase and capture are exciting in themselves, but also because they are deemed to be worthwhile police work. After the pre-match patrols of the more eventful games, the officers compare stories over what happened with their vans that afternoon and maybe laugh over how they eventually caught some of the offenders (Smith and Gray 1985: 340). The fights seem to give them a peak, or 'flow', experience (Csikszentmihalyi 1975), and they are disappointed if one did not materialise when they had expected it. During the patrols the MSU officers swear, talk about going drinking later, regale each other with stories of previous nights out, discuss football (many are supporters themselves), and make fun of the higher ranks in the police force (they seem to distrust authority). Considering what has been written about football hooligans previously (Giulianotti 1996, Armstrong 1998), these police traits do not seem all that far removed from those of the hooligans. This is not to suggest that the MSU officers would go out and initiate fights if given the chance or that they routinely break the law. However, considering the above it appears that Goffman's strict boundaries between teams do not fit here.

A similar argument can be made for the detectives. When visiting detectives/spotters are present, both groups of detectives refer to the hooligans as 'our lot' and 'your lot', terms of possession and familiarity. 'Our lot' refers to the hooligans that the detectives know to be from their hometowns while 'your lot' are those from the others'. On at least one occasion, the visiting detectives seemed to almost sympathise with their hooligans and said that they (the visiting detectives) were 'the friendliest faces (the visiting hooligans) have seen all day'. One of the visiting detectives even knew a hooligan from his PC days when the hooligan was a young boy. Some of the local detectives are strong supporters of certain Scottish football clubs and share in the regional loyalties and rivalries those clubs espouse. This sometimes features in the way they talk about the detectives or spotters from that region. For example, the strong rivalry between the home city's football club and another football club was mentioned as one of the reasons these detectives did not get along very well when policing a match together. In addition, the detectives enjoy smoking, drinking, discussing football with each other, and invite their detective/spotter counterparts from other forces to join them in pursuing the hooligans. These are traits also associated with the hooligans who occasionally band with other hooligans groups to fight a common enemy (such as the case with the National Firm).

What this seems to be suggesting is that the detectives and MSU officers at football share a common subculture with the hooligans there, even if they do not like or even respect the hooligans. Manning (1980: 41) also observed that detectives share the symbolic, linguistic, cultural and social world of those they regulate. This makes the detectives more autonomous from the police department and from the public, and it also makes their work with the criminals more successful (1980: 51). This is similar to the argument made by Hobbs (1988). In his work with detectives and criminals in the East End of London, he noticed that both groups acted as entrepreneurs. This was the culture of the East End, and to be a successful detective one had to adopt this culture as well. Doing so brought rewards, not only with those policed but also from the police force itself. This reward incentive is also present in football policing. The MSU officers can receive overtime pay for their work there and experience 'flow' when chasing hooligans. The detectives seem to enjoy the challenge of the match day more than their usual desk work during the week. The police in turn provide the hooligans with an added element of danger in their day. So not only do they share (to some degree) a subculture with the hooligans, but the MSU officers, the detectives, and the hooligans have incentives to continue their association with each other. This weakening of team boundaries (through a common subculture) and interdependence of these groups suggests that Goffman's definition of team may need to be reconsidered. However, this will be fully achieved after the discussion on the regions of dramaturgical action in football policing, as that will add the final element to my argument.

Regions: MSUs

Goffman (1959: 109) found that interaction usually occurs in highly spatially and temporally bounded regions. There are four aspects to the regions of interaction between the MSU officers or detectives and the supporters at football. These are temporal, physical space, symbolic space, and the backstage area. The first three are part of the 'front stage' of interaction, or, that aspect of a team's performance that the audience is supposed to see. The backstage is where the performance is prepared and the team relaxes, allowing actions to happen that would otherwise discredit the performance if the audience were to see them (Goffman 1959: 114).

Temporal region

For the MSU officers, the temporal structure of a football match day is largely dictated by the scheduling of the match, the scheduling of their briefings and the actions of the supporters. These things are out of their control. The briefings are held a certain amount of time before the beginning and ending of the match depending on previous supporter behaviour at this fixture. If the two sides are usually hostile to each other, the briefings are held farther in advance than if the two sides are largely ambivalent to each other or if the supporter group is small. However, if there is activity in the city centre that needs MSU involvement while they are still in the briefings, the officers will leave to attend to them. When determining the level of potential disorder for each game, the police often consider whether or not it is a holiday weekend. If it is, less violence is expected from the hooligans because if they were arrested they would be in jail an extra day. The courts are closed on Bank Holiday Mondays so the more aggressive supporters tend to be quieter on those weekends.

There were only a couple of occasions when the MSU officers had any control over the temporal region of interaction with the supporters. The first has been mentioned previously in this chapter. This was the time the National Firm coach of visiting hooligans was apprehended. MSU officers detained the occupants of the bus who did not have tickets to the game for the duration of it and then allowed the coach to leave the city. The other occasion included control of physical space as well, the next aspect of interaction regions that I will consider, and so will be discussed next.

Physical space

At one point during my fieldwork, the local football club was not doing very well. The fans were upset at the team's record and decided to hold a demonstration after one of the matches, as was briefly mentioned before. The police had heard rumours that this may occur, but did not know it was certain until after the match. They erected barriers around the stadium's corporate entrance and a few senior officers and stewards stood in front of it. MSU officers and PCs were present at the fringes of the group and watched as the crowd shouted and sang. The core of the protesting group seemed very angry and passionate while the people around the fringes were watching the commotion quietly and not really participating. After a while the Match Commander made an announcement to all the fans and the PCs and MSU officers were instructed to start moving them up the road to go home. The fans resisted a bit at first, but soon dispersed.

This demonstrates well the negotiation of power between the two groups (police and supporters) through temporal and spatial regions of interaction. In this case, the fans decided when to hold the demonstration and where to hold it. The police could not have prevented it nor dispersed it quickly. After an appropriate amount of time had passed and some fans began to leave though, the police decided to end the event and start pushing the fans back and up the road. Thus both groups had some element of power through the time and space they could control, but were eventually subject to the will of the other as well. The physical force of the MSU van and the timing of its intervention were key to the police operation during this event.

MSU officers have far more influence over supporters through the use of physical space than they do through time. The van itself is large and suggests a strong police presence. Vans are placed in areas that need a stronger influence than that which a PC can provide. For example, on one occasion the MSU officers parked by and stood in front of the barriers around the hill in back of the football ground. Only by the MSU officers and their van physically being there were supporters deterred from taking the short cut over the hill that would have impeded segregation. When an MSU officer arrests a person, that custody loses his or her access to free space and becomes confined to the back of the van. One custody attempted to resist this restriction on his space by defying the officers' instructions to sit on the floor of the van while it was en route to another incident and driving fast. He sat on the bench instead and complained about being bounced around during the chase to assert some degree of free will. However, this is about the extent of the control any custody has of physical space in a police van.

Another good demonstration of police use of physical space is the structure of the charge room in the main police station. As in Goffman's *Asylums* (1961a), there are rituals and procedures each new inmate must experience before fully entering the institution. When custodies are first brought in, they are already handcuffed and wait in a holding area together until one of the charge counters is free. The arresting officer and the custody then walk through a door on the opposite wall to get to the counter. On the other side is the sergeant or one of the police officers on duty in the cells. He or she accesses that side of the counter through a separate door. On the floor is a platform that causes this booking officer to stand slightly higher than the custody and the arresting officer on the other side of the counter. Personal possessions and information are taken and recorded according to set legal procedures. There are forms the custody must sign and CCTV records all actions here. The Police and Criminal Evidence Act 1984 (PACE) in England brought about great changes in these formal booking procedures and made non-compliance a serious offence for a police officer. PACE does not apply in Scotland, however, but many of the same sorts of legal rules are in place there and these are what the officers I observed were following.[29] Access to a second charge counter is separate from that of the first counter so that no custodies encounter each other during the actual booking process. This official performance is enacted each time someone is charged and makes clear to the person in question that he or she is lower than the police and subject to the will of the bureaucratic state. At all times custodies are either in confined spaces or carefully supervised by an officer. I did not see any hooligan successfully challenge this invasion of their physical space. But symbolic space does leave some doors open for contests, as I will discuss next.

Symbolic space

In addition to physical space, the use of symbolic space is also important here. This is a term I use to refer to the area immediately around a person, their possessions, clothing and body (a combination of the terms that Goffman developed [1971: 29–40], which he calls the 'territories of self'). It also refers to things that are not tangible but are valued, like personal information. MSU officers can enter the symbolic space of a supporter when they are trying to control that person. For instance, I have seen an officer touch a suspected hooligan (who was sitting) on the knee when he was trying to get the person to give his name. Officers sometimes swear at the supporters when they get agitated, but the supporters never try to touch the officers and are not allowed to swear at them. Custodies have ways of challenging this invasion of their personal space, however. Some tactics, such as asking for handcuffs to be loosened, getting the MSU officer in the van to argue, custodies asking for things when in the cells, require the officer to stop what he or she is doing and come to the custody to meet his or her needs. Thus, the arrested person enters the police officer's symbolic space a little and is perhaps able to regain some of the control he or she lost through the formal booking process and the associated loss of physical and symbolic space. However, there was another tactic I noticed that contested the invasion of a custody's symbolic space. This time, when the arresting officer asked for the custody's personal details, he gave out the information as though he was inviting the officer over for a party and he needed to know the address. The hooligan was very relaxed, spoke clearly, spelled names and made it clear that this was not an invasion of his privacy at all and that the officer was not really gaining any ground on him this way. These techniques discussed above are similar to what Goffman terms 'secondary adjustments' (1961a: 270). These are the tactics one uses to subtly challenge the constraints of the total institution and thus retain some sense of self. These actions are not intended to bring about change, but to demonstrate a 'rejection of one's rejectors' (1961a: 276).

Backstage

The final aspect of MSU interaction regions I will discuss here is the backstage area. This was difficult to discuss in the previous chapter with the uniformed PCs as they were out among the public the majority of the time I was with them. However, the MSU officers are in an enclosed van or at the station a good portion of the time, and thus can relax around each other more. In the van, one of the favourite pastimes of the officers is to comment on and usually make fun of the people that they see (Westmarland 2001). However, if someone approached the van or needed help they were treated politely. Occasionally supporters shout and make gestures at MSUs, so this running commentary on the public when it was out of earshot could be one way to get back at them. The officers will also talk openly to each other about how much they like or dislike whatever job they were about to do. But again, once they are out of the van and in the front stage, they appear impartial and professional. This confirms Goffman's (1959: 114) suggestion that the backstage is an area where the performance is knowingly and routinely contradicted.

In the charge room of the station there was more opportunity for backstage interaction, even though several custodies may be close by. During a football match the charge counters can be busy so there are occasionally several custodies and arresting officers waiting for a chance to go through processing. Occasionally, the officers would have a quiet word with each other so the custodies could not hear. This is when the backstage communication would happen. At one point after a hooligan had given an explanation as to why he should not be there, an officer came up to me and said very quietly, 'Isn't it amazing how it's always the innocent ones who get caught?' The hooligans also had some degree of backstage communication with each other. I saw one hooligan who was coming out of the charge counter wink at one who was just going in. So it would seem that even in the most confined and regulated regions, backstage interaction can still happen. This also suggests that unlike the total institution of Goffman's study, the mortification of self here is not total and not permanent. Mortification of self refers to the process by which a person becomes fully absorbed by the institution and it involves severing ties to the outside world, taking personal possessions from the inmate, issuing new clothes, taking personal details, etc. (1961a: 24–6). This process in the holding cell of the police station is not as extreme and thus not as complete. As is suggested above, the custodies do seem to retain a very distinct idea of self and do not fully incorporate the institutional identity given to them. This is also suggested by Armstrong (1998: 244) who describes cells and courtrooms as an opportunity for rival hooligans to chat with each other and keep in contact.

It was noted in the previous chapter how supporter activity in the city centre could interrupt the backstage of the PCs in that they had to stop what they were doing and run out to attend to violent incidents. All these examples above also suggest that there can be a closer link between the front and backstage than what Goffman suggests. Hooligans secretly communicate in cells and courtrooms (usually used as front stages), police have quiet conversations with each other in front of their custodies and fans influence how long PCs are on a break. My work thus suggests that the spatial barrier between the front and back regions (Goffman 1959: 115) is not always needed to keep one's audience at bay, nor does it successfully separate a team from its audience. Front and back regions can exist in the same space at the same time and the actions in one can influence the actions in the other.

Regions: detectives

The most significant regional interaction that occurs with the detectives is in the symbolic spaces and the backstage. I will briefly discuss interaction in time and physical space first, however. Like the MSU officers, the detectives do not have much control over the temporal organisation of the match days. They begin their patrols after considering the past actions of the hooligans during this particular fixture and any intelligence that they may have. Their job generally ends when the visiting supporters leave the city, as the local hooligans are not likely to find any opposition. If the hooligans attend the game, the detectives do, too. If the hooligans leave the match early, so do the detectives. Thus for the detectives at football, their *temporal* involvement is largely reactive (but the work they do within those time constraints to follow the hooligans and gather information on them is itself proactive).

The detectives also do not have much control over the physical space of their interactions with the hooligans. As was mentioned before, the detectives openly follow the hooligans and even tease them when doing so in their car. If they see hooligans in a place where they should not be (like on the visiting supporters' route to the football ground) they will call to have an MSU or other nearby officer check the hooligans' details. But these are really the only spaces over which they have control, and even then it is not a total control. Once when the detectives and I were parked in the road that leads to the ground, a hooligan approached the car to have chat with the officers. He took an interest in me and frequently reached his hand in to shake mine. By entering the car, even if it was just his arm, the hooligan seemed to suggest that he had some control of the situation and was not afraid of the detectives. He was entering one of their 'territories of self' (Goffman 1971: 29–40). Goffman writes that the greater the rank, the more control one has over territories of self (1971: 40–1). It would appear though that this hooligan was challenging any idea the detectives may have that they are the higher-ranking actors. While the detectives have more autonomy in their use of space than the MSUs or the constables, as with time, the detectives' use of physical space is mostly in reaction to the movements of the hooligans.

Symbolic space

However, when it comes to the region of symbolic space, the detectives and the hooligans are on a more level ground. The detectives do not usually get involved in the more intrusive symbolic space interactions that the MSU officers do. They may ask the hooligans for their names and their plans for the day, but this is usually in an amicable exchange. The detectives will tell the hooligans their own names, as well. The two groups often make physical contact with each other, such as grasping arms or giving pats on the back. Granted, not all interaction between the detectives and the hooligans is this civil, but it happens with much more frequency with them than any other police team at football. Part of the reason could be that any attempt to 'mortify the self' (Goffman 1961a: 24–6) of the hooligans is doomed to fail. These actors have accepted their social stigma willingly and as such have nothing to lose if it is openly displayed. This is in contrast to Goffman's assertion that stigma is always damaging to self (Goffman 1963b: 13). In the case of football hooligans, it is a negative attribute they have worked to achieve. It is still a *stigma*, however, as non-hooligan members of the public see hooliganism as discrediting, and the actors themselves know this and relish in it (Armstrong 1998: 310).

The only time I saw the hooligans maliciously use symbolic space was when visiting hooligans were chatting to local and visiting detectives/spotters. The hooligans made a lot of comments about the clothes and appearance of the detectives and me, one of which was that I was 'trendy as f**k'. I do not think this was said in seriousness and so it seemed to be a way of trying to even out the power level between the two groups by taking the discussion to a much more personal level. While interaction with supporters and hooligans can involve negotiation of time and space for the PCs and MSUs, for the detectives and hooligans it mostly involves negotiation of symbolic space. Aside from that incident above, interaction between hooligans and detectives on a symbolic level was usually a demonstration of equity and good humour, while interaction for the PCs and MSUs with supporters can often be aggressive or challenging. The reason for this becomes clear when we look at the backstage of the detectives at football.

Backstage

The relationship of the hooligans and the detectives is a game for the hooligans, according to the detectives. The hooligans see the detectives' role in their football day as part of their fun (Kerr 1994 also suggests this). When away from the hooligans and in the backstage, the detectives admit that football spotting is very enjoyable. They like it when the hooligans are active and thus more of a challenge to police. Although the detectives do not enjoy violence and would never condone it, it certainly makes their day more interesting when it does happen. This would suggest that that detectives and the hooligans have something of a symbiotic relationship, even though they may not even like each other that much (see the section on typologies). The hooligans need the police to be close by so they do not get too seriously injured or need to risk losing face if a fight happens, and they need the police for an extra element of chase and escape during the football day (Armstrong 1998, Marsh et al 1978). The detectives need the hooligans for intelligence gathering purposes and to provide a challenging yet enjoyable policing experience. As Marx (1988: 159) noted, undercover agents are more dispersed and free from the usual uniform constraints and thus controlling them is more difficult for supervisors. They do not have to worry about getting bogged down with arrest procedures or following the more rigid policing plans for the uniformed officers. And football policing itself can be especially enjoyable for the detectives, as Armstrong and Hobbs (1995) discuss. It relives the boredom of usual detective work, appears glamorous and dangerous and so helps the police to compete for resources, dramatises the fight against crime and so is a good political tool. Football hooliganism is a very visible modern 'evil' (1995: 176). This is similar to Goffman's definition of 'game' as discussed in *Encounters* (1961b). For him, it involves 'a problematic outcome and then, within these limits, allow(s) for a maximum possible display of externally relevant attributes' (1961b: 68). The hooligans and detectives do not know how their potentially violent encounters will end and both can use it as a way of demonstrating their strengths. Thus football detection could be the ideal policing situation. This will be explored further in the summary.

Summary

On the surface, the MSU officers and the detectives at a football match appear very different. One group wears the police uniform and rides in a large police van. The other wears plain clothes and drives an unmarked car with no police equipment other than a radio. However, these two groups are similar in that their main focus during the match is the football hooligans, and both have the element of mobility that the PCs lack. This makes their experience of the football match much different from the other police officers I have considered so far. However, all these officers are members of *the police* and so do have some important connections to each other. Despite this connection and the similarities in some of their audience members and interaction regions though, the MSU officers and the detectives do indeed experience football policing in very different ways.

For the MSU officers, negotiation of control over the situation with the hooligans is a constant feature of their day. This may be a product of the uniform they wear. Manning (1980: 50) found the lack of uniform important in the detectives he studied as the uniform distances one from the criminal. The MSU officers at football represent a strong force of state order and control (Reiner 2000a: 6), especially with the large vans they operate and thus the space they can command. They are not out to get to know the hooligans or just observe them, but to control and arrest them if need be. The football experience is much different for the detectives. They approach every encounter with the hooligans in the same relaxed manner and this is reflected in the plain clothes that they wear. They are not really attempting to control the situation, just to gather information and some of this involves being friendly with the people they are observing (unlike the approach of the MSUs).

The MSU officers and the detectives have different definitions of what constitutes a hooligan though both would seem to agree that they are not like 'normal' people. Even so, there seems to be more similarity between the police and the policed than would appear on the surface. In the section on teams above, I discussed how the detectives and the MSU officers seem to share subcultural meanings with the football hooligans. The police culture keeps any formal identification with the hooligans and supporters in check. However, after examining the interaction of the MSU officers and detectives with hooligans, it became apparent that more was happening here than the usual audience/performer team interaction, especially in the backstage region. Considering the symbiotic nature of these teams' interactions and the section above on regions lead me to a new reading of Goffman's 'team' concept.

For Goffman (1959: 116), the backstage region is usually an area safe from the intrusion of members of other teams. This is not entirely the case here, although the backstage area does still exist as I discussed previously in this chapter. While football hooligans could never be allowed fully into the backstages of the police and vice versa, the groups do have some degree of knowledge about these areas. The hooligans and the police have a long-standing relationship with each other. They have been encountering each other on Saturdays (usually) for the majority of each year, every year. The hooligans will have seen the police act fail on occasions and so will know them as fallible persons, not just officers. They have seen the inside of their cars, vans, and police stations. The police have some degree of personal information about the hooligans and some intelligence on their plans and their favourite places to congregate. They know some of the hooligans personally and have watched them over the years. So while their backstages are not open to each other they are not totally closed to each other either.

Thus while the MSU officers, the detectives and the hooligans are not all members of the same team, their teams are not completely separate from each other. In this respect, one could say that instead of performing *for* each other as alternating performers and audiences, they are performing *with* each other. Each team: stadium and city centre MSU officers, local and visiting detectives/spotters, and hooligans have separate roles to portray, but they are all involved in the same play. As discussed above, the hooligans do not reject their stigmatised (Goffman 1963b) role as the antagonists, but welcome it and perpetuate it through this performance. The audience for this play thus becomes other football supporters and the general public (through the eyes of the media). The police and hooligans are not adversaries, but partners in one large production, though this may not be something of which any of them are aware. Although they may present themselves as involved in a 'war' with each other, none of them actually want to win. They all need the play to continue for the reasons discussed above. Instead of considering the local and visiting detectives/spotters, stadium and city centre MSU officers and hooligans as separate teams when they encounter each other, they should be seen rather as protagonists (detectives and MSUs) and antagonists (hooligans) in the same play. This ability of teams to stage the same play, to be interdependent, and to have flexible boundaries are aspects of interaction this research has revealed that Goffman did not consider in *The Presentation of Self* (1959).

This chapter has also presented some new insights for the informal police occupational hierarchy. In the previous chapter it was suggested that football policing could be seen as the ideal police situation. I would suggest here that the role of the MSU officers and the detectives are evolved forms of that, with detective work as the epitome. The MSU officers do not have to stand around in what is frequently a boring game and watch people eat pies and shout at the pitch. They are constantly on the move, looking for trouble and getting there fast should it happen. Admittedly, their job is not always very exciting either but it has a more proactive feel to it than that of the PCs.

The detectives and spotters are a step above this, though. They do not have to get bogged down with arrest procedures and are largely self-motivating compared to uniformed officers. They decide where they will go and when based on their interpretation of the intelligence that they have gathered, not on the orders of a superior officer. They feel they know who the main troublemakers are, where they are likely to be and when, who their antagonists are, and what to expect when these groups get together. Football's pre-determined schedule and predictable traditions help make this the ideal policing situation. As many authors have commented, the police tend to have a shared myth as to what constitutes 'real police work'. This involves the battle of good versus evil, with the police officer in the middle, catching the bad guys and helping make society a better place (Manning 1997). In fact, the police have very little control over their environments and the people in them, but this ideology is propagated as it gives the officer an aura of calm and order in an otherwise chaotic world. As the football hooligan has become demonised in contemporary Britain, the actions of the plain clothes detective are at the epicentre of this recent morality war, and a good opportunity to demonstrate policing skills (Armstrong and Hobbs 1995). No other situation that calls for a police presence occurs with this amount of regularity, media attention, and predictability. Thus the feeling of control the police may have in this situation is easy to understand as it is one of the rare occasions where the police *can* live up to their image (to a large extent). However, it would seem that the hooligans have their own element of control and order as well. In some situations, they may even have more control than the police (such as in the temporal region of interaction).

It would appear that the idea of unified police forces tackling mindless hooliganism is an inaccurate one. Rather, it could be suggested that isolated police groups seek out people who fit the typologies they have constructed and interact with them in routine ways. The football supporters and hooligans themselves however, have their own methods for order and control and in fact are not all that different on a personal level from those who are policing them. This has developed to an extent that challenges Goffman's idea of what constitutes a team and a performance. As we have seen here, it is possible to have interdependent teams staging the same play for a general audience: the public via the media or the non-aggressive supporters near by. In addition, the front and back stages can exist in the same space and time, which facilitates this interdependence of these teams. But do these factors continue in the ranks of the senior officers? What kind of supporter typologies do they hold and how do they deal with them? The answers to these questions will be explored next.

5
Senior Officers

This chapter will continue my analysis of interaction between football supporters and the police. The previous two chapters considered interaction with uniformed police constables, Mobile Support Unit officers, and the football spotters. This chapter will also examine interaction at football matches, but will focus on the senior police officers. I have included sergeants in this category as well as inspectors, chief inspectors, superintendents and chief superintendents. The police do not normally consider sergeants as senior officers, but I have included them here because, as I will demonstrate later, they have a degree of control and responsibility beyond that of the constables. They are supervisors of other PCs as well as police officers themselves so their interactions with supporters are different.

Reuss-Ianni (1983) has found distinct differences in the occupational culture of senior officers than of more junior ones. She discusses an occupational culture, not of rules, but of what she called the 'cop's code' which is comprised of maxims. These are things like, 'don't give up another cop' or 'hold up your end of the work' (1983: 13–14). The code defines relationships with other cops and there is one set of maxims for relationships with peers and one for relationships with superiors (1983: 13). Senior officers have a separate 'cop's code' because their loyalties are more with their political allies than with their constables (Reiner 2000a: 103) and they respond to almost all situations differently than the constables feel they should. For instance, police constables see supervision as a negotiated and reciprocal relationship. Management officers would like supervisors to act on rules on procedures alone. Management sees constables experiencing job stress as potential public relations problems who need to be controlled. Police constables would see such colleagues as ones that need protection (Reuss-Ianni 1983: 4, 62, 77). 'The inevitable result appears to be continuous disintegration in communication, morale, and effectiveness, due to the fact that there is no longer a common context for interpretation or action. Instead, each culture (each side) selectively interprets events to justify its own position' (Reuss-Ianni 1983: 118). They are involved in a game, trying to outsmart each other, as they know they can never control the other. So even though management officers and rank-and-file police officers usually have common cultural backgrounds (Reiner 2000a: 103), their ranks and resultant loyalties mean they will always be divided sub-culturally within the force.

I found similar differences between senior and other officers' interaction teams at football. Senior officers in general cannot be considered as members of the constables' interaction teams, if for no other reason than that they are often the audience for PCs' performances and as such cannot be their teammates. This chapter will, however, explore other reasons why this is case. To do this, I will follow a similar structure when discussing the senior officers that I did in the previous two chapters, by examining their informal rules of interaction and how these are enacted. This will be detailed below. Senior officers do not fit the usual mould when it comes to team interaction at football and are not accepted as teammates in other police teams. This chapter will examine their unique experiences of interaction at football and demonstrate these differences.

While the senior officers may set out the procedures and rules to be followed on a match day, they are still subject to the informal rules of interaction that manifest themselves during the policing of a football game. Although senior officers are present at football in mainly supervisory capacities, they do have a need to present a good performance to their audiences, as I will discuss first. I will then examine the typologies they have constructed about this event and the people in it, and the rules of engagement that they follow when interacting with the supporters, both directly and indirectly. The last two sections will investigate how senior officers perform as members of a team, and the regions in which their interactions occur. There were a few female senior officers involved in the football matches I attended, although not many. Thus, I will be using both 'he' and 'she' in this chapter when referring to senior officers. However, please note that female senior officers are an exception, rather than the rule (see Silvestri 2003 for more on policewomen in leadership positions).

Performance

In order to give a convincing performance, Goffman (1959: 32) suggests that one must operate within a specific setting and with a controlled personal front. One must also give an idealised performance and manage any discrediting information (1959: 44, 59). These will each be discussed in turn, starting with setting and personal front. For the senior officers at football, the setting depends on which subdivision they are working. The city centre senior officers start their day in their offices, preparing for the events ahead. They then gather in the assembly hall or the muster room to give the briefing. After that, they are either in the CCTV room, driving or walking around the city centre for the pre and post-match patrols. During the match they go back to their offices or to the canteen to chat to the other officers. Stadium sub-division senior officers spend the majority of the match either immediately outside or inside the ground. After the game ends, they walk with the fans for a while until the Match Commander calls over the radio that all football patrols can return to the station.

The personal front of the senior officers is comprised of their appearance and manner (Goffman 1959: 34). Senior officers place much importance on physical appearance, for both themselves and their officers. Senior officers are dressed in the same uniform as the police constables, but have special markings to reflect their rank (such as a stripe on their hats and stars or crowns on their shoulders). Often in the briefings they will give the other officers instructions on their appearance, although not in the strict fashion they received as recruits (Fielding 1988: 61). Senior officers thus help direct the constables in staging their own performances. However, the officers themselves ultimately decide what kid of performance to give when out of the station and away from their supervisor's view. One of the most recurring instructions is that the constables should not gather at junctions during the dispersals after the match and chat to each other. They should continue to walk with the supporters and keep themselves spread out. Senior officers feel it looks unprofessional in front of the general public to have a gaggle of PCs on street corners. Another common appearance discussion concerns the black knife-proof vests the officers now wear. They were originally intended to go under the yellow reflective jackets so that the police would not be any less visible but still more protected. However, the yellow jackets are often too tight to allow this so some officers wear the vests over the jackets. Some senior officers allow the PCs to decide for themselves how to wear the vests while others insist that the vests go under the jackets. Senior officers are allowed a degree of discretion in how they instruct their officers in the less crucial matters of police conduct.

Just as the senior officers' opinions on appearance can vary, so do the manners they espouse. Some senior officers approach all people and situations at football in the same gruff, no-nonsense manner. They seem to suggest that they are the ones in charge and they have the final word on everything. Other officers tend to take a more relaxed and friendly approach to people and situations until the event calls on them to be more serious. Some even go out of their way to chat to supporters and be friendly to them. For example, two young girls who needed tickets to the game approached a sergeant. He had been given one earlier by a supporter who did not need it and so he offered it to them. They gave him a hard time because he did not have two. He said he would have given them money to buy another, but he did not have any cash on him. The girls grudgingly took the ticket, as if the generosity he had already shown them was contemptible. Senior officers are aware that they present varying appearances and manners. In the higher ranks especially, discretion of this kind is seen as their right.

Senior officers are also keen to present an idealised image of their role to others (Goffman 1959: 44). This entails remaining calm and controlled no matter what the situation. Police at matches are sometimes taunted and jeered by the supporters. On one occasion, a visiting supporter shouted at an inspector that he was protecting the wrong side and that if you can not get a job you should join the police. The inspector ignored the supporter and said to me that they get that a lot. On another occasion, a different inspector was discussing an upcoming game between the home team and the team he supports. He said the game would be 'good' and the other officers teased him by saying that he would be in with the visiting fans, cheering away while he was working. He looked genuinely excited about the prospect of the game, but said he was glad he was not going to be working at it. I asked if he is ever tempted to join in with those fans while working, and he answered a stern 'No' without hesitation. No matter what their personal feelings, senior officers do not allow themselves to *appear* partial to any side as that would go against their role as neutral and calm law enforcers (Jefferson and Grimshaw 1982: 95). However, their attention to police duties may wane at times during the game and this is discussed further in the later section on teams.

A performance can fall through if discrediting information about the performers becomes apparent (Goffman 1959: 59). This is the same for

LIVERPOOL JOHN MOORES UNIVERSITY
LEARNING SERVICES

the senior officers as it was for the PCs and other police groups. But as senior officers have the added element of supervision they must also appear competent to lead (Manning 1997: 145). One chief inspector handled this by 'cracking down' on break-ins into cars and houses around the football ground. He was doing so by using officers who were familiar with the area and the people in it. This resulted in fewer break-ins and he said this helps 'keep his stats down'. Had a high level of break-ins continued this would have been reflected in his statistics and his ability to be an effective senior officer might have been questioned. Unlike PCs, senior officers must directly answer to outside political pressures so controlling mistakes is a vital part of their performance (Reuss-Ianni 1983: 50, Fielding 1988: 181).

Typologies

In the previous two chapters I have discussed the many and varied typologies of supporters that the police officers use during their football duties. These categories help make what might otherwise be an unpredictable and confusing event more organised and understandable (Reiner 2000a: 95, Manning 1997: 202). Senior police officers are no exception to this. In fact, they have more opinions on supporter (non-hooligan) typologies than any other police group. The main four categories they suggest are general supporters, visiting supporters, troublesome supporters, and hooligans.

There were many characteristics within the category of general fans. Some officers said that the majority of football supporters were there to have a good time and did not cause any trouble. Others said that supporters come to the match to get a release and take their frustrations out on an authority figure, which the police represent. Others said (like some of the PCs) that supporters are animals or are operating on tribal instincts. For example, a sergeant jokingly called the supporters in cells at the station 'chimpanzees'. Two officers even mentioned the work of Desmond Morris (1981) as being applicable to football supporters at this ground.[30] One inspector suggested that supporters are fickle. Sometimes they will do anything to help and other times they are determined to cause trouble. Most of these categories seem to stress emotion over rationality as the main motivator in the behaviour of general fans. Senior officers have also said that supporters are not smart and that they are often involved in criminal activities outside football.[31]

Senior officers suggest that they can get a 'feeling' for potential trouble between groups of fans. Manning (1997: 265) has noted that crucial to the police role is making sense of the interaction they observe in order to ascertain its meaning (and ultimately decide if it warrants arrest). For senior officers at football, this takes into account the particular team that is playing, as each visiting support side is seen to have a different mentality. Senior officers feel that Rangers and Celtic fans are the worst behaved. As was mentioned in Chapter 3, the visiting supporters and the home supporters nearest to them in the stadium have the heaviest police presence, while the family and executive sections have only a couple of officers in each. This suggests that visiting supporters are one of the main concerns for the senior officers. One sergeant said that they often come to the city early with their families to do some shopping. Then the 'lads' go to the pubs for a while and later the game. So visiting supporters are a concern not only in the ground but also for several hours before that in the city centre.

There did seem to be a distinction in the minds of many of the senior officers between football supporters who cause trouble and football hooligans. The troublesome supporters only become so due to a number of factors. According to the senior officers, it is because they are young men, under the influence of alcohol, in a crowd with their best friends at an event that is very important to them. This leads them to be more boisterous and troublesome than they would usually be. One sergeant said that nine out of ten supporters do as the police tell them. However, one out of ten will not because he has never done as he was told anyway. It is on these few that the police focus their energy within the ground. Senior officers also feel that evening kick-off times contribute to behaviour problems at the games because the supporters have more time to drink. So according to senior officers, it is both external and internal factors that determine whether fans will become troublesome.[32]

When discussing the hooligans themselves, opinions of the senior officers varied from calling them cowards who are afraid of the police to right-wing extremists. On one end, some senior officers suggested that hooligans were just a group of 'likely lads' who drank a lot and did not wear club colours. They never really engage in fights, just dance around each other and throw things (in a similar vein, Armstrong [1998: 220] found that not all encounters between rival hooligan groups end up in violence and few serious injuries are incurred; see Giulianotti [1996] for the choreography of hooligan encounters). One sergeant feels that the word 'hooligan' is used too easily among the police (Coalter 1985) and that the men in question do not do the amount of damage that they could do if they wished. They just use football as an opportunity to be anti-social because they cannot be anti-social anywhere else. On the other end of the spectrum, some senior officers feel that the hooligans are organised enough to have developed a national network (see Giulianotti 1999: 50–1 for more on this), as do many of the police football spotters. Hooligans from various parts of the country and Scotland are believed to team up to fight common enemies. This 'National Firm' seems at times to be more of a concern to the senior officers than the local hooligans are. Regardless of where a senior officer falls on the spectrum, they all tend to feel that they know who the individual hooligans are or could identify someone as a hooligan based on that person's appearance and the context in which he is encountered. This is similar to Fyfe's finding (1992) that police officers look for continuity in social activities, time and space. People are more likely to be picked up by the police if they demonstrate a contradiction in any of these categories. For example, working class men walking through a middle class area at night are more likely to be questioned than if they had been walking through a working class area. However, whether the senior officers have as fine-tuned a sense as the detectives or spotters do when it comes to picking hooligans out of a Saturday crowd is another matter.

Not only do the senior officers have many different typologies than the PCs, MSUs and detectives/spotters do when it comes to football; these typologies seem to be static. For example, a senior officer deemed one group of visiting supporters to be relatively harmless and did not expect them to cause much trouble that day. However, the last time that team was in the city for a match it brought a significant number of hooligans who caused the detectives a lot of concern throughout the day. This shows the lack of communication between the various police interaction teams. When speaking to members of an MSU, one officer said that the older officers still 'panic' at the word 'hooligan' because they remember the days when there were running battles in the streets (Fielding 1988: 177). So even though violence at football is relatively uncommon now, hooligans at the games are still a major concern for some of the senior officers organising the policing of it.

The differences in the typologies the senior officers employ could be symptomatic of the different methods they espouse to police the hooligans. As I have shown here, some senior officers suggest that football hooligans are not really a huge problem, while others seem to view them as the biggest threat to modern community safety, with only the police as a 'thin blue line' between order and chaos (Holdaway 1989: 65). As such, these different senior officers may instruct their constables and detectives to use different degrees of proactiveness when policing the hooligans.

Rules of engagement

This section will consider the underlying rules of engagement between senior officers and supporters (the actions which Goffman [1959: 27] labels as 'parts'). As senior officers are usually in a supervisory or advisory role, they do not always have that much direct interaction with the supporters. However, they can influence interaction on the ground between the supporters and the PCs, MSUs, and detectives/spotters through their briefings and policies. Senior officers intend to set the tone for the day so have a part to play in the events that take place and the rules of engagement that are followed. Consequently, the first part of this section will consider the briefings and instructions that the senior officers give to other officers at a football match. The second part will look at some of the few interactions that do take place between senior officers and supporters.

Briefings and policies

The general briefing is one of the key duties of the senior officer in charge at a football match. It is through this that the other officers learn what their duties are for the day, how they should go about executing them, and what intelligence there is to aid them (O'Neill 2004: 97, Rubinstein 1973: 54). Quite often the senior officer takes what he or she calls the 'firm but fair' approach. This instructs the officers to treat all fans well and help them where they can, but not to take any hassle from anyone. At the first sign of trouble, the person should be dealt with appropriately. This is especially the case with the hooligans. The senior officers often recommend a very hard-line approach with these fans and urge the officers to be 'vigilant'. Officers at the ground should throw them out right away if they give any trouble and search them for weapons or controlled containers if 'they need it'. If it is not possible to arrest all the people involved in an incident either in or outside of the ground, the PCs should arrest the 'ringleaders' or just a few supporters to serve as a warning to the others (O'Neill 2004: 97–8). As previous chapters have demonstrated however, the police do not actually hold universally recognised definitions for 'hooligans', or 'ringleaders', although the senior officers seem to assume that they do. PCs must then rely on their own definitions, which may not be the same as those of their supervisors. This supports my continuous argument that these officers do not occupy the same interaction teams, for while they speak the same language their meanings are different, and no one really acknowledges this openly (O'Neill 2004: 98). Reuss-Ianni (1983) has also noted this lack of communication between the two police groups. 'The inevitable result appears to be continuous disintegration in communication, morale, and effectiveness, due to the fact that there is no longer a common context for interpretation or action. Instead, each culture (each side) selectively interprets events to justify its own position' (1983: 118).

There are also occasions where senior officers suggest policing techniques that are not strictly within the rule of law. The main example here is with open containers of alcohol in the city. At the time of research, the main city I studied did not have any law that prohibited drinking in public spaces. However, during a football match senior officers would sometimes suggest to the PCs that they approach supporters drinking outside and ask them to pour out the contents of their containers. Supporters, especially ones from other cities, may not have realised that they were not obligated under law to do this, and so followed the officers' instructions. The officers tended not to volunteer the information that the supporters were not violating any city regulations. Bittner (1967) discusses similar techniques by the police on skid-row who arrest people more for their own good than for legitimate legal reasons. At times the peacekeeping officer and the law enforcer are difficult to separate. Police will occasionally give supporters instructions in an authoritative manner that are for the supporters' own good and produce overall social tranquillity, even though the supporters are not legally obligated to follow them. Police refer to this kind of action colloquially as the 'Ways and Means Act' (Reiner 1997: 713).

Senior officers can not only influence interaction at the match through their instructions, but also through the policies that they follow. At the training course they are taught only to interfere in a situation if necessary; that sometimes it is better to let small infractions in the stadium go if addressing them would only cause more hassles (Fielding [1988: 151] also mentions that it is not always advisable to make an arrest). So, if an officer calls in to the control room to find out if he or she should act, the response may often be 'No'. Arresting depletes resources and so is only done inside football grounds when absolutely necessary. The senior officers on the football training course were also advised to promote the use of a 'happy face' among their PCs whenever they can. A good attitude is felt to go a long way in preventing some situations from occurring at all. They should try to help the supporters have a good time, as that is the point of the game anyway. Sometimes flags will be allowed into the ground (or not removed) if they are not harming anyone and help bring about a fun atmosphere.[33] So senior officers can have an indirect influence on interaction at the match through their briefings and policies, but this is not absolute. The constables themselves may choose not to follow these guidelines and instead rely on their own interpretations of the situation, which could be just as effective in maintaining what they deem to be 'order' (O'Neill 2004: 98).

Actual interaction

Most of the direct interaction I observed between the senior officers and the supporters was in the football ground. Senior officers in the city centre were there as supervisors and observers and so tended not to have much opportunity to engage with the supporters walking past. The one main occasion I witnessed where a senior officer did encounter supporters in the city centre was when the coach of National Firm hooligans was apprehended. The superintendent boarded the bus and announced that he was invoking his emergency powers and was detaining all those who did not have football tickets until the game ended. He told me later that the hooligans were not too happy about that and that he has no such thing as emergency powers, but he would find a legal reason to justify detaining them later. However, the plan worked and there was no major violence that day between the hooligans. Young (1991: 175) notes the way police handle a situation that falls outside of specific legal statues. In his case, a man was arrested for flashing a simulated penis made from wool and nylon at a woman. Many officers carefully searched through the reference books to find a way to quantify the offence. In the end, they fell back on 'insulting behaviour whereby a breach of the peace can be anticipated'. He writes that 'the whole incident is really outside of the central tenets of the system, but the (police) men and women search to make it fit known patterns of disorder'. Reiner (1997: 730) also discusses legal justification after the fact and other aspects of police discretion and Chatterton (1989) describes how police officers use paperwork to cover up creative uses of their powers.

Inside the ground some senior officers will speak to the PCs about the supporters around them, but not try to whisper or disguise what they are saying so the supporters cannot hear. More often than not what they are saying (usually about the inherent nature of football supporters) is not flattering, but if the supporters hear they do not show it and the senior officers did not seem too concerned if they do. But whenever a supporter does approach them, the senior officers are always friendly and polite. And the supporters in turn are sometimes helpful to the officers, such as by picking up their hats if they blow off. Most people, such as PCs and MSU officers, would probably wait until they were in the backstage to make critical observations of this kind as this information could threaten the performance the person is trying to give (Goffman 1959). However, as some senior officers do not see the need to do this, their low opinions of supporters must not be a regarded as secret or discrediting information. Their image of control and power may even be enhanced by their ability to hold contempt for those they are policing and yet treat them as fairly and politely as they do everyone else. Senior officers do not work with supporters on a daily basis, so they have no personal need to try to maintain a good rapport with individual people. They are demonstrating that they not only have control over others, they have a good deal of self-control as well. In this case, the senior officers seem very aware that they are putting on an act for the supporters.

The strict approach the senior officers advocate in the briefings is not always the approach that they themselves follow inside the ground. They too, use the kind of discretion for which constables are infamous (McBarnet 1979, Reiner 1997: 723–52). On one occasion a father approached a sergeant and an inspector and asked if his son could stand behind the last row of seats in the concourse if it started raining. According to the ground and police rules, all fans must be in their seats during the game unless they are getting food or going to the toilets. However, the senior officers in question did not say no to the father, but only that they would wait and see how busy it was later. Their firm advice on arrest and keeping out drunken fans is also not quite followed to the letter. One senior officer told me that visiting fans are usually ejected rather than arrested. They are too much hassle to process as arrests. It would thus seem that previous observations that police are easier on visiting fans are somewhat justified.[34] A sergeant described an occasion to me where he refused entry to a drunken sup- porter, but the supporter kept coming back in different clothes to try to gain entry. Eventually the sergeant allowed him in because of the sheer ingenuity of his approach and because 'he was sober by then'. The sergeant told me this story to demonstrate that the police are not heartless and appreciate humour in fans. This, and the other examples in this paragraph show that despite the fire and brimstone preached by senior officers, they too are subject to the interaction rules of engage-ment as were described in this chapter and use their own discretion even when they would formally instruct another officer not to do so.

Teams

Like all the previous discussions of interaction in this book, the 'team' has been the main unit of organisation. Senior officers are no excep-tion to this but, as this section will demonstrate, their personification of the 'team' is different to all those yet discussed. To analyse the senior officers' interaction teams (Goffman 1959: 83) I will discuss the membership criteria of each team, the audience to which each team performs, the definition of the situation the teams espouse and script the teams follow. In this way it will become apparent the unique way in which senior officers work with others to maintain their performance.

In deciding the membership criteria of senior officers' teams, the first thing to consider is rank. This plays an important part in determining the duties and actions of the particular officer. In this vein, sergeants from each subdivision can be considered members of the same team. They do not always work together at the matches, but their level of responsibility sets them apart from the constables. They present them-selves in a similar way: not quite full senior officers, but not quite con-stables anymore either. Manning (1980: 101–2) has also noted this middle role that sergeants occupy, describing them as the 'axis around which enforcement rotates' (1980: 101) as they must negotiate the demands of both sides (see also Fielding 1988: 176 and Reuss-Ianni 1983: 9, 63). Their perspective on the police force and football is unique within their subdivision due to the liminal role they occupy.

Goffman suggests that teams are usually comprised of more than one person. However, it is possible to have a team of only one member (1959: 86). This seems to be the case with the more senior officers. In the football context, there are not many of them present, especially within the ranks of superintendent, and they do not work together. Match Commanders and section supervisors (usually inspectors) can set their own rules as to the behaviour of the other officers and sup-porters (within the wider guidelines of the football script, which will be discussed later) and so do not tend to (and are not required to) have a unified approach to football policing. Thus, they cannot be considered members of one team, but have become their own one-member teams. This is what differentiates their interaction during a football match day from that of the constables, MSUs and detectives or spotters. Their teams are formed in a completely different way, based on their right to autonomy, which leaves them rather isolated.

However, the difficulty with this is that police officers have an underlying association with each other. Though as we have seen here and in previous chapters, the individual ranks and roles may operate differently, they are still 'the police' and were all trained in the same way and instilled with the same institutional values (for example, see Fielding 1988, Young 1991 and Manning 1997). So while the higher-ranking senior officers at football are all one-member teams, they are also fellows of a greater police community. This community may not operate as a team in Goffman's sense, but to the wider public it appears as though it does and the police encourage this view (Manning 1997: 25–7). It gives the appearance of a unity that does not exist, but the underlying loose association among all police officers is no less real. This police community also makes it difficult for the members to take on non-police team roles. When off-duty officers come to football matches, they frequently stand in the back of the stand and socialise with the on-duty officers. In my experience with the police they seem to have strong friendships with each other and frequently socialise together outside of work (Fielding 1988: 36). Thus, any discussion of teams within the police must also incorporate this underlying police community.

Determining the audience for the actions of the senior officers is also problematic. Some senior officers are football supporters themselves and so may have trouble setting themselves apart from the fans. One sergeant said that he and all supporters are 'moaners', and that they are not happy unless they have something to moan about. He also admits that sometimes he does not always watch the crowd but the match instead (an example of Cain's 'easing behaviour' [1971: 72]). In this case, the fans are not really the audience for the actions of this sergeant as he often sees himself as one of them. Higher-level senior officers have two main audiences: the supporters and the other officers. As was mentioned in previous chapters, the police sometimes perform more for each other than for the public and senior officers are no exception to this. They must give briefings to the PCs (and this is a case where they really are 'on stage'), assign responsibilities, and make difficult decisions in an authoritative way. A commanding officer cannot appear to be unsure of himself or herself in these situations and so must give a convincing performance to the other officers. Once they are out in the city centre or in the ground, then they too must also make sure the performance the supporters see is just as calm, controlled, and assured as the rest of the police teams.

In addition to the definition of the situation suggested above, the senior officers in the city centre also present the situation to the supporters as one that is not all that different from normality. They instruct their officers to follow groups of hooligans if they are spotted, break them up into smaller groups if they can, try to prevent them from running, keep them on the pavement, and not to hesitate to arrest them if need be. They and their officers make sure general supporters are not too loud and boisterous and bothering people unrelated to football. This is a difficult task, but they try to make sure the supporters know that the world does not stop and start for them and that obnoxious behaviour will not be tolerated. Skolnick has also found that the police tend to have a more conservative definition of 'order' than the public does (1966: 47–8) and this is certainly the case for football match days. The senior officers around the ground also try to catch the 'troublemakers' before they get in, as ejecting them once they are inside is difficult. They look for people who are obviously drunk or people they recognise as being a problem in the past. They try to structure the crowd itself and thus influence the definition of the situation in that way. Football is presented as an arena where the police have the final say and only the 'true' supporters who are there to see the match and not cause problems are let in. Smith and Gray (1985: 336) also found that senior officers tend to speak in general terms like this when discussing policing objectives.

The final aspects of team level interaction I will consider are the scripts the teams follow. For the highest-level officers in football this is more clear-cut. The script they must cover in briefings is predetermined and generally the same for each match. They tell their officers what behaviour to expect from the fans, what will justify an arrest, which supporters are the most troublesome, what the emergency procedures are, what the intelligence is for the match, where they are to stand, what groups they will be in, where they move to and when, etc. (O'Neill 2004: 97, Rubinstein 1973: 58–60). However, each senior officer (one-member team) interprets this script in his or her own way and so the instructions for one match may be quite different in some respects to those for other matches. For example, the level of contact the detective or spotter is to have with the hooligans depends entirely on the superintendent assigned to the game. Some want the detectives/spotters to be very distant and others want them to watch hooligans closely. Other senior officers (below that of match commander or overall supervisor in the city centre) follow the script of their own experience in football. Many have been doing this for years and each senior officer has a clear idea of how the policing should go in his or her own area (Manning 1980: 16). At times this may conflict with what was discussed in the general briefing (see Fielding 1988: 85 for more on lack of communication within management).

One common feature among all these scripts is the use of military language. For example, one supervisory officer said he would go 'survey the troops', another called the number of arrests a 'body count', and debris around the ground was referred to as 'ammunition'. This leads one to think of a football match as a military operation between the ordered and powerful police and the anarchic and violent supporters. Chatterton (1979: 83–4), Reuss-Ianni (1983: 21) and Hobbs (1988: 78–9) find that the military model is an attractive one for senior officers as it presents an apparent way to control the lower ranks. It can also help to keep the public at a safe distance in that one police commander defended his lack of public consultation by saying 'No good general ever declares his forces in a prelude to any kind of attack' (Harman 1982: 47). Referring to the military is not just restricted to the senior officers, either. Fielding (1988: 61) found that new recruits likened their experiences in the job to being in the army. Reuss-Ianni (1983: 37) also found that patrol officers see themselves as a kind of occupying military force. However, I only ever heard senior officers use militaristic terms during my fieldwork. This simplistic metaphoric language seems to be a common feature of institutions of social control. Young (1991: 76) writes that the army itself uses concepts of bodily pollution to refer to other regiments or units. The uniform styles thus mark a significant difference between the pure 'us' and the polluted 'them'. As I have shown here, however, interaction at football is far more complex than the army metaphor allows.

Regions

This final section of my analysis of senior police officers and supporters will consider the regions in which their interaction occurs (Goffman 1959: 109). The earlier section on the 'setting' of interaction discussed the basic areas where interaction takes place, regarding it more as a backdrop. This analysis will look at how the actors use those areas. In this case, the regions of interaction and the use of space have their own role to play in the encounters between senior police officers and supporters. Thus, analysing these regions will help clarify the interaction that results. I will consider senior officers' use of physical space outside and inside the ground and their use of symbolic space.

Physical space

One of the primary concerns of the senior officers at football, especially those with a command role, is to control the physical space the supporters use or to which they have access inside and outside the ground even though there is no formal mandate compelling them to do so in the city centre (segregation in the ground *is* a formal strategy, however). They feel this will reduce the chances for disorder and thus influence the behaviour of the supporters. This section on physical space will examine if that is actually the case. Outside the football ground the PCs and Mobile Units are strategically placed to help guide supporters down certain paths to the ground, depending on whether they are home or visiting supporters. This is the main reason behind having PCs in the streets before a match and it is the senior officers who decide the exact positions of the officers to maintain segregation of the fans. Sometimes barriers are erected to prevent opposing supporters from encountering each other and compromising these segregation tactics. This is where the officers encounter hostility. They cannot totally control where people park or where they want to walk, and do not like making exceptions to the rules for those who persist in arguing their cases. One senior officer said that everyone should be treated the same for safety reasons because 'even if someone looks nice, they may not be'. Some of those who cause the most problems are people from the home city who support the visiting team. They tend to not come to the ground from the same direction as the other visiting supporters and make maintaining segregation outside difficult.

Physical space is also used to attempt to control the hooligans. There are a few 'flashpoints' in the city where fights are more likely to happen because rival supporters' paths come close together or because the area is difficult to police. In the main city I studied, there is an area across from the hooligans' favourite pub that is one of these flashpoints. If the hooligans are leaving this pub in a large group, the police will try to hold some back so that they are broken into smaller groups. Occasionally the bouncers at the pub will help by closing one of the exit doors so that the hooligans must leave in single file. Senior officers feel that this tactic reduces the chances of a fight occurring across the road because the hooligans are not in a large number. Occasionally, the football ground itself is used to control the hooligans. One Match

Commander said he preferred to have the hooligans in the ground where he could keep an eye on them than have them wandering around the city centre where they could meet up with other hooligans. This is rather ironic, as it was not too long ago that the police were doing all they could to get the violent fans *out* of the ground.[35] However, in recent times organised football hooligans have tended not to be very disorderly inside the ground (Garland and Rowe 2000). Their organised fights are usually restricted to areas within the city (Giulianotti and Armstrong 2002) so senior officers do not have anything to fear by keeping them inside the ground.

The other group of fans that the senior officers wish to control spatially is the visiting supporters. One football ground I studied does not have parking facilities for visiting supporters' buses, so they are usually parked about fifteen minutes' walking distance away. This freedom of movement makes the police nervous as anything could happen to the fans in that time. Also, visiting supporters in the city centre before the match could be easy targets for home supporters wishing to start a fight. The senior officers never relax at a football game until the visiting supporters are on their buses and out of the city. After that, the main target of football aggression is gone and the controls can be eased.

Inside the ground, the spatial control of supporters is an even greater concern. The main issue again is segregation, for which there are a variety of techniques to keep the home and visiting supporters apart. It seems that in general for the senior officers, supporters and freedom in space are linked in their minds with danger.[36] In order to keep the peace and ensure safety, supporters and their movements must be controlled, prescribed, and monitored at all times. If a new issue comes up in crowd control, the usual response from the police seems to be to constrict supporters' space even more. As Mary Douglas (1986: 92) has suggested, institutions (like the police) respond to problematic situations only within the limited range of their experience. 'If the institution is one that depends on participation, it will reply to our frantic question: "More participation!" If it is one that depends on authority, it will only reply: "More authority!"' Thus if the police feel their mandate of control is threatened, they tend to respond by trying to exert even more control.

However, it appears on closer investigation that segregation and the other means of physical control only work because they have the consent of the majority of the fans. As was demonstrated in a previous chapter, the supporters have many ways of circumventing the controls placed upon them. If they really wanted to get to each other and fight, there is little the police could do about it. For example, in one ground I visited, the home and visiting supporters share a concession area and usually do so without trouble or segregation. However, when a particular team that has a traditional rivalry with the home side visits, barriers are brought into the concession area and there is usually a lot of hostility between the groups at half-time. So it would appear that the spatial control the senior officers demand is largely an illusion, but perhaps it is an illusion that the supporters need as much as the officers. To be able to make threatening gestures at other fans and yet know you will be safe from retaliation is easier to put down to segregation tactics than lack of gumption on your part to get around them. This allows the supporters to have their fun and yet be safe and save face (Goffman 1967: 9). The senior officers need this illusion of control to maintain their authority in this arena, justify their presence there and continue the premise of a supreme moral order (Manning 1997: 120, Armstrong and Hobbs 1995: 190–1). Thus interaction in the realm of physical space has special salience for senior officers who are answerable to a wider political sphere (Reuss-Ianni 1983: 55–6), but they cannot present themselves as successful to this sphere without the assistance of the policed. These groups have become interdependent to some extent.

Symbolic space

In order to regain some of the control they have lost in physical space, some supporters may use symbolic space (a term I have derived from Goffman's 'territories of the self' [1971: 29–40]) to gain an advantage over senior officers. For example, one supporter was angry that a senior officer would not let him through the barriers to go back into the ground after a game and find a jacket he had lost. The only recourse he had was to announce the senior officer's name loudly when he overheard a PC say it, and promise to report him. By doing so the supporter made clear that while he may be powerless to get to the ground, he could enter the officer's symbolic space by attacking him personally if need be. By doing so he violated the senior officer's 'face'. According to Goffman in *Interaction Ritual* (1967: 5–7), this is the self-image one claims in reference to accepted social values, which include status. Thus this football fan refused to support the high status a senior officer can expect and tried to make him lose face by treating him as a subordinate he needed to report. However, the senior officer did not look concerned.

As Bale (1994) has suggested, the football ground itself can come to have a symbolic and emotional significance to some supporters. One Match Commander referred to the front entrance to his ground as 'Mecca' because the supporters flock to it to 'worship' whenever an exciting event happens with the team. In addition to this topophilia (love of a space), football grounds have spaces that may become points of honour to some supporters, as the following example demonstrates. One ground I visited uses metal barriers to keep the exiting groups of opposing supporters apart after a match. However, instead of taking the long way around, one group of home fans prefers to wait until all the visiting fans have cleared and the barriers are removed to walk home. According to the senior officers, the fans would rather be delayed than allow the opposition to make them change their route. Senior officers have to make sure this corner is carefully policed because of the segregation issue and the build-up of home fans that routinely occurs there. If anyone violates that barrier, he or she will be arrested.

Summary

This chapter has considered the role of senior police officers in the running of a football match day. Despite being the leaders and co-ordinators of the football policing efforts, senior officers do not seem to occupy a team themselves. The only ones who might be considered a team are the sergeants. Their marginal position (as they are no longer PCs but not senior management either) within the police hierarchy means that they have similar performance experiences and the same audiences for their actions. However, senior officers above the rank of sergeant approach their duties largely independently and as so do not seem to identify with anyone. They have become one-member teams (Goffman 1959: 86). This is how senior officers are unique when it comes to interaction at football. They work largely alone in their isolated or marginal teams. Because of this, senior officers each have their own approaches to the football match day. This has resulted in a very detailed typology system among them, especially on the concept of a 'supporter'. Like a C.E.O. who has never met his or her customers some senior police officers may rarely encounter football supporters directly, but all have opinions on how supporters behave, why, and what their inherent nature is like. As senior officers have no team members with whom to collaborate on their performance, they must have a belief system, i.e. a system of myths, to guide and inform their actions.

Manning has written at length about the 'police myth' which 'alleviates societal crises by providing a verbal explanation for causes, meanings, and consequences of events that might otherwise be considered inexplicable' (1997: 279). It is a way of putting order to chaos. The supporter typologies the senior officers use helps them predict what supporters will do and why. This informs their decisions on how to instruct their officers.

This then raises the question of how appropriate these instructions about methods for policing the supporters may be. Some constables seemed to suggest that the senior officers have outdated ideas on football policing and football hooliganism. They urge their officers to be vigilant with 'hooligans', but without defining who may qualify for each category. It is assumed that the officers know whom they mean by each, but this may not necessarily be the case. As has been demonstrated in previous chapters, the definitions of these terms can vary widely from one officer to another. In addition, violence at football is relatively rare now, but still seems to be a major concern for the senior officers. Because the police operate as separate teams they do not communicate with each other well and so cannot challenge each other's outdated notions. The use of military terms in their briefings also gives the football policing system an aura of simplicity that it actually lacks. Senior officers may do this because they mostly have indirect interaction with supporters and so do not have a lot of personal experience on which to draw. Constables do not always follow senior officers' instructions (and neither do some of the senior officers themselves). However, order may still be maintained through each team's own negotiations with the supporters. So the instructions senior officers give are only one version of how things are 'supposed' to be.

The above examples illustrate one type of indirect interaction the senior officers have with supporters. Their briefings set the tone for the police officers that day, who in turn encounter the supporters with this in mind. Another kind of indirect interaction is the way senior officers structure the actual crowd at the football match. Not only do senior officers determine which constables are positioned where in the ground, but they can also refuse entry to those they feel would be disruptive to the game. They use their typologies to weed out the supporters who have undesirable personal attributes that may influence their behaviour. As such, they have a hand in moulding the football experiences of the people inside the ground by keeping certain people out. When they do encounter supporters, senior officers are friendly with them but often make loud judgements about supporters to other officers. So unlike most constables, they do not feel the need to keep these comments in their backstage area.

In addition to avoiding certain types of person, the senior officers also manipulate space in the ground to avoid certain types of external factors that they feel can influence supporter behaviour. The main example here is segregation and the distance that needs to be maintained between support sides to ensure the least amount of trouble. As was suggested in the text, the tactics the senior officers employ appear to be successful, but this could be more due to supporter consent than any inherent value to the tactics themselves. Supporters use the segregation at football to appear 'hard' when they taunt each other, but they do not lose face by failing to actually fight with each other. However, there are many techniques the supporters can, and sometimes do, use to get around the spatial control the senior officers seem to exert over them. Thus, this analysis of senior officers at football has illustrated the importance of studying interaction from the perspective of teams. Senior officers still need to negotiate with other officers and with the supporters themselves to be effective. They need to make sure they are presenting themselves in appositive light to their outside political observers, but they can only have influence if these other groups let them. Therefore, the power in football policing does not just flow from the top down, but also from the very bottom upwards. Senior officers are just as subject to the influence of interaction as everyone else is. However, their experiences are different from that of the PCs, MSUs and detectives for the reasons discussed above: they have different typologies, they do not hide their opinions of supporters, they have outside political pressures to meet which they achieve through an interdependence with supporters in the use of physical space, they have more indirect (rather than direct) interaction with fans and they are comprised of one-member teams.

Senior officers I interviewed refer to football as a 'planned major incident'. Officially, it is treated just like any other major public order event. However, one wonders if this is actually the case. Football supporters seem in police thinking to be quite distinct from other members of the public. In addition, the officers, especially senior officers, are not removed from the event at hand. As was discussed above, they influence the football game day by manipulating the football crowd through consideration of the internal and external factors they feel contribute to football violence. They cannot be seen as neutral observers to the action like they might be at other large public gatherings like a festival or horticultural exhibit.

Football has too turbulent a history for the police to approach it completely objectively.

This and the previous two chapters have demonstrated the intricate relationships many police teams at football have with football supporters. However, the way these teams relate to each other is also important to consider. As we have seen, there are many different performance teams within any police force. But unlike many other teams in our society, police teams belong to one underlying community. Even though they have different definitions of the situation and different audiences, they are still all considered (by themselves and the wider public) to be *the police*. They train together and often socialise together, so while they are not all teammates, they are all fellows of the same police community. Some of these teams are less well integrated into the fellowship than others, as I have demonstrated here with senior officers. This outsider experience will be seen in even greater detail with the subjects of the next chapter, women police constables (WPCs).

6
Women Police Constables

This chapter will examine the role of female police officers (known as women police constables, or WPCs) at football. As they were a very small proportion of the police officers present at the matches my analysis of their interaction with supporters will not be as detailed as that in previous chapters. However they are still important to consider, and to consider separately from other officers, as their interactions were different from their male colleagues and because they represent a unique development of Goffman's (1959) 'team' concept. This will be developed later. I will begin this chapter with a look at some previous discussions of WPCs and will then move on to my own analysis of their work at football. This chapter will conclude by returning to the idea of the 'underlying police community', which was introduced in Chapter 5, as the experiences of WPCs show well how this concept works by giving the illusion of a united police service which does not actually exist.

Previous research on WPCs

There has been much written in the past about the police occupational culture and the various adaptations that officers have made to it (see for example Muir 1977 and Reiner 1997). Most of these analyses did not consider the unique experiences of policewomen, however. WPCs have had to make very different adaptations to their role and status than male officers. Martin (1979) was one of the first writers on women police officers, and she identified two extremes in how these women coped with their situation. She called these the POLICEwoman and the policeWOMAN. The former refers to someone who adopts the police role entirely and the male approach to it, shirking associations with femininity. The latter refers to someone who sees herself as a woman first, a 'lady in uniform', and avoids confrontation. These are two ends in a continuum rather than distinct categories, but show the roles that she felt the women had to constantly negotiate in order to be accepted. Brown and Heidensohn (2000: 128) argue that the policeWOMAN category does not really exist anymore, but was more for those leftover from the days of the separate policewomen's departments (to be discussed later).

In her study of policewomen from the US and the UK, Heidensohn (1992: 118–55) developed several 'organising ideas', or focus points, for understanding the experiences of female officers. Some of these are: a sense of mission, pioneers, transformation scenes, professionalism, soft cops and top cops. Previous writers have also identified a sense of mission among the police (Reiner 2000a), but Heidensohn (1992: 125–6) argues that the one the WPCs espouse is different from that of male officers. Their mission involved more personal struggle than that of the men to gain acceptance. These women also saw themselves as pioneers as some are still finding departments or ranks that have yet to have a female officer in them (Heidensohn 1992: 135, Silvestri 2003). Transformation scenes relate to those incidents where a policewoman was able to demonstrate her competence to her male colleagues and gain acceptance. All officers have to go through processes of initiation, but it is especially difficult for the women as they have more to prove and thus these scenes can be vitally important (Heidensohn 1992: 143). Many policewomen in this study identified 'professionalism' as key to their success. This involved 'going by the book, doing things properly, treating the public, including offenders, well, and working extremely hard' (Heidensohn 1992: 145). While some of these concepts overlap and may even be contradictory, they were crucial in the minds of the policewomen as key to demonstrating their skills. 'Soft cops' refers to the social service role that police officers are increasingly being asked to play. Policewomen are likely to be expected to not only be involved with this work, but to be good at it. Some felt despair at this, while others were very committed to the work (Heidensohn 1992: 150–2). The final category of 'top cops' refers to those women who have been able to gain significant promotions. Many of them mentioned how they had to rely on their own resources to get there, as there were so few role models to guide them. None found it easy to gain promotion and said there are formidable demands from senior men (Heidensohn 1992: 153–4, Silvestri 2003: 99–100). So while Heidensohn did not produce the clear-cut typologies that other authors have devised, it is clear that the policewoman's experience of and response to the demands of the police role will be different from that of the men. They accept the values of policing as much as the men do (Heidensohn 1992: 121), but respond to it in their own ways.

It has been argued that the police occupational culture in general is one designed with men in mind. Smith and Gray (1985: 372) found a 'cult of masculinity' among police officers as reflected in their attitudes and norms. Violence and physical courage are glamorised; excessive drinking demonstrates worth and masculine solidarity, even if one's colleague is in the wrong, is vital. These tests tend to exclude women and affect how the officers perceive female members of the public. Fielding (1994) developed this link between the masculine police ideology and its consequences for behaviour in that the occupational culture highlights:

(i) aggressive, physical action; (ii) a strong sense of competitiveness and preoccupation with the imagery of conflict; (iii) exaggerated heterosexual orientations, often articulated in terms of misogynistic and patriarchal attitudes towards women; and (iv) the operation of rigid in-group/out-group distinctions whose consequences are strongly exclusionary in the case of out-groups and strongly assertive of loyalty and affinity in the case of in-groups. (1994: 47)

Not only is desirable police work and behaviour seen as masculine, but also the undesirable has become associated with the feminine in police ideology. Hunt (1990: 8–11) identified a series of dichotomies that police officers use to structure and define their experiences through implicit cultural codes. These include an assumption that 'real' police work involves action and force, and thus requires male skills. Anything else is anathema to that. For example, the academy, social service, paperwork and cleanliness are associated with the female, and thus are 'not us'. The street, rescue activity, crime fighting and dirt are the valued male preserves. The thought of allowing women police officers into that dirty male arena not only challenges the police notion of the 'moral' woman but creates a perceived threat that the women will expose male indiscretions and will end the myth of police work focusing on crime-fighting (Hunt 1990: 12–15). Hunt feels that if policewomen are ever to be accepted they have to create a new category for themselves that removes them from these dichotomies (1990: 26).

The police see their purpose as being crime-fighters (Fielding 1988) and this involves skills that policewomen are not perceived to have.

Primarily, male police officers stress the need for psychical strength and 'presence' (or authority) to handle police work and they argue that policewomen are thus not capable officers. This is despite the fact that police rarely need to use physical force anyway and that managing a hostile situation need not involve strength (Fielding and Fielding 1992: 211–13, Brown et al 1993: 121–4). As a consequence, policewomen discuss experiencing overly chivalrous behaviour from male colleagues who try to 'protect them', which suggests that the women cannot do the job on their own and put their partners in more danger (Fielding and Fielding 1992: 209, C. Martin 1996: 520, Bryant et al 1985: 239). Policewomen find that if they are able to do their job well, male colleagues see them as unfeminine and the success of one woman does not carry over to all policewomen. However if a policewoman is seen to fail in her work, all policewomen are judged to be inept at policing. (Bryant et al 1985: 239–40, Reuss-Ianni 1983: 61). Many policewomen find that there are only two identity categories open to them at work. Bryant et al (1985: 239–40) argue that these women are either 'prudes' or 'butch'. Hunt (1990: 19) and Heidensohn (1992: 108) found 'whores' and 'dykes' to be the more common cultural categories. Regardless of which are more accurate, it is clear that male colleagues try to reduce the power and effectiveness of policewomen by treating them in sexually based ways, rather than as officers in themselves.

Policewomen used to be restricted to their own specialist departments within forces to deal with issues involving women and children, the more social service aspects of policing. Those departments have been disbanded after the Sex Discrimination Act in 1975 and women are supposed to be fully integrated into police work (C. Martin 1996). However, Bryant et al found that many policewomen are still expected to handle these types of cases, sometimes in addition to their other duties (1985: 237). They argue that women are also less likely to be assigned to the more action-oriented events or be in situations likely to lead to an arrest. Social service type work is still undervalued in policing, even though it is becoming more a part of routine duties. Consequently, policewomen are not getting the kind of experience one needs to build a portfolio for promotion (Brown and Heidensohn 2000: 98–100, Fielding and Fielding 1992: 206, Brown et al 1993: 130, Silvestri 2003 99–100). In the days of the women's departments they were able to gain promotion through that kind of work, but it is argued that that is more difficult to achieve now (Bryant et al 1985: 236). In addition, C. Martin found that taking time for maternity leave could also hamper a policewoman's career prospects as women often find they have lost their previous posts in favour of more administrative ones. While the equal opportunities legislation that lead to the integration of women into policing has had a marked affect on their experiences, it was vague on how to handle maternity leave and returning to the job (1996: 518, 521). As a consequence, policewomen may have to work even harder to progress through the ranks (Bryant et al 1985: 242, Silvestri 2003).

Westmarland (2001) recently conducted an ethnographic study of gender in policing and came to somewhat different conclusions from the above writers. She found several policewomen who had positive experiences of promotion without needing to be overly 'masculine' in their approach to the job, as well as women who did not encounter a large degree of difficulty re-integrating into the force after maternity leave or deciding to work part-time (2001: 31–2). She also found in the area of general patrol work that women are not differentially deployed (2001: 44). She does admit, however, that women do tend to be more likely to deal with victims of sexual offences (2001: 84, although this is not the same as working with women and children, where Westmarland found little differential deployment, 2001: 44) and that women are still excluded from the overly masculine and symbolically power-loaded specialist units such as in firearms or traffic departments (2001: 188–9). So while there may be some disagreement as to the exact nature of women's experiences in the police service, it is clear that they have yet to achieve equal status with their male counterparts in practice, although not in policy.

Fielding (1994: 51) warns not to assume that all officers adopt the overly masculine occupational culture completely in all stages of their careers. Biased police behaviour is more likely in some situations than in others, for instance, with young male officers in urban settings keen to gain 'street' knowledge. However, as Heidensohn (1992: 121) has argued, women police constables do tend to adopt the male police culture rather than form their own. They accept the generally held values of what is a valid policing experience and 'cop culture'.[37] It is suggested then that the problem is not so much getting the organisation to accept women in its ranks, but to challenge the masculine-centred nature of policing culture, and to see 'real' police work as encompassing what has hitherto been known as 'women's work' (Fielding and Fielding 1992: 217, Heidensohn 1992: 202). Removing these preconceptions would allow women to be accepted as legitimate agents in the police culture.

Before moving on to look at the exact experiences WPCs had during football policing, it is important to briefly mention the role of ethnicity in the police culture. Ethnic minorities have also experienced difficulty in gaining acceptance in the police ranks as the 'canteen culture' can include racist, as well as sexist, imagery. Holdaway and Barron (1997: 145) argue that it is the routine and common aspects of the occupational culture that construct 'race' and sustain racialised relationships between the officers. For instance, teamwork is integral to the success of a police officer, but black and Asian officers find it more difficult to gain full team acceptance. As was discussed above, social drinking is an accepted and expected way to bond with one's colleagues. Some Asian officers do not drink for religious reasons and so are excluded from this route. A black officer found that he gained acceptance from his peers once he proved he could 'handle himself' in a violent situation. He had not been fully accepted before this incident as he was racially stereotyped, but then gained acceptance by succumbing to another stereotype, that of being *the* officer to have on hand in a dangerous situation (Holdaway and Barron 1997: 129–30). Other examples were joking and general banter. White officers tended to view racist banter as 'part of the job', even when it was said in front of black and Asian colleagues and did not realise the offence it caused them. They assumed that the ethnic minority officers have put up with it all their lives so it will not be an issue. The message seemed to be that if they did not put up with it, they would be isolated from the wider police group, which would make their working environment even worse (Holdaway and Barron 1997: 123, 138–9). Lord Macpherson's inquiry into the police handling of the murder of Stephen Lawrence (1999) accused the Metropolitan Police Service (and by implication all UK police services) of institutional racism, and made several recommendations for addressing this aspect of the police occupational culture. However, despite many formal policy changes in police forces across the country and the work of Black Police Associations (Holdaway and O'Neill 2004, O'Neill and Holdaway forthcoming) there is still doubt over whether or not much has actually changed (Cashmore 2002).

This was a deliberately brief look at the experiences of ethnic minorities in the police force, as racial issues among the police and supporters did not play a significant role in my own research (Giulianotti and Gerrard 2001: 31).[38] But I mention it here to note that it is not just the female officers who struggle with and are often excluded by the occupational culture. Homosexual members of the police force are also becoming a focus of research and experience their own difficulties in gaining acceptance (Burke 1993). It is important, however, to explore the combined effect of race and gender in the occupational culture. These issues should not always be viewed in isolation, as Martin (1994) argues. According to her research, it is easier for black men to integrate into a police force than it is for women of any ethnicity, as any man will fit the ideal police model better than a woman will. The discrimination that women face is different for the white and black officers, though. White policewomen are stereotyped as being fragile and needing protection. Black policewomen are treated as being either overly sexual or lazy. White women and black men are more likely to try to gain acceptance from the white male majority and thus tended not to challenge these stereotypes or overtly support the black women. Zhao et al (2001) add to this argument by showing that policewomen of different ethnicities have different reasons for being encouraged or discouraged to join the force. For example, environmental factors, such as the size of the city, had an effect on the decision of ethnic minorities to join the force but not on white women. Thus, these groups of women cannot be assumed to be facing the same issues in their decisions. All of the women police constables I observed at football did not seem to be members of an ethnic minority, so my analysis of their experiences to follow needs to be read with this in mind.

WPCs at football

Officially, women police officers are fully integrated members of the police force. The Sex Discrimination Act 1975 and a letter from the Secretary of State to all Chief Constables in the same year ordered that all women be entitled to the same opportunities as men and that separate departments for women police officers should cease (Young 1991: 227). Analysing the interactions of WPCs and supporters is difficult because while they are officially equal members of the police, there still are not many of them in forces generally and even fewer at football matches. Lewis (1982: 420) feels there are two main reasons why so few women officers work at football matches. First, he sensed a prejudice among the male officers against working with women at the games. They feared hooligans were more likely to attack a woman than a man (which Lewis doubts and my later discussion challenges) and that the male officers would abandon their crowd control duties if a female colleague was injured. Lewis feels this latter prejudice is probably correct, and other writers as mentioned above have also noted this chivalrous tendency. The second reason Lewis gives for the lack of

WPCs at matches is that football is primarily a male leisure activity in the UK so women officers are not as attracted to the possibility of watching the match as male officers are. Heidensohn (1992: 241) takes this a step further and argues that male officers do not wish to share the control of male order with women, as they see this as their special preserve. This could be another reason I saw so few policewomen at the matches, so the following is a short summary of the main observations I had while working with those WPCs I did encounter at football.

In general it seemed that interaction between football supporters and WPCs is different from that with supporters and male officers. However, this is not to suggest that it is better or worse. Some of the women with whom I spoke suggested that it can be discrediting for male supporters to be ejected or otherwise disciplined by a female officer. One woman said that a male supporter will give her a lot of hassle in front of his friends, but then apologise once he has been ejected and they are outside the ground. Fielding and Fielding (1992: 209) also found some support for this argument in their research. A male officer they interviewed said it does not go down well for men to punch women, so WPCs can be an asset in that respect. It also seemed to me on at least two occasions that the male supporters were trying to be flirtatious with the WPC near them to make her less inclined to eject them should they start to cause problems (Brown and Heidensohn [2000: 56] discuss the fear among male officers that WPCs would be too friendly with criminals in custody). In this respect, they were not supporting her performance as a police officer, but were interacting with her role as a woman. Whether or not they were successful I do not know but (for this audience) her gender spoiled her intended police performance (Goffman 1959). However, one WPC suggested that female officers can be better at diffusing situations than male officers. She says that male PCs might feel like they have something to prove (perhaps because both sides of the encounter would be male and thus would feel a need to dominate the other), whereas women do not (because women do not seek dominance but order).[39] Heidensohn (1994: 300) also found that negotiation is seen as a particularly feminine trait that some policewomen feel they use more effectively than men, but because it is seen as feminine it is not sufficiently valued by the police organisation.

When discussing the types of people who attend football, the WPCs held many of the same typologies as the PCs. However, one also mentioned a category of 'girlies'. These are women who go to football dressed as if they were at a nightclub: in full makeup, heels, and tight clothes. She thought this was very funny, as there was no way in her mind that the men at the game would be looking anywhere but at the pitch. PCs never singled out women in their typologies of supporters except to say that girlfriends may have a calming influence on their football-supporting boyfriends. This gender-based view of the fans was echoed by a WPC who said that football would be a better form of entertainment if it were more family orientated. She felt there was too much 'testosterone' there now. Murphy et al (1990) have also discussed the possible positive influence of the family (especially women) on football supporters. Lord Justice Taylor's report (The Home Office 1990) on the Hillsborough disaster suggested that women and children could be a calming influence on the crowd. However, many writers have argued against this view, especially as women have been known to participate in football violence themselves (Finn 1994: 123n). Another WPC associated all her sport experiences with a man, be it her father, husband, or grandfather who took her to matches or got her to watch his favourite sport on television. I did meet at least one WPC who was a passionate supporter in her own right, but she seemed to be exceptional.

Relationships between the women police officers and their male colleagues also tended to be highly gender based, although WPCs did seem at times to be accepted as equal partners with their male colleagues (Fielding and Fielding 1992: 209). One WPC who was new to the force said that her male police partner always keeps her involved in what they are doing. He would not be doing her any favours if he told her to stay in the car. However, there are other times when the WPCs seem to almost be a joke with the male officers. A group of PCs before a match was discussing a WPC they knew from their training days. Apparently this WPC was very short and had a high squeaky voice. The idea of her trying to be an effective officer was very funny to them. This may be because they see physical strength and 'presence' as essential to good policing (Brown et al 1993: 121–4). This is the only occasion I can recall where PCs questioned the ability of someone of their own rank. Usually their criticisms are reserved for those in other ranks or the detectives.

Interaction between WPCs and senior officers is not much better (Fielding and Fielding 1992: 206). WPCs generally seem to be seen as women first and police officers second. As Young (1991) has observed with police officers and Eisenhart (1975) with American Marines, a 'true' police officer or soldier is the one who shows complete *masculinity*. Weakness is equated with womanhood and officers who are believed to be below par are called varies names that suggest they are feminine or homosexual (see also Hunt 1990). In such an environment, it is not surprising that women officers are not taken seriously. The scheduling process for police at a football match is in practice selective and individualistic, although officially a scheduling officer will say that he would put anyone anywhere. One scheduling officer I interviewed will not put WPCs in certain situations in which he feels big aggressive-looking male officers would be more effective. Another scheduling officer said he is just over protective of the WPCs and would not position two of them in the same area of the ground for their own safety. He would insist that one of the pair is a male officer.

My work with the WPCs highlights the extreme gendered basis of the Scottish football experience of both the police and the supporters. The male supporters are seen to be there to get out aggression, have a laugh with the lads, and act like the uncivilised 'animals' they are. The few women who attend football matches are assumed to be there with a man or are trying to be noticed by one.[40] Even WPCs are seen (by others and at times themselves) as women first and constables or supporters second.[41] These observations are by no means the rule for everyone at the match, but seem to be the typologies held by many. Therefore, while WPCs do not comprise their own team, they are not fully accepted into those of the male officers. Even the fact that they have their own title, '*Women* Police Constables', suggests that they are outside the realm of 'normal' police officers. Young (1991: 197) writes that where integration of women into the police force 'appears to have been achieved it is often only skin deep, or is accompanied by a symbolic transference of gender which temporarily ascribes the female with male categories so that she can operate as "one of the boys"'. As such, any reference to a WPC's gender immediately will call her performance into question, as to be a true police officer one cannot be a woman. This then presents a challenge to Goffman's reading of teams (1959: 83–108). He does allow for individuals to stage their own performances (1959: 28) and thus not be seen as team members. However, I do not think that is the case here. While WPCs with whom I spoke have unique perspectives on football and football policing they are still trying to be a part of the police team (and *not* their own women's team) but are not allowed to be (Silvestri 2003: 14). If their performances fall short of what the team wants, it does not reflect badly on the other members as it would for a full team member (Goffman 1959: 168). Rather, as Bryant et al (1985: 239) discuss, if a WPC demonstrates a failing it is not seen to be a personal one (as it is for male constables) but instead reflects badly on all policewomen. Thus we have here an example of how one can be a member of no team and yet not an individual performer either, something for which Goffman did not allow.

The experiences of WPCs also demonstrate well the final topic I will address in this chapter, that is, the way the police operate in practice as several separate interaction teams (or isolated individuals in the case of WPCs) but yet present themselves to the outside world and each other as a united force. For WPCs, they have been fully integrated members of the police service since 1975 as far as policy and outward appearance are concerned, but in practice their experiences suggest ongoing marginalisation and prejudice. I have called this phenomenon the 'underlying police community', a topic I introduced in Chapter 5 but will more fully develop here.

The underlying police community

Several authors have noted internal divisions within policing (Reiner 2000a: 220, Van Maanen 1978: 328, Rubenstein 1973: xiii), which I have further developed with Goffman's (1959) 'interaction team' concept throughout this book. This has shown that even within the same rank there are further internal divisions that more accurately portray how police officers actually work. But while these teams are separate, they do still belong to an underlying community of police officers. The teams operate independently, but do have some residual ties to each other (Manning 1980: 94, Reuss-Ianni 1983: 70). 'The underlying police community' refers to the common bond that ties the various separate police teams together. I will first discuss how it works and thus presents a false image of a united police team to the public and to the police officers themselves. I will then examine it critically by drawing together observations from the various police teams noted elsewhere in this book. While this police community is important for the morale of the officers, it does not always operate in a supportive or advantageous way. It is these reasons that keep the police community from becoming a team in the full sense of Goffman's (1959) term.

Creating an underlying police community

The 'underlying police community' is my term to describe the usual taken-for-granted association between the individual members of the police. These officers belong to separate teams within police forces, but they are still perceived as all being 'the police' by outsiders and often by themselves (Manning 1980: 20, 94). The mid-twentieth century conception of the police has developed into a presumably inevitable and essential aspect of western culture (Reiner 1997: 716). This is even reflected in the early research on the police, which never questioned what the police are or if their mandate is appropriate (Cain 1979). Thus, this false sense of unity is functional in that it helps to ensure the survival of the police organisation. It is this assumed notion of 'the police' that forms the basis for my discussion of the underlying police community.

Aspects of their training, work and social activities help bond police officers in this common fellowship (Fielding 1988). Even if officers of a particular force do not end up members of the same team (in Goffman's terms) they will all train together for months. This is particularly important in Scotland where all police officers undertake their initial training at Tulliallan Police College. Thus new recruits and older members about to retire will all share a similar memory and experience from when they first became members of the police force. This common history includes the history of the force itself, which has experienced many changes over the years and is continuing to do so. Each new police officer can consider him or herself to now be a part of that history. Their old status claims are stripped away and they are invested with a common new one (Fielding 1988: 16). Social activities are a key part to an officer's life (as many told me during my research). Not only do the police chat with and tease each other during their working hours, but they also socialise with each other outside of work (Rubinstein 1973: 435). I heard many stories at football matches about their previous and upcoming social activities.

During working hours, many of the various police teams are dependent on each other for information sharing (Smith and Gray 1985: 564–5). For instance, a superintendent who wants to take further action against some violent football hooligans needs to hear from the constables who intervened in the altercation. The CCTV operators need to communicate information they have from their monitors to the officers on the ground to make them more effective. This working co-operation even extends to ignoring another officer's rule breaking (e.g. speeding tickets are often cancelled) or refraining from breaking a rule if a nearby officer would get reprimanded by the public for not responding to the infraction (e.g. not making an illegal turn in an unmarked car when police officers and civilians are present) (Rubinstein 1973: 439, Reuss-Ianni 1983: 50). Even though the teams are separate, they still need and rely on each other in their training, socialising and work, and they are successful in doing so. Despite any criticisms they may have of each other, football policing usually occurs without incident. This would explain why one sergeant described the police to me as being 'one big family'.

The underlying police community can be determined not only from what the police officers are and what they do, but also from what they are *not* and what they do *not* do. As Giulianotti (1995) has found with his work on Scottish football supporters abroad, defining what you are not (in that case, not English) can be just as useful a source of identity formation as defining what you are. In my experience, police officers find social workers, the courts, and football hooligans to be anathema to their being.[42] Social workers are felt to sometimes be sympathetic with the criminal or otherwise engaged in 'soft' measures of social control. Police officers feel that the courts are not always as supportive of them as they should be. Judges are difficult to contact on evenings and weekends when search warrants are needed most, and giving evidence in court is risky for officers. They receive training and tips on how to do this so that they do not end up being held accountable for the events that took place. For example, one officer told me he was instructed to memorise what is in his notebook as to consult it in court would open the possibility that it could be examined as evidence. Football hooligans are seen as folk devils, not only by many police officers, but by the general public as well, and so form another 'outside' group. By communally identifying these various groups of people as threatening, police officers can better define their own community's boundaries and thus be sure of what they are by clearly marking off what they are not (Westley 1970: 49).

Consequences of the underlying police community

So if the police officers in a force have so many different ways of joining together, why are they not more unified? Why do they have the appearance of being one team but actually function as a fellowship of several? Previous chapters and this one have demonstrated how strong the boundaries are between the various police teams within a police force. After rank, team membership is the most common basis of an officer's identity. Each team tends to be critical of other teams within the force as well to varying degrees, thus reinforcing its own team identity. For example, police constables seem to find much about other police teams to their dislike, although the main subjects of their disdain are the senior officers. Frequently they are regarded as not really knowing what they are doing or as being contradictory in their instructions (Fielding 1988: 138, 177). The MSU officers tend to be less critical of other police teams. This may be because their team boundary (as marked by the police vans) is already very clear and their position within the police force is secure. They seem to have less uncertainty over who they are and what their role is. However, even within that strong group there are still some boundaries. During my discussions with an MSU, the officers would usually let the sergeant respond to my questions. However, when he was not there they tended to speak more openly to me about their opinions. This did not impair their ability to work as a team, but it suggests that the backstage (Goffman 1959) may have levels within it and only certain members can access them all. Only people of the same rank can have full backstage access. Detectives seem to have many negative comments to make about the other police teams. They comment to each other that the PCs or MSUs are not where they should be, that other teams are not responding to requests for assistance from the detectives fast enough, that their messages to other officers are getting changed by the radio controller (Westmarland 2001: 121, 123) and that other police teams are expecting the detectives to perform tasks that are not in their remit (Smith and Gray 1985: 553). Senior officers who do the scheduling for matches add to police divisiveness by being selective in where certain officers are placed during a football game. Thus some officers, especially WPCs, are not accepted as full police officers because they are not considered to be able to handle any situation. Team membership is very important to an officer's identity and security (Westmarland 2001: 155–6).

Not only are the various police teams clearly demarcated, but they also have misconceptions about what the other teams do or are supposed to do. This may be due in part to the police assuming that they will all operate as a unit (the assumption the underlying police community gives off) while in fact they do not. The detectives especially seem to get upset when another police team does not do what the detectives assume it will. These strong team boundaries and inaccurate assumptions about the roles of other teams ensure that the police will remain divided. Their own team boundaries are too secure to allow other police officers in, especially ones they may not fully respect. Identity and loyalty were probably important factors to emphasise in initial training (Fielding 1988: 90). However, it seems that they have developed into divisive tendencies that are reflected in their differential interactions with football supporters and each other.

Summary

In this chapter I have also considered the role of WPCs at football matches. They are the only group at football who do not belong to any interaction team, thus they are truly outsiders to interaction in this arena. This is a development of Goffman's work in that he did not previously consider that a person could be a member of no team and yet not an individual performer either. It also appears that WPCs interact with supporters differently than male constables, but this is not to suggest that they are better or worse at this task. It would seem that they relate to the supporters (both male and female) on a gendered basis, whereas male PCs tend not to do so. However, more research needs to be done specifically on WPCs at football to develop a more thorough analysis.

The discussion of WPCs demonstrated well the underlying police community, the subject of the latter section of this chapter. While it is easy for outsiders to assume that there is a group called 'the police', with women officers as fully integrated members, this is really just an underlying association that binds together very separate police teams and isolated WPCs. Sometimes this association is supportive and it gives individual officers a shared history and bond. However, this association is often not supportive in that the separate police teams within it can be very critical of each other. It has also developed to the extent of denying women police officers full membership of any team, no matter how hard they may try to be accepted as equals, so that they are permanently in the role of outsiders. It is through studying the police at football that these team formations and interactions have become apparent. It also suggests that until police teams can interact with each other on equal terms and see each other's point of view, there cannot be a unified police performance at football. Supporters will continue to receive different definitions of the situation depending on the police team with which they interact at that moment. While this analysis was conducted with football policing in mind, an understanding of team interaction will have salience for wider discussions of institutional change in the police. Other writers have written more extensively on the issues of sexual and racial discrimination within policing and the institutional changes needed to address these (C. Martin 1996, Walklate 1996, Reiner 2000a, Chan 1996, Silvestri 2003). My work here can be seen as complimenting this ongoing debate.

The next and final chapter of this book will look at CCTV operators and stewards, and their interactions with football supporters. While they all have important roles to play in the policing and safety of a football match they are also excluded from membership of the police teams with which they work. This will be developed into a discussion of the informal occupational hierarchy operating at football, in which stewards and CCTV operators are at the very bottom.

7
CCTV Operators and Stewards

The previous two chapters were a look at the types of police officers who have a rather marginal status when it comes to football policing (and in the police occupational culture generally), senior officers and women police constables. This final chapter will consider the other 'outsiders' of football policing, CCTV operators and stewards, and what all these peripheral players can tell us about the informal police hierarchy of 'real' officers and 'real' police work.

Contemporary Britain has seen an explosion of surveillance technologies in the past thirty years (Norris and Armstrong 1999: 18). This has included DNA profiling, mandatory drug testing of athletes and criminals, electronic monitoring of employee computer activity and the collection of consumer information for targeted marketing (Norris and Armstrong 1999: 20). Closed Circuit Television is a further example, and the one most applicable to football. Although the operators of the CCTV cameras do not have much, if any direct interaction with football supporters, they are important to mention here because of their indirect interaction with them. Although there are one or two police officers present in the CCTV room as supervisors and as a link to the police force, the men and women who monitor the supporters and the police during a football match are civilian employees. The cameras that are important to consider during a football match are the ones in the city centre and the stadium. The police feel the presence of these surveillance devices has had a noticeable impact on supporter behaviour, especially in the ground. It is the experiences of these non-police personnel I will discuss first to analyse their contribution to the interaction at a football match.

Stewards are the only security/safety group at football matches who do not have police officers as part of their operational unit and are the second group I will consider in this chapter. However, at modern football matches more and more stewards are employed to ensure the smooth running of a game. Stewards cost the club considerably less to employ inside the ground than police officers. In addition, the Taylor Report (The Home Office 1990) recommended that clubs recruit and retain a sufficient number of stewards that are fit and capable of performing their duties to a national standard, as listed in the *Guide to Safety at Sports Grounds* (The Home Office 1997). This guide lists many responsibilities for the stewards, and they must work with the police to ensure the stadium is safe and orderly. As their role is connected to that of the police and they have frequent contact with supporters, they need to be considered in my analysis of social interaction at football.

While CCTV operators constantly work with police officers in a mutual sharing of information, they are not accepted as part of any police interaction 'team' in Goffman's sense of the word (1959). Stewards work next to and often with police officers in the ground, at both the seating level and in the police observation room where supervisors from both groups tend to be based. However, none of these stewards, of any rank, are a part of a police interaction team. While the work of CCTV operators and stewards is important to the smooth running of a football match, theirs is not considered 'real' police work. The final section of this chapter will examine in more depth the informal hierarchy of 'real' policing and police officers when it comes to football and how this is different from that described by previous writers on the police.

CCTV operators

Before detailing CCTV's role in the football ground during my research, I would like to discuss Foucault's (1977) use of Bentham's 'Panopticon' and its relevance here. The Panopticon was designed to be the ideal prison in that officers in a central watchtower could observe all prisoners at once because they would be held in individual cells in a ring-shaped building around a central watchtower. This would have Venetian blinds so that the prisoners could not see in and thus never know exactly when they were being watched (1977: 200).

> Hence the major effect of the Panopticon: to induce in the inmate a state of conscious and permanent visibility that assures the automatic functioning of power. So to arrange things that the surveillance is permanent in its effects, even if it is discontinuous in its

Loan Receipt
Liverpool John Moores University
Library Services

Borrower Name: Peers, Elora
HSSEPEER
Borrower ID: ********

The strong arm of the law : armed and
public order policing /
31111014994584
Due Date: 16/05/2018 23:59:00 BST

Policing football : social interaction and
negotiated disorder /
31111011703681
Due Date: 16/05/2018 23:59:00 BST

Total Items: 2
09/05/2018 14:55

Please keep your receipt in case of
dispute.

action; that the perfection of power should tend to render its actual exercise unnecessary; that this architectural apparatus should be a machine for creating and sustaining a power relation independent of the person who exercises it; in short, that the inmates should be caught up in a power situation of which they are themselves the bearers (Foucault 1977: 201).

Eventually, the authority figures would not need to exercise their disciplinary power directly as the inmates end up doing it themselves. It has been argued that football grounds and other areas in contemporary society (such as shopping malls and the high street) have elements of the Panopticon in them through the increasing use of CCTV. In fact, the football stadium was an early testing ground for surveillance technology in the UK (Giulianotti 1999: 81–2). However, Norris and Armstrong (1999: 6) warn against making this connection between CCTV and the Panopticon too quickly. The power to watch must also be coupled with the power to discipline in order for the link to work, and it is debatable whether or not CCTV has that disciplinary power. There is no one CCTV system in the UK, but several small ones, each used for their own reasons and with their own degrees of effectiveness (Norris and Armstrong 1999: 7). While the work of CCTV operators during my research did sometimes lead to the police intervening in an ongoing situation in the ground or city centre (to be discussed below), the majority of their work did not result in this type of activity. Even during the few occasions when surveillance did lead to police interaction with supporters, strict disciplinary action was not always the end product. Thus my observations of CCTV use during football would support Norris and Armstrong's statement above that the Panopticon is an inaccurate analogy. However, it is in these moments when CCTV operators did influence what happened between police officers and supporters on the ground that makes it important to consider their role in social interaction on a football match day.

The CCTV operators I observed in the city centre said that they use the cameras to follow the movements of the supporters before and after the match in order to alert the police to any potential or current altercations (but as mentioned above these altercations were usually infrequent). In this way, the CCTV operator's definition of a 'hooligan' is important. They tend to follow large groups of young men wearing baseball caps (Norris and Armstrong 1999: 120). Police officers will also call in to the CCTV room and ask that the cameras follow specific people whom they suspect may become troublesome. If an incident does occur, the CCTV operators piece together a tape of the event from all the cameras that caught it. As they are doing the editing, the CCTV operators have control over what eventually ends up in court as evidence. So while the operators may not be on the ground in the action, they can have a great deal of influence over the eventual outcome of police and supporter encounters (Armstrong and Giulianotti 1998: 129). An investigation of the procurator fiscal in 2000 into the content of CCTV footage submitted to the courts has highlighted this issue. A football supporter claimed that police officers used a heavy-handed approach to control violent football fans, but evidence of this appeared to have been omitted from the CCTV tapes used to prosecute the football supporters in question (Walker: *The Scotsman*, 3 October 2000, p. 1). This points to the often-overlooked human element of this new and pervasive technology. Norris and Armstrong (1999: 93–4, 165) have argued that what the camera operators are actually doing can have a large bearing on how effective CCTV is. They are often low-paid, overworked and transient employees (1999: 102–3), which does not bode well for producing an ever-alert surveillance team. So just because CCTV is there does not mean it is being used well. In addition, Norris and Armstrong (1999: 109) found that CCTV operators tended to focus on the activities of young men wearing casual clothes. 'Thus the most frequent reason that an individual is targeted is not because of what they have done, but because of who they are, and operators identify them as belonging to a particular social category which is deemed to be indicative of criminal or troublesome behaviour' (Norris and Armstrong 1999: 112). In this respect, those who fit the operator's idea of a football 'hooligan' are more likely than all other people to be watched during a football match.

CCTV in the stadium is used a little differently than that in the city centre. The police there often ask for the cameras to follow them if they are about to approach a group of supporters to reprimand them or eject them. If a hostile reaction results, the cameras should have the encounter on tape to save the officer from blame. Cameras in the ground can also zoom in on groups of fans and take still photos of them for intelligence purposes (Armstrong and Giulianotti 1998: 130, Norris and Armstrong 1999: 50). If supporters in a certain section are being disruptive and the police there have not seen it yet, the CCTV operators or Match Commander (if he or she is in the room) may direct officers to the area. So while CCTV is not as forceful a presence in football interaction as the police officers themselves are, it does have a role to play in the performance of the various police teams. In addition, the cameras in many grounds are not disguised so the supporters are certainly aware of them. Some may even play up to a camera if they see the lens pointing at them (Norris and Armstrong 1999: 145). Thus through this inanimate object some interaction between the CCTV operators and the fans can occur.

I have yet to consider one other important influence that CCTV has had on the behaviour of football hooligans. Armstrong and Giulianotti (1998: 131) argue that 'the policing of fan violence has a material effect on the phenomenon itself, as the hooligan "object" attempts to evade its capture'. Segregation tactics have been effective in reducing violence in the football ground, but they tend displace it to areas outside (Coalter 1985). CCTV has compounded this displacement in that football hooligans must now be as organised as police officers in order to avoid surveillance (Armstrong and Giulianotti 1998: 117). They may communicate with each other via mobile phones to meet in places away from the watchful eye of a CCTV camera, like motorway service areas (Armstrong and Giulianotti 1998: 131). So while CCTV may be an effective policing tool in the short term, the police could be making their job more difficult in the future through the pervasiveness of CCTV in modern cities.

While an examination of how CCTV can influence interaction between police officers and supporters is important to conduct, so too is an analysis of interaction between CCTV operators and the police officers themselves. CCTV operators can be considered an interaction team (Goffman 1959) of their own for all the same reasons that have been given elsewhere in this book about the various police interaction teams. CCTV operators work together in one room for an extended period of time, they have separate training from police officers and a separate uniform. They do not attend police daily briefings. While their work often involves liasing with police officers (especially in the CCTV room in the city centre where they are supervised by a police sergeant) their role and thus their performance is clearly separate from that of the officers. The audience for their performance is also different from the other police teams I have considered so far, and this involves their unique use of the 'backstage', that region of interaction where actors test out their performances and relax with each other, usually away from the gaze of the audience (Goffman 1959: 114–15).

CCTV operators do not get many opportunities to leave their posts (Norris and Armstrong 1999: 93, 102), but they do not encounter the football supporters directly either. So they do the majority of their interaction within the backstage by communicating with officers on duty via the radios to help direct their interactions with supporters. Both CCTV rooms (city centre and stadium) are relaxed places where jokes are shared, teasing of each other is common, and sometimes where snack foods are kept (Roy 1960). While the CCTV operators get along well with each other, other police officers frequently visit them in a social capacity as well. PCs and other officers on duty during a match (either policing it directly or in another part of the city) will come into the CCTV room to see what the football score is and what is happening in town. During these visits the CCTV room takes on a temporary 'front stage' capacity as the CCTV operators are now performing directly for the police officers present.[43] But the rest of the time it is a permanent backstage area (sometimes operators will shout at people seen on the screens in a non-flattering way that they would never do in a front stage encounter, see Norris and Armstrong 1999) and yet the site of (usually indirect) interaction with other teams as well, supporters and police officers. CCTV has made backstage action relevant and important for front stage encounters. This is a novel use of the backstage that Goffman could not have considered in his 1959 discussion. It could also be seen as an ideal site for interaction as one can relax among teammates and yet still be an effective actor.

Interaction between CCTV operators and other police teams is generally friendly. However, there are times the CCTV operators do not like the way senior officers are running things and they say so to each other. There are also occasions where it seems that the various police teams do not have an accurate understanding of each other's roles. Sometimes officers call in and ask the CCTV operators to follow a particular bus or group of supporters and they assume (incorrectly) that the operators know which ones they mean. The CCTV operators see their role as informing (on their own initiative) other officers of the whereabouts of football hooligans. Other police teams see the role of CCTV as responding to their requests for the cameras to follow certain people or vehicles for them (see Norris and Armstrong [1999: 174–96] for more on the relationship between the CCTV operators and the police). So we can see that the CCTV operators are an interaction team in their own right, separate from the police teams, but they have a unique way of interacting with them. CCTV interaction with supporters is indirect (via their influence on police action) and takes place entirely in the backstage. Their interaction with police teams is either from a distance via the radios in their backstage environment, or in the CCTV room when it takes on a temporary front stage capacity.

Stewards

There has not been much specifically written about stewarding at football matches. Instead, the most relevant literature concerns the private policing of 'mass private property'. The study of private policing, or the private security industry, began in the UK in the 1970s, although it did not gain prominence until the 1990s (Jones and Newburn 1998: 21). By then private policing's unregulated growth had been causing concern for many, thus bringing it to academic attention. Shearing and Stenning (1983: 496, Kempa et al 2004: 570) developed the term 'mass private property' to describe large privately owned facilities in which public activities increasingly take place. Examples they give are large shopping malls or leisure complexes, all developments of the late twentieth century. Stenning (2000: 327), Loader (1997b: 146) and Kempa et al (1999: 203) also mention sports stadia as examples of this kind of property. However, Wakefield (2003: 24–5) has argued that if one actually considers types of ownership (public or private) and degrees of urban space 'openness', then sports stadia are in fact restricted private spaces, as they are privately owned and charge admission fees. Spaces like shopping centres, while also privately owned, do not charge admission and so may be better examples of mass private property. While Wakefield's analysis raises important issues, it is the only one to specifically address the topic of urban space 'openness' and so the rest of the mass private property literature can still be useful here.

Mass private property owners tend to employ security guards (private police) to police their complexes, either through established companies or through hiring them directly (Loader 1997b: 146). As these are not publicly owned spaces, the public police do not enter them unless requested to do so by the owners. Thus large areas of public life are increasingly falling under the control of private corporations (Shearing and Stenning 1983: 496–7, Kempa et al 2004). We can view the stewards at a football ground as the private police of that area. Previous to the Taylor Report (The Home Office 1990), stewarding was left up to the individual club to organise, and could often result in poorly trained and poorly paid employees who were really there just to see the game for free (Livingstone and Hart 2003: 163–4). More recently, private companies have been employed to recruit, train, and supply stewards to the grounds. They also supply steward supervisors and their own radio controllers in the CCTV rooms. This has resulted in a complex division of labour between the police and the stewarding company. The stewards now perform tasks that used to belong to the police (Shearing and Stenning 1983: 497) and are able to eject supporters from the ground. The police and the club are urged to agree on a statement of intent to make sure all parties know exactly what their specific duties are (from both the Taylor Report and *The Green Guide*). However, the police Match Commander still has ultimate control over the way the event is run. Only recently has legislation been introduced in the UK to start regulating this industry.[44] The Private Security Industry Act 2001 mandated that the Security Industry Authority (SIA) be formed to issue and manage licences for people working in private security and to develop an approved contractor scheme. This latter task involves maintaining a public register of approved security firms. SIA's work is rolling out gradually over a number of years in several areas of the private security industry. It currently applies to only England and Wales, but procedures for including Scotland are also being developed. Northern Ireland will have its own separate scheme (from the SIA website, www.the-sia.org.uk). While the stewards in place today at football are undoubtedly better prepared for their task than their predecessors were and the SIA will help further improve the situation, private security is still an under-trained and underpaid job with poor prospects (Loader 1997b: 147–8, Lister et al 2001).

Like CCTV operators, stewards comprise their own interaction team (Goffman 1959), as they are not accepted as part of any police team. However, as we will see they are a team with some problems. Many stewards work just about every match in a particular ground and so get to know each other over time through chatting before and during their duties. Their main backstages are the changing room where they sign in and collect their coats, the stadium concourses before and after the match, and any opportunity to speak to each other out of earshot of the supporters. The front stage for their performances is the stadium when supporters and police are present, as these are their primary audiences. The main jobs the stewards have are to keep the corridors and concourses open (i.e. tell people who are standing around to return to their seats) and direct people to the toilets, concession areas, and their seats. They often intervene if a dispute arises over the owner of a particular seat. In case of an emergency, the stewards help direct people to the exits and ensure an orderly evacuation of the ground. So like the police, stewards are concerned with the use of space in the ground. Stewards are not at matches to act as police officers, but they are not there as supporters either (at least officially). This middle team role seems to be difficult for some of them. One said that they have to be mean to people sometimes and he is not used to doing that. A steward supervisor said that they must keep their emotions bottled up inside until after the game, and that is hard for them to do. However, on a few occasions I did see stewards reacting to events on the pitch more like a supporter than a calm steward. It would appear that the stewards are not as practised as the police are in the use of the front and backstage for interaction at football (Goffman 1959).

While stewards may know each other well, they do not always seem to know the exact nature of their duties or the official procedures for carrying them out. For example, there are established procedures that the stewards follow before ejecting someone from the ground, usually a series of warnings and then the ejection. This is similar to the tactic used by other private police in that they are more likely to deny access to goods and services to prevent future breaches of security than to employ the criminal justice system to prosecute someone (Stenning 2000: 334). However, when I asked various stewards and supervisors what the exact procedure was, I received different answers. Some said three warnings, some said none, some said back-up or permission was required, others said they were not. Many stewards I encountered said they had no or very little classroom training (Wakefield 2003: 149–50). A 'training officer' walks around during the match and asks certain stewards (such as all new staff) questions about procedures for steward-ing to test their knowledge. This is a rolling programme so that the training officer eventually questions all stewards throughout the year. I was told that the private company who hires the stewards in the grounds I visited usually trains them off-site in large groups. If people sign up to become a steward they may be assigned matches to work before they have a classroom-based training session if there are not enough new people at the time to justify one. They are given instruc-tion books for each ground, but not all stewards had them while they were working. Often at briefings, stewards are told that they would be following the 'usual procedure' for things. However, what exactly is entailed in the usual procedure is not always mentioned and one wonders if all the stewards know what this means.

The stewards with whom I spoke did all agree though that in any situation, a steward should just use 'common sense' to handle it. This term is often used by police officers to describe how they approach unexpected situations, but as Jefferson and Grimshaw note (1982: 93–4) this term is not a consistent one and often contains contradic-tions. As Loader has mentioned in his work, private security officers are not very well paid (1997b: 147–8, Wakefield 2003: 68) and this, coupled with patchy training, suggests that these team members are probably not very committed to the team or the performance they are supposed to espouse. When discussing problems they have had with supporters in the past, many stewards say that they are not paid enough to take a lot of hassle from supporters and will call on a police officer to deal with the situation. This all seems to suggest that the steward role is ambiguous. In Goffman's terms, the team does not have its performance prepared very well. With their own uniforms, procedures, radio controllers and supervisors stewards are trying to present themselves as a second type of professional crowd controller (Noaks 2004: 270–1) but as yet lack the skill the police have developed in maintaining their performances in the face of challenges.

When it comes to interaction with supporters, more experienced stewards have developed their own informal rules with the fans, which guide them in their work (Noaks 2004, for a similar discussion on the work of 'bouncers', see Hobbs et al 2002). Some stewards are positioned in the same section of the ground for each match. They get to know the supporters there and build a rapport with them. This is especially important in areas of a ground where the opposing support sides sit adjacent to each other across a segregation divide. These are traditionally the most aggressive and vocal areas in the ground. According to the stewards, these are also the areas where the 'hooligans' sit (Hobbs et al 2002: 356).[45] Usually a formidable steward is put in with the home supporters here and one of these told me that the supporters know how far they can push him before he will eject them or start warning them. He feels the fans learn their limits and the situation works well. Sharp and Wilson (2000) researched a private security firm in Doncaster that was owned and operated by a formal criminal. His reputation seemed to be his key selling point as would-be burglars would know which houses his company was patrolling by the stickers in the windows and would stay away, afraid of his retaliation (2000: 120–1). In the same way, the supporters in the aggressive areas were familiar with this particular steward and his limits. There is also a lot of shouting between the two support sides in these sections and one steward said that the visiting fans pay more attention to the home fans than to the match. This is allowed as long as the supporters stay in (or, if they are standing, in front of) their seats and do not try to injure anyone by throwing objects or direct their aggression at the stewards themselves. During one match a supporter assaulted a steward and was promptly arrested, but the steward refused to press charges because he knew the man personally and was afraid of retribution. Thus it seems that this steward at least was aware that his quasi-professional performance does not last beyond the match.

Despite the challenge of the aggressive areas, some of the stewards feel that football is too boring now and they want the 'old days' of football back (when disorder in the stadium was more common, see Smith and Gray [1985: 340–1] for similar feelings among the police). In contrast, many of them also work at rugby matches and suggest that it is an entirely different atmosphere from football, as it has no segregation and no violence in the stands. The stewards feel that if football was desegregated, a 'war' would result. In general, visiting supporters are felt to be friendlier to the stewards than the home supporters are. They give the stewards more respect while the home supporters take their aggression out on the stewards. Overall, the attitude of the fans is dictated by the outcome of the match. If the home side is winning then the home supporters are friendlier. If they lose, the stewards get a lot of hassle from them on their way out. In relation to the police though, some stewards feel that the supporters give stewards more respect than they do to the police constables.

However, interaction between the stewards and the police teams themselves are often problematic (Wakefield 2003: 44–8), despite the observation in the stewards' handbook that they are 'the eyes and ears of the police'. Stewards feel that the police sometimes do more harm than good in trying to calm disruptive supporters. Officers who arrest only one or two members of an aggressive group 'to serve as a warning to the others' make the job of the nearby steward more difficult. The supporter or supporters' remaining angry friends do not hold back in expressing their disapproval of the situation to the steward.[46] There were also a few occasions where the stewards needed police support, but the police were slow to respond because the situation was not a usual police responsibility. For example, on one occasion a temporary gate was erected near some turnstiles (because the original one had been removed due to violating safety regulations) and the stewards were having difficulty keeping the supporters from getting in for free through this vulnerable area. The police nearby just watched. In general, the attitude seems to be that the stewards are responsible for making sure the football ground rules are followed and the supporters are safe. The police are there to uphold the law. However, the exact responsibilities these categories entail are not clear and at the time of my research had not been established in any formal way[47] (Stenning 2000: 326–8). These two groups may find themselves doing the other's job, e.g. police officers showing supporters where the toilets are and stewards ejecting someone for foul language. In some grounds the stewards search the supporters' bags for illegal items, but they do not have the power to take any action if they actually find something. Thus while the stewards and the police are certainly members of different teams, the boundaries between their performances are not always apparent (Shearing and Stenning 1983: 497). Their interactions with each other are not always negative, though. Before the match and at slow points during it the stewards and nearby police frequently chat to each other amicably.

'Real' police work and 'real' police

Although stewards and CCTV operators are an integral part of the safety and security operations in a football ground, police officers do not usually highly value them and the work that they do. They are not police officers and theirs is not police work, thus many officers I encountered see them as being of a lower calibre than themselves (Livingstone and Hart 2003: 162). Throughout my discussions with all the police officers at football matches, it became apparent that the official police hierarchy (uniformed constables at the bottom, Chief Constable at the top) is not the same as that which exists in the minds of the officers themselves (Westmarland 2001: 92). They also seem to hold a hierarchy of police tasks in which some of their mandatory duties are regarded as not 'real' police work. This final section of the chapter will discuss these informal hierarchies of work and officers in more detail, the role of CCTV operators and stewards in them and their possible influence on police interaction at football matches.

Real police work and officers generally

First I will consider what exactly the police regard as 'real' police work generally. Reiner (1997: 735) suggests it is mainly apprehending criminals and general crime fighting. Police officers are very committed to producing results in this vein and resent any obstacles to doing so. Crime fighting is action-oriented (chases or direct confrontation with suspects) so paperwork or other dull tasks are disliked (Chatterton 1989). Public service duties, like football policing, are among the tasks police officers regard as a waste of their time (Fyfe 1992). They feel there are many more useful things they could be doing than standing around on a Saturday afternoon for four hours.[48] But from my own experience at the matches it is apparent that while officers do not like football duty, they recognise the need for their presence there. As with the rest of their duties, they feel that chaos would ensue were they not present (Holdaway 1989: 65). Cain (1971) notices a paradox in the idea of 'real' police work among officers. 'It seemed that foot patrol work was at the base of the police pyramid, and yet that the norms generated in that setting penetrated the whole structure... There was a feeling that the beat men, together with the (detectives), were the real policemen; yet the beat men had to face the fact that many of their actual tasks...required little skill' (1971: 76–7). So while constables are at the bottom of the formal police hierarchy, their work is the most valued throughout it, even if it requires the least skill.

Young (1991: 189) has developed a detailed model of the criminal justice world that places its various members along a spectrum of clean-ambiguous-dirty categories. He developed this based on the behaviour and opinions of the officers with whom he worked. This includes far more groups than I will consider here, but it does illustrate how members of the police force itself can be seen as not quite 'real' officers. According to Young, the true police officers are the uniformed PCs who do the most direct work with the public and consider themselves to face the most danger on a routine basis. Detectives and administrative senior officers are on the next level down in the hierarchy. PCs regard themselves as doing the real dirty work of policing while detectives come in later and get all the glory. Senior officers are too desk-bound to be real police officers as they are detached from the current world of policing. People like social workers and sociologists are right above the criminal category. They are liberal non-police people who tend to sympathise with the criminals and may try to alter the way police do things (Young 1991). Young describes how police constables feel that the traditional (and ideal) binary world of the real police officer and the real criminal ('prig') has eroded:

> This is a world which should remain the concern of the two sides, but increasing interference from the social worker, the politician, the do-gooder, the press, the 'prig' solicitor, the magistrate or judge, the television pundit, the police administrator, and the chief officer in his 'ivory tower' merely intrudes to destroy the exclusive and rigid arenas of action which are preferred (Young 1991: 185).

In this account, effective policing has been perverted by the influence of non-real police officers, liberals and outsiders, and it is the 'true' constables who have suffered.

Real football policing

Football policing produces a slightly different informal hierarchy, however, according to my fieldwork experiences and discussions with the officers there. As the football hooligans are the main demons of the day (Armstrong and Hobbs 1995), all policing efforts are focused around them and this changes the stacking of 'real' police officers. In effect, the football policing hierarchy is based on *the amount of direct contact an officer has with the football hooligans.* In this case, the lowest people on the ladder are the stewards as they are not members of the police and are often regarded as not really knowing what they are doing. The stewards themselves recognise that they are subordinate to the police and should always do what an officer tells them. Traffic wardens are next on the list. They are also not police officers and while their role is important for a smooth flow of people and cars before and after a match, they are still held in contempt and regarded as not very intelligent. Traffic police officers are above them, as they are members of the police force. However, as they focus their duties on traffic matters, they are seen to be below calibre when it comes to serious police work. Above traffic officers are the CCTV operators and the radio controllers. These police officers and civilians are important in finding hooligans and communicating their whereabouts to other officers. However, as they are safely tucked away in the police station or observation room of the ground, their role will never be highly regarded.

Senior police officers come next on the list. Senior officers who have desk jobs during most of the week are regarded with the least amount of respect. Their jobs are too 'cushy' and it is felt that they have no common sense (Fielding 1988: 177, Smith and Gray 1985: 536). Senior officers who are overweight or do not otherwise 'look' like police officers (e.g. how they carry themselves, if they wear their uniform properly, etc.) are also not well respected. Uniform officers feel these senior officers would be useless if a real emergency happened because they could not run very far or very fast (see Manning [1980: 50–2] for more on the importance of appearance for uniformed officers). An academic history is also a barrier to acceptance from lower ranking officers (Young 1991). There is a programme in Scottish, English and Welsh police forces to promote some of the new recruits with relevant university degrees through the ranks quickly (called the Accelerated Promotion Scheme for Graduates). PCs do not like this programme, as it could mean people with minimal practical experience would be in charge (Fielding 1988: 137–41). Other senior officers are usually treated with respect if they work outside the office most of the time and appear competent in their duties. However, it seemed to me that anyone who started on the promotion ladder immediately lost some respect. That person would be getting too close to the reviled administrative senior officers (Fielding 1988: 85).

Sixth on the informal hierarchy (from the bottom) for football policing are the uniformed police constables. These are the first officers who are truly engaged in 'real' police work (Manning 1997: 145). They deal with the public and the supporters directly and make arrests or ejections when necessary. They are sometimes involved in the apprehension and control of football hooligans. However, a good portion of their day at the football match is concerned with standing around and either watching the fans or conducting steward-like duties such as telling people where their seats are. These aspects of the job are not highly prized and as such reduce their place on the police hierarchy. Thus this view of the policing world is different from that suggested by Young (1991). MSU officers occupy the next highest level. A good portion of their job involves finding, following, and sometimes arresting football hooligans. Although they are in uniform, their duties are detective-like in nature. But they must still follow the orders of a senior officer and are further restricted by briefing schedules and force boundaries.

The detectives or football spotters occupy the highest level of the informal football policing hierarchy. They are self-directing, wear plain clothes (Manning 1980: 51), and use intelligence gathered previously to seek out hooligans and intercept any meetings they may have with other hooligans (Armstrong and Hobbs 1995). From the conversations I have had with officers at games, it is this role that is considered to be most associated with 'real' police work. The detectives or spotters do not have to stand around on street corners or in the football stadium for hours. They do not have to answer inane questions from supporters. They are purely consumed with seeking out the folk devil of football: the hooligans. This is 'real' policing at its finest.

Women police constables were not mentioned here, as due to not being members of any police team they do not tend to specifically feature in police thinking when it comes to the hierarchy. They are subsumed within the other ranks despite having quite different experiences when it comes to football policing. This informal hierarchy can extend beyond the local police force boundary and include other forces as well. When speaking to officers from around Scotland, it became clear that national stereotypes exist. For instance, some officers from the Strathclyde police force consider themselves to face more danger and challenge than their counterparts in Grampian do. Glasgow has more 'real' police work and police officers than does Aberdeen, according to these officers.

Despite the potential crime-fighting aspect of football policing, the majority of the officers have little direct involvement with the hooligans and so they do not feel they are involved in 'real' police work. This could be why football supporters and football matches are not seen as a part of normality. Many of the officers feel that they are not doing important duties and should really be somewhere else. Football is marginal to their 'real' work, (Fyfe 1992) and is not 'normal' policing. This is despite the fact that football matches happen about once a fortnight from August to May at least. Thus when interacting with supporters and each other, police officers at football may already feel resentful for having to be there in the first place. In addition, the officers may not be inclined to take their football duties as seriously as they would their other police work. This may be why football policing seems to be such a good social opportunity for the officers.

The tendency to build an informal hierarchy also occurs among military personnel. Mack (1954) surveyed airmen at two U.S. Air Force bases. He found that both bases held the same rankings of squadrons based on 'best' to 'worst'. Operations and command squadrons (such as bombers and wing headquarters) were ranked far higher than service squadrons (such as medical and food services). In addition, each squadron ranked itself higher than the other squadrons did, showing a unilateral loyalty to one's own group. Ground troops in World War II also developed an informal hierarchy (Stouffer et al 1965: 292). Specifically, support services, or those in the 'rear', were viewed with disdain and antagonism. Front line soldiers allotted themselves a higher status, although research suggests that many of them would have gladly given up their more dangerous positions for the far safer ones in the support services. But as with the police and Air Force examples above, officers who received the most respect were those involved in 'real' combat or active policing/detecting situations.

Summary

This chapter has considered the non-police personnel (the other 'outsiders') involved in the safety and security of football matches, CCTV operators and stewards, and their role in the informal police hierarchy of 'real' police work and police officers. CCTV operators are probably the most removed from interaction with the supporters, but that is not to suggest that they are unimportant in the performances that occur. Officers both in and outside the ground use CCTV to gain an advantage over supporters during their relations with them. However, this results in another definition of 'hooligans' being introduced to the match, which may influence on whom the officers focus their attention. CCTV operators are unique in football interaction as their performances are conducted entirely from their backstage arena. This presents a new development of Goffman's (1959) conception of the backstage, in that it can be used to interact, albeit indirectly, with one's audience. CCTV is the subject of much recent research[49] and I would encourage this, especially during interaction at football policing to find out the full influence CCTV has on the outcome of events. CCTV operators are outsiders in football interaction as they are not police officers and thus are not completely accepted as a competent team. Those police officers who supervise CCTV rooms are also outsiders, as they do not work directly with the public as the constables in the stadium or city centre do.

The second part of the chapter examined football stewards, who are becoming a major force in the experience of a football match. Their role is a unique one in that they are often football supporters themselves, but are not allowed to appear so during the match. They also have many responsibilities that are similar to those of the police, but yet do not have the power of arrest or the forceful appearance that the police do. The police have suggested that there are fewer officers in the ground now because more duties are being handed to the stewards. However, during my time with them I was concerned at the apparent lack of or minimal training each steward receives. Some of the ones I met had been to several matches but had yet to receive any training beyond the briefing at the start of each match. They also do not receive much money for the work they do. These factors may make it more likely that the stewards will identify with the supporters at the game rather than with the police officers or as a group in themselves. More training and higher pay would help to make their team identity stronger and the boundaries of their roles more distinct. At the moment though, it is difficult for stewards to sustain the performance they are supposed to give and breaches are not infrequent (such as openly celebrating goals). Again, more empirical research is required here to fully develop this analysis as so far football stewards can only be studied as part of the wider private policing literature, which is itself still a largely underdeveloped area (Wakefield 2003: 46 and 66, Davis et al 2003: 199–200).

Like senior officers and women police constables discussed in previous chapters, CCTV operators and stewards are 'outsiders' when it comes to football policing. They do not feature very highly in the informal hierarchy of football policing, the topic of the last section of this chapter, due to their lack of ability to chase and capture football hooligans. The plain clothes detectives and spotters are thus at the top of this list with stewards at the very bottom. The informal football policing hierarchy is different from that of general police duties as discussed by previous writers, where the work of police constables is usually deemed to be the most 'real' police work. Both informal hierarchies value the ability to chase and capture the 'criminal', but when the criminal is question is a football hooligan, the stacking of 'real' police work changes. This demonstrates that not all police work and police situations are viewed as the same, thus the importance of continuing ethnographic research on policing and the value of researching football policing specifically. Both of these hierarchies also differ from the formal rank structure, reinforcing that the image the police present to outsiders is not the same as how interaction actually works in practice.

While I would not argue that football policing represents a separate police occupational culture, this informal football policing hierarchy does suggest that the occupational culture is more variable than many previous writers have argued. The debate around the exact nature of the police occupational culture as well as a more detailed look at what my research can add to it will be developed further as an aspect of the book's conclusion. The other findings to be taken from my work will also be detailed next.

Part III

Conclusion: The Big Implications of Small Teams

The purpose of this book has been to present my long-term ethnographic study of interaction between police officers, football ground stewards and football supporters during both calm and disorderly moments on football match days. It has also considered the way police officers interact with each other and how these internal relationships influence their behaviour with outsiders. Participant observation, detailed field notes and informal as well as semi-structured interviews with police officers and football stewards provided the data for this research, which was conducted largely during one football season in Scotland (1998–99). I visited three football grounds and secured the participation of three police forces in this study. Police constables in uniform, plain clothes spotters, senior officers, mobile units and stewarding staff were observed before, during and after the matches to allow me to piece together an overview of interaction between the football spectators and the agents of social control they encounter. It revealed that while football supporters are indeed a rule-governed group, the rules in question are not the formal ones known publicly, but a more informal and unofficial group of rules developed in conjunction with the police. The police themselves are a much more crucial part of a football match day than they appear and that when in the football context, their internal hierarchy is different than is officially the case. Police officers actually work as several separate interaction teams, not as a unified force, although their work at a football match can be used to present themselves to outsiders as an effective and cohesive group and thus sustains this illusion.

This approach to the sociology of football has never been attempted in such depth. In addition, this aspect of policing has never been directly analysed. Using Goffman's work (largely that of his earlier works, especially *The Presentation of Self in Everyday Life* 1959) to do this not only aided these endeavours, but it also developed Goffman's dramaturgic metaphor and signalled its continued utility for understanding contemporary life. For example, it presented the possibility of two teams staging the same performance as protagonists and antagonists, as well as the possibility of front stage and back stage co-existing in space and time. This was an investigation of particular social patterns and relationships that are constantly changing and evolving. But despite their uniqueness, the lessons that have been learned about general social interaction can be applied to other sections of society.

Implications for interaction

Three main conceptual themes emerge from the findings of my research. These are the significance of the mundane, the interdependence of boundaries and the flow of power through those boundaries. I will discuss each in turn, starting with the significance of the mundane. By this term, I am referring to the subtle yet vital negotiations and interactions that take place between police officers and supporters (and between police officers and each other) during calm, orderly and relatively uneventful moments of football match days. These negotiations produce the informal rules of interaction by which the performers involved align their actions. It is these rules, not the formal sanctions in the law, which keep order in place. It is only when the informal rules are violated (such as when supporters direct their aggression at specific police officers or stewards or ignore police instructions which may not necessarily be based in law) that formal rules and statutes are brought into play and fans are arrested or ejected. Thus orderly interaction here is contingent upon following the understood rules of engagement. This shows again why Goffman's work is relevant here: mistakes are interesting in that they highlight the rule that was violated.

Because these negotiations are a constant feature of interaction at football, they have become normal. The police and the fans expect to challenge each other in subtle ways each time they meet and so are constantly reinforcing or modifying the understood behavioural guidelines. Thus a small element of trust is involved in these proceedings. The police and the fans know what to expect from each other and so know how to handle the situation. However, the definition of 'normal' depends very much upon the context of the encounter. Inside the ground the negotiations mentioned above are dominant. However, outside the ground the fans are not allowed nearly as much leeway in their actions. Many officers expect them to behave as if they had no connection to the football match. They are not to shout, chant, run or otherwise be boisterous and so there is really little room for negotiation here. Because there is no one definition of normality it is easy to see why some supporters get upset when they follow the informal football ground rules outside the stadium and get in trouble with the police for it. One important aspect of context in this case is the particular police team the supporters in question encounter as each team creates their own definition of the situation.

All the police officers involved in a football match day can be located within an interaction team (except for WPCs who are not fully accepted in any team). As such, these officers have very clearly defined and maintained boundaries between each other, which transcend the formal ranking system. They are not always sure of the exact duties and responsibilities of the other teams; they just know they are not a part of them. Yet despite this clear sense of 'us and them', the police are an integral part of football culture. While each team may approach it in a different way (and thus exude a different definition of 'normal' fan behaviour), they all need to be involved in football and are needed by the fans in return. For the police (as individual officers and as an institution), football provides an opportunity to earn some extra money, to get away from paperwork for a while, and even to demonstrate to a national audience (via the media) how good they are at their job in this ideal policing situation. The supporters in turn need the police to be there to give them an extra target for their ritual insults, to protect them from hurting each other (but allow them to act like they are not afraid of the possibility) and to make their day more fun with games of cat and mouse. The police look for distinguishing features among the fans and mentally categorise them into pre-established typologies. They then base their interactions on the type of supporter in question, not the specific individual. However, despite all these boundaries and markers, the police and fans are often not so different from each other; many police officers are football fans themselves and enjoy several of the same (legal) pastimes as the fans. In addition, the spatial boundary between the front and backstages of interaction between police and supporters is not always necessary. Their different types of performances (front and back) can be closely linked in time and space. All these similarities above suggest that the overall boundaries between the police and supporters can be seen as interdependent. Police and fans need each other in order to define themselves and yet the personal crossing of identity and performance boundaries means that they can understand each other. The football hooligan spotters and the MSU officers take this to the extent of performing (in the Goffman sense) *with* the football hooligans, instead of *for* them. And while the police themselves work very hard at maintaining their internal boundaries, they have a degree of interdependence as well, as the next theme of power flows will discuss.

While all these distinct police teams stage different performances for the football supporters and each other, they are bound together by the underlying police community. One purpose of this community is to present the image of a unified police presence to the outside world. This image incorporates the official police hierarchy in which the Chief Constable is in charge and the police constable is the lowest member. The flow of power in this image is from the top down to the constable, who then uses the power he or she is given to arrest members of the public if need be. However, my research has shown that not only is this view of the hierarchy misleading, so are the images of prestige and power that it suggests. In football policing, the detectives or football spotters are at the top of the informal prestige hierarchy because the other officers respect detective work the most and because detectives have the most control over their day. These hooligan spotters are involved in 'real' police work because they focus their actions on catching the football hooligans while the rest of the officers are more involved with non-hooligan supporters or desk jobs. Football stewards are at the bottom of the informal prestige hierarchy, as not only are they not police officers and do not do 'real' police-type work, but they are often viewed as being no better than supporters in yellow jackets.

Not only is the implicit police prestige hierarchy different for football, so is the flow of power through that hierarchy. Weber (1968: 53) describes power as the amount of influence someone or a group of people can have over another. Lukes (1974: 22–3, 32) challenges this view as it focuses too much on actual individuals (instead of including institutions) and also requires overt conflict. Lukes feels that it is possible to exercise power over another by preventing conflict from ever materialising in the first place, i.e., by keeping it latent. This can involve manipulation or authority, without deliberate coercion or force. As long as there is some form of conflict of interest (overt or latent) and/or the threat or use of sanctions, power is being exercised. I would argue that this is what is happening at football. Police constables have power in that they do not always follow the instructions they are given. There is a degree of interpretation and discretion involved that no senior officer can change. Thus constables have a degree of power in that they manipulate senior officers into thinking they *are* following their instructions, as their own techniques for maintaining order (which are not necessarily the prescribed ones) work and thus keep potential conflict between the ranks latent. This was made clear by studying how the constables interact with each other and others at football. In the same vein, football supporters and football hooligans have many ways of circumventing police controls they do not like (usually through manipulating time, physical space or symbolic space) or they can decide to obey the controls they are given and so allow the senior officers and constables to feel they are effective in their jobs. Supporters thus have the power to threaten sanctions (disorder in the ground) against the police if they do not like the treatment they get and so can keep their conflict of interests latent through their use of manipulation.

Supporters and hooligans can be seen to operate as two large inter-action teams, staging performances for (or with) the police and a national audience via the media. This is not to suggest these two interaction teams are wholly homogenous, nor to deny the possibility of internal variations within these teams or indeed unique local mani-festations of supporter and hooligan teams (King 2001a, Stott and Reicher 1998a, 1998b). However, for the purposes of analysing police and supporter/hooligan interaction from a Goffmanesque team per-spective, one can regard the supporters and the hooligans as two large interaction teams who have very well rehearsed and established team performances (although this may not be something of which they are consciously aware). The police, however, work as several small interac-tion teams who do not always communicate with each other well or even like each other. Cain (1971: 84) has written that 'those who control the channels of informal communication, if they are them-selves a tightly knit group, can project their definition of a situation on to a less closely integrated group. Such a group would have no means of formulating its own agreed definition, nor would it have mechanisms of enforcement'. I argue instead that the football sup-porters and hooligans are indeed tightly knit groups, through their common and strong identities as (in the case of hooligans, aggressive) supporters of a particular club, and that the police are not as tightly knit as they usually appear. Thus they can all project definitions of the situation, rather than just the police doing so, as the supporters and hooligans have a mechanism of enforcement through their threat of disorder.

While this may be how things work at football, to the outside world the image of a strong official police hierarchy remains. An important reason why this is so is the implicit hierarchy of accountability. Senior officers must take responsibility if anything goes wrong during their shifts, and the Chief Constable must answer on behalf of the force as a whole if it makes a grave error in executing its duties. Senior officers must perform to external audiences (including the public via the media) who can have a great deal of influence over them. This may be why the police constables are reluctant to change the way the police system works, even though they often say how much they do not like it and its hierarchy. They are reluctant to take on the responsibilities that official power brings, and the audiences that those official performances involve.

Implications for the occupational culture

My research into football policing brought these three main interaction themes (the significance of the mundane, interdependent boundaries and the flow of power) to light. However, how my findings relate to the infamous police occupational culture is also important to address. There have been many debates over the years as to the exact nature of this phenomenon, which I will briefly examine here. While I do not propose that football policing is its own occupational culture, I do feel that it sheds new light on this old concept and is able to unite some contrasting theories.

Many writers, especially some of the earliest ones, describe a rather monolithic police occupational culture. This culture has central features to which most (if not all) officers are seen to adhere. For Westley (1970), three main police attitudes can be identified: the perception of a hostile public, isolation and secrecy (which lead to solidarity). For him, these form the main influences on police action. Rubenstein (1973: 435–6) picks up this theme of isolation, though in his work it did not arise because of a perceived public hostility. He sees the police as isolated because of the nature of their work. He also finds pervasive secrecy in the force, but unlike Westley who saw the police group as secretive against outsiders (1970: 141), Rubenstein sees individual officers as being secretive against everyone else, including other officers. In order to relieve tension with the other officers from whom one is withholding information, jokes, pranks and insults are 'normal features of squad life' (Rubenstein 1973: 445). Skolnick (1966) has proposed the idea of a police 'working personality', which is generated by a combination of three elements of police work: danger, authority and efficiency. He acknowledges that not all police officers are alike in this personality, but that it is reflective of distinct cognitive tendencies in the police as an occupational group. In addition to the attitudes discussed above (isolation, secrecy, suspicion and solidarity), Reiner (2000a: 89–101) also identifies five others as common among police officers: a sense of mission, a love of action, cynicism, pessimism and pragmatism.

Some writers have also gone on to describe within-rank variations on the police occupational culture, usually when analysing police constables. For example, Muir (1977) discusses the effect of coercive power on police officers and identifies their four general behavioural responses: the enforcer, the avoider, the reciprocator and the professional. Reiner (1997: 737–8) found that all studies like Muir's discuss basically the same four categories of police constables. In his terms, these are peacekeepers, law-enforcers, alienated cynics, and managerial professionals. Chatterton (1976: 119) looks at two main approaches that police officers can take when it comes to arrest: those who act as judge and jury and so decide if they *should* arrest (based on finding the 'truth' of the incident), and those who just do it whenever possible (and let the courts sort out the 'truth'). These latter officers get the nickname 'snatchers'. Overall, while these studies present some interesting internal variations and interpretations of the occupational culture, the concept itself as one that is largely the same in all police forces is not challenged.

Two other oft-cited aspects of the universal police occupational culture are sexism and racism. Many studies on this were described in an earlier chapter and so will not be repeated here. In short, a police career is seen as one ideally dominated by the white aggressive male, and this is the image to which all other officers are to aspire. If they cannot do so they are viewed as inferior in some way, although these judgements may not necessarily be conscious ones (see for example Martin 1979, Smith and Gray 1985, Fielding 1994, Hunt 1990, Heidensohn 1992, Burke 1993, Holdaway and Barron 1997 and Westmarland 2001). Some writers have argued, however, that it is more productive to see the occupational culture as being *different* for women and ethnic minorities (such as Heidensohn 1992, Holdaway and O'Neill 2004, O'Neill and Holdaway forthcoming), rather than seeing these groups as unfortunate and helpless outsiders to it. For example, recent research on Black Police Associations has argued that it is no longer the case that ethnic minority officers see themselves as police officers who 'happen to be black' (Holdaway and Barron 1997), but that many now see themselves as 'black police officers'. In this sense they do not try to 'blend in' to the majority police culture but have developed a parallel culture unique to officers and staff of ethnic minority groups. While this is still very much a *police* culture, it is one more attuned to the social and cultural perspectives of these groups (Holdaway and O'Neill 2004, O'Neill and Holdaway forthcoming).

Another challenge to the monolithic view of the occupational culture comes from writers who have looked at differences between the ranks. As described in a previous chapter, Reuss-Ianni (1983) discusses an occupational culture organised around maxims (rather than rules) to guide action, which are different for more senior members of the organisation. The separate 'cop's code' for senior officers means that they will respond to events differently than those in the lower ranks, as their loyalties usually lie with political allies rather than the constables. Silvestri (2003) has challenged the long-held view that the occupational culture sees the work of senior management as 'feminine', or not 'real police work'. The senior policewomen she interviewed pointed out the 'competitive masculinity' of the higher ranks and that in order for one to succeed in them, one had to adopt a 'corporate' male attitude (2003: 41–2). Thus while this attitude is different to that held by the lower ranks, it is no less 'macho'.

Other more general challenges have also been made to the idea of a universal police occupational culture. Reiner (2000a: 85–6) argues that variations exist between forces relative to their unique environments and histories. For example, Cain (1971) found marked differences in the occupational cultures between an urban and a rural force, Manning (1980) notes differences in the occupational cultures of the vice squads of an urban and a suburban police department and Chatterton (1989) found distinct differences in the approach to paperwork between two sub-divisions in one force. Fielding (1988) argues that police officers mediate the influences of the formal and informal socialisation processes they experience in training. Recruits construct 'an "organisational reality" special to themselves from these various sources of influence' (1988: 9). He also views the occupational culture as a resource, rather than as a pervasive ideology. Officers can use it, among other influences, to guide their action or justify their behaviour should they wish to do so (1988: 204). Chan (1997) has taken this a step further and argues that police officers have a role in transforming their occupational culture; that is it not something they blindly accept but that it is one that they continuously create and modify. Waddington

(1999) has even argued that the police do not have a unique sub-culture at all, but a series of understandable reactions to the tasks they face in their occupation.

In this book I have organised my discussion of the police around their interaction teams (in Goffman's sense of the word, 1959: 83). While other authors have indeed noted internal divisions within policing (Reiner 2000a: 220, Van Maanen 1978: 328, Rubenstein 1973: xiii, as well as some of the authors above), what makes my analysis different is that it does not rely on formal demarcations of rank or grade to structure these internal divisions. While rank did play a part in the criteria for team membership, other factors were also important and these brought about separate police interaction teams within the ranks as well as between them. So in order to get a complete picture of police team boundaries one must look beyond the formal structures of the organisation. These interaction teams are recurring (in that they appear in the form I noted at all football matches, as well as possibly existing outside of football) but are not permanent (some teams will disband as members move up the ranks or into other police force areas). They are also organic groups that will grow and develop with each performance.

But despite the strong boundaries of team membership and teams' continuous development, all police officers do have universal yet resid-ual ties to each other through the underlying police community, which cuts across interaction teams (Manning 1980: 94, Reuss-Ianni 1983: 70). This presents the image of a unified force to the outside world and gives police officers a common pool of attitudes, percep-tions, symbolism and history on which to base their performances. While each team will ultimately develop its own definition of the situ-ation and performance, the resources on which they draw to do this are similar (Chan 1996). Thus my analysis of police interaction at foot-ball has shown that it is possible to have the appearance of a mono-lithic police occupational culture while still accepting the internal and external variations of that. This is what makes studying the interaction of the police so interesting: their capacity to appear to be a strongly loyal and unified group and yet also operate with very strict internal demarcations that often seem to contradict that loyalty and unifor-mity. This contrasts Waddington's (1999) argument that canteen chatter (his location for police culture) has no influence on police action and thus there is no utility in discussing a police culture. My research shows that police culture can be located in police *action*, not just talk, and is therefore still a viable concept.

Implications for Goffman

This book was not just an analysis of football policing and police team interaction, but also an exercise in the application of Goffman's key concepts to a new social context. These concepts, while proving very useful in guiding the analysis, have also not gone unchallenged by my findings. First of all, interaction does not necessarily conform to the 'officially accredited values of the society' as Goffman suggests (1959: 45), but to the values and norms of the situation. Each interaction team and its audience can develop their own expectations for acceptable behaviour (such as PCs in the stadium and football supporters) and conforming to those may actually be in violation of what 'society' would deem acceptable. The above discussion of power is also something that Goffman does not directly address, as well as the hierarchical relationships between teams. So we can see that not only is interaction between teams important to consider, but also how those teams are related to each other and can influence each other and the definition of the situation. One way I found this influence could take place is through the manipulation of time and space. Goffman identified these as markers to indicate a performance's regional boundaries. My research suggests that these boundaries can actually be challenged and altered to change the definition of the situation. The relationship between senior officers and supporters illustrates both points in that senior officers need the supporters to accept the rules they impose on the use of space to appear effective in crowd control, but cannot guarantee that the supporters will actually do so. Regional boundaries are thus more flexible than Goffman considered. My work has also offered a new level to team interaction, that of protagonists and antagonists. As we see with the football spotters, MSUs and the hooligans, performance teams can work with each other to present the same play to a general other audience. So while these police officers and supporters were never on the same team, they were both presenting the same definition of the situation to the same audience. This shows that teams can be more flexible and interdependent than Goffman allows. In addition, rather than shying away from a stigmatising role as the violent and deviant antagonists in the play, hooligans welcome and help cultivate their stigma. Goffman (1963b) presented stigma as always discrediting and thus something to be hidden if possible, whereas here we see a group who welcome it.

WPCs indicate a further development of Goffman's work in that some people can have no real team membership at all and yet are also not individual performers. These officers, on account of their gender, were excluded from full participation in the team of which they present themselves to be a part. A few instances in my work also suggested that the backstage can be interwoven with the front stage: they do not need to be physically separate. One space can act as front and backstage simultaneously, if the actors are careful in how they communicate to each other. For example, in the charge room subtle jokes or looks between police officers or between hooligans are backstage exchanges in the frontstage. Actions in the front stage can also influence those in the back without an actual physical invasion of the audience. Thus, it is not always the haven that Goffman suggested, such as when officers must stop their break early to attend to incidents in the streets. The reverse is also true in that CCTV operators are in a permanent backstage area in relation to football fans but can influence the interaction that occurs in the frontstage with these supporters by their communication with the officers there. Senior officers have proven Goffman's brief statement about the possibility of one-member teams (1959: 86). These officers are too far removed from each other and from the other officers to consider them teammates and so conduct their own performances with their own scripts. But unlike WPCs, they do not try to present themselves as members of any team. This work has also added some support to Jenkins' (1992: 90–1) claim that people can have more influence in their life worlds, in their habituses and fields, than Bourdieu allows.

Context is very important in Goffman's study of dramaturgy, and by definition the setting in which the interaction takes place and the people involved will shape how it progresses (see p. 62 for more on setting and actors in an interaction performance). However, many of the issues police officers face at football matches are similar throughout the country, as are the controls the supporters experience and the general culture they have developed (albeit with local variations). It is reasonable to see this study of interaction at football as one end of a continuum of similar interaction. In my study, interaction in the Scottish Premier League (its top level of competition) between the police and the fans was highly symbolic and ritualistic. Understood rules of decorum guided the behaviour there and actual violence was rare (but not entirely absent). However for football teams in other parts of the country, such as those in the English Premier League (the top level of competition in England), actual football violence may be a more common occurrence.[50] In this case the symbolic aspect of violence is minimal compared to its realisation and this would place it on the other end of the continuum. However, football policing in the English Championship (formerly the First Division, the second-highest level of competition) may be more similar to that which I witnessed in Scotland and so would occupy a similar place with it on the scale. In any case, there will always be some degree of interaction and negotiation between police officers and supporters (including the football hooligans).

In addition to these small and intricate levels of interaction, this research has implications for more macro sociological studies. Social control, order, territory and performance are topics that can apply to any social setting. My work has highlighted the symbolic nature of these and urges a greater analysis of the subtle differences possible in common understandings of 'normal', the flexibility inherent in seemingly rigid boundaries and the subtle levels of mutual influence possible in any power-charged relationship. Although our front stage performances may suggest that we are highly powerful or orderly or different from 'them', there is room to negotiate these definitions in a more subtle and symbolic level. Our own teams may not be as well defined as we think.

Notes

Introduction: Football, Policing and the Excitement of Mundane Sociology

1 In this book, the word 'football' will be used to refer to the sport also known as 'soccer'.

2 See Young 2002 for an analysis of North American sports crowd disorder throughout the twentieth century.

3 Alcohol was officially banned at matches in England in 1985.

4 English football supporters/hooligans attending international matches are a different matter, however. See Stott et al 2001, Stott 2003.

5 Some issues of a policy or tactical nature have emerged during the course of this study and have been presented to the main force I researched in a separate report. This is in keeping with my promise to them to do so.

Chapter 1   Previous Research

6 This type of behaviour is also called 'hooliganism' in England, especially in recent years when the term 'casual' has fallen out of use.

7 Smith (2000) has critically evaluated King's work and questions its theoretical basis. He is not a sociologist of sport himself, but a Manchester United supporter who was offended by the work King did on that particular group. King has responded (2001b) by critiquing not the content of Smith's article but the manner in which he formed this critique.

8 An exception is Ian Taylor (1971) who initially uses a Marxist perspective to prevent negative stereotyping of hooligans.

9 It should be noted that academic writers on hooliganism have downplayed the role alcohol has in 'causing' football violence. Many have pointed out (such as Dunning et al 2002: 11–12) that not all supporters who drink become violent and not all violent supporters are drunk.

10 For a more detailed look, please see Giulianotti (1999).

Chapter 2   Government Reports and Football Legislation

11 Please see Home Office Circular 34/2000 for a complete discussion of football related legislation in England and Wales, including the forms and procedures for banning orders. This is available on the Internet at: http://www.circulars.homeoffice.gov.uk.

12 This has already happened once in the Football (Disorder) (Amendment) Act 2002. These provisions are now in place for another five years.

13 It should be noted, however, that in early 2005 the Scottish Executive proposed a new Scottish Police Bill that includes provision for football banning orders for Scottish supporters. Individuals who have shown a pattern of

football violence and/or bigoted abuse could be subject to bans of up to 10 years. Those who have never been convicted of football disorder could still have a ban imposed after a summary application by a Chief Constable (Scottish Executive 2005).

14 This is The Police and Magistrates' Courts Act 1994.

Chapter 3   Uniformed Police Constables

15 This rivalry began in the 1980s when Aberdeen became one of the top teams in Scotland, thus challenging the dominance of Rangers. It reached a climax on 8 October 1988 during an Aberdeen vs. Rangers match. An Aberdeen player, Neil Simpson, badly injured Rangers' Ian Durrant. His playing career almost ended, and a new hatred between the two sides was born. It continues today (Cosgrove 1991).

16 This very old rivalry is based on the religious affiliation of each team, with Celtic having a Roman Catholic history and Rangers having a Protestant one. See Murray 1984 for a full discussion.

17 Generally, if a police officer is on duty for football, he or she does not respond to other criminal activities in the city. Thus anyone who is not associated with football is not really their concern and more easily regarded as 'normal'.

18 More recent writers might suggest that the trend has reversed itself, however. See Garland 2001.

19 Scotland's supporters present themselves as very fun-loving and jovial and rarely involved in confrontation with other supporters. It is an image that has been carefully cultivated for a number of years. See Giulianotti 1991 and 1995.

20 Although this may be changing, see Garland and Rowe 2000.

21 The distinction between hooligans and supporters is discussed in the introduction and earlier in this chapter. I am using the term 'hooligan' here to refer to those people who intentionally engage in violence with other hooligans during a football match day. They will be discussed further in the next chapter.

22 Glasgow Rangers' supporters tend to have Unionist political leanings and sometimes carry pictures of the Queen with them. They generally oppose an independent Scotland (Murray 1984). 'Flower of Scotland' is very nationalistic and anti-monarchy. (Bradley 2003: 18).

Chapter 4   Mobile Constables, Detectives and Football Spotters

23 Since the time of my research, the main force I studied has changed its tactics to use this latter approach where plain clothes spotters work match days and follow detectives' instructions.

24 The Football Intelligence Section (FIS) of the National Criminal Intelligence Service (NCIS) collates the intelligence reported to them from the various police forces and shares it with other forces. At the time of the research, Scottish police forces were not a part of this system but did consult with the FIS occasionally.

25 It is interesting to note though that the hooligans are still considered violent even though they do not actually engage in fights very often.

26 This was partly due to being apprehended in their coach by the detectives before a match, as mentioned earlier.

27 This appears to be the view of the government as well. As was discussed in Chapter 2, the Football (Disorder) Act 2000 allows the courts to ban *suspected* hooligans in England and Wales from attending international matches and hold their passports during specified periods. The police are able to stop people they suspect of football violence from leaving the country and refer them to the courts for a ban.

28 At that time, entrance to the visitor's section cost less than the home sections. It was not unheard of to get home fans in the visitor's section for just that reason.

29 For more on the actual Scottish Acts that direct the arrest and processing of prisoners and their individual rights, see *Renton and Brown's Criminal Procedure* (6th ed. by Sir Gerald Gordon, 1996) or Alistair Brown's (1996) *Criminal Evidence and Procedure*. For more on PACE and its implementation, see Reiner 2000a.

Chapter 5   Senior Officers

30 See discussion of Morris' work in Chapter 1.

31 See discussion in Chapter 4 about hooligans and criminal activity.

32 See discussion in Chapter 1 about the role of alcohol in football violence.

33 Flags are a controversial subject in British grounds. The *Guide to Safety at Sports Grounds* (The Home Office 1997) and all current legislation do not mention them so it is up to the discretion of the Match Commander to decide whether to allow them in or not. Some Match Commanders allow them as long as they are not on poles and do not carry sectarian messages or imagery, whereas others do not allow them at all.

34 See Chapters 3 and 4.

35 In fact, the Football (Disorder) Act 2000 encourages the banning of disruptive supporters from both domestic and international football matches.

36 This is not without justification, however. In addition to the Hillsborough Stadium disaster in 1989, there have been a number of other football tragedies that were caused by the uncontrolled movement of many supporters. For Scotland, the main one is the 1971 crush at Ibrox that killed 66 people. A last-minute goal lead some of the fans who had been exiting the stand to turn around on the stairs and try to go back to the terraces to see what was happening. The weight of the congestion that ensued was too much for the barriers on the stairs and they collapsed, crushing the people beneath them. See Chapter 2 for more on this.

Chapter 6   Women Police Constables

37 This may no longer be the case or may not be the case for long. The 'Gender Agenda', a push for change from several British and European police action groups, was launched in 2001 (Silvestri 2003: 14, 20n).

38 This is not to suggest that there was no racism or racialised interactions occurring during the matches. However, as there were little if no ethnic

minority police officers present during my research I have insufficient data to enter into a discussion of the matter.

39 Words in brackets are my deductions about the meaning of her statement.

40 The exact number of women who attend football matches is difficult to calculate. Previous surveys estimate that between 10% and 12% of match goers are female (Malcolm et al 2000).

41 For more on gender issues with football supporters, please see Giulianotti (1999).

42 Young (1991) lists many more categories of persons that the police class as 'other'. The ones I consider here are just the groups that were mentioned during my fieldwork.

Chapter 7   CCTV Operators and Stewards

43 This supports an observation I made on p. 125 about how the charge room in the police station can be both a front and a back stage. This is further proof that the spatial barrier between the two (Goffman 1959: 115) is not always needed.

44 For more on the debate as to whether there should be regulation of private security firms (including how they do their training) see Stenning 2000, Johnston (1999), Loader (1997c, 2000), Kempa et al (1999), Davis et al (2003), and O'Connor et al (2004).

45 Uniformed PCs in the ground would agree with this, but the detectives would not. See previous discussions on the variable definitions of 'hooligans' in Chapters 3 and 4.

46 An officer mentioned in Chapter 3 acknowledged this problem as well but senior officers, mentioned in Chapter 5, see this technique as good practice.

47 Since the time of my research, however, the main club and stewarding company I studied have written up a statement of intent as to their duties and responsibilities during the match. These largely involve matters of safety and the pledge to report to the police when problems are encountered. This has been given to the police, but there is no corresponding statement from the police to the club and stewards.

48 However, as Muir (1977) and Reiner (1997) suggest, not all police officers feel this way. Some like the social work aspect of the job and some are eager to be involved in police administration. These internal typologies of police officers were not prevalent in my research. The majority of the officers I spoke with seemed to be of the 'law-enforcer' type that Reiner describes. Thus, I have restricted my discussion to the police teams, rather than typologies, as these were very prevalent in football policing.

49 For example, see Norris et al (eds) 1998, especially the chapter by Armstrong and Giulianotti.

Conclusion: The Big Implications of Small Teams

50 See for example the BBC television series *MacIntyre Undercover*, aired in 1999, in which an undercover journalist became a member of a group of active hooligans from Chelsea Football Club (BBC News, 8 December 2000).

Bibliography

Allan, J. (1989) *Bloody Casuals: Diary of a Football Hooligan*. Glasgow: Famedram.

Anderson, B. (1990) *Imagined Communities*. London: Verso.

Archetti, E. P., and Romero, A. G. (1994) 'Death and violence in Argentinian football' in R. Giulianotti, N. Bonney, and M. Hepworth (eds), *Football, Violence, and Social Identity*. London: Routledge.

Armstrong, G. (1993) 'Like that Desmond Morris?' in D. Hobbs and T. May (eds) *Interpreting the Field: Accounts of Ethnography*. Oxford: Clarendon Press.

Armstrong, G. (1998) *Football Hooligans: Knowing the Score*. Oxford: Berg.

Armstrong, G. and Giulianotti, R. (1998) 'From another angle: Police surveillance and football supporters' in C. Norris, J. Moran, and G. Armstrong (eds), *Surveillance, Closed Circuit Television and Social Control*. Aldershot: Ashgate.

Armstrong, G. and Harris, R. (1991) 'Football hooligans: theory and evidence', *Sociological Review*, 39: 427–58.

Armstrong, G. and Hobbs, D. (1994) 'Tackled from behind' in R. Giulianotti, N. Bonney, and M. Hepworth (eds) *Football, Violence, and Social Identity*. London: Routledge.

Armstrong, G. and Hobbs, D. (1995) 'High tackles and professional fouls: The policing of soccer hooliganism', in C. Fijnaut and G. T. Marx (eds) *Undercover: Police Surveillance in Comparative Perspective*. The Hague: Kluwer Law International.

Armstrong, G. and Young, M. (1997) 'Legislators and interpreters: the law and "football hooligans"' in G. Armstrong and R. Giulianotti (eds) *Entering the Field: New Perspectives on World Football*. Oxford: Berg.

Armstrong, G. and Young, M. (2000) 'Fanatical football chants: Creating and controlling the carnival', in G. P. T. Finn and R. Giulianotti (eds) *Football Culture: Local Contests, Global Visions*. London: Frank Cass.

Bale, J. (1994) *Landscapes of Modern Sport*. Leicester: Leicester University Press.

BBC News (2000) 'Hooligans jailed after TV exposure', *BBC News Online*, 8 December 2000, <<http://news.bbc.co.uk/1/hi/uk/1061244.stm>>.

Becker, H. S. (1963) *Outsiders: Studies in the Sociology of Deviance*. New York: The Free Press.

Birrell, S. J. (1978) *Sporting Encounters: An Examination of the Work of Erving Goffman and its Application to Sport*. Unpublished PhD thesis, University of Massachusetts.

Bittner, E. (1967) 'The police on skid-row: A study of peace keeping', *American Sociological Review*, 32(5): 699–715.

Box, S. (1971) *Deviance, Reality and Society*. London: Holt, Rinehart and Winston Ltd.

Bradley, J. M. (2003) 'Images of Scottishness and otherness in international football', *Social Identities*, 9(1): 7–24.

Bramshill Police Staff College (1985) *Specialist Group Report on Hooliganism at Football Matches*. Sixty-fourth Intermediate Command Course.

Branaman, A. (1997) 'Goffman's social theory', in C. Lemert and A. Branaman (eds) *The Goffman Reader*. Oxford: Blackwell.

Brick, C. (2000) 'Taking Offence: Modern Moralities and the Perception of the Football Fan', *Soccer and Society*, 1(1): 158–72.

Brown, A. N. (1996) *Criminal Evidence and Procedure: An Introduction*. Edinburgh: T&T Clark.

Brown, J. and Heidensohn, F. (2000) *Gender and Policing: Comparative Perspectives*. London: Macmillan Press Ltd.

Brown, J., Maidment, A. and Bull, R. (1993) 'Appropriate skill-task matching or gender bias in deployment of female police officers?' *Policing and Society*, 3: 121–36.

Bryant, L., Dunkerley, D. and Kelland, G. (1985) 'One of the boys?', *Policing*, 1(4): 236–44.

Burke, M. E. (1993) *Coming Out of the Blue*. London: Cassells.

Cain, M. (1971) 'On the beat: Interactions and relations in rural and urban police forces', in S. Cohen (ed.) *Images of Deviance*. Harmondsworth: Penguin.

Cain, M. (1979) 'Trends in the sociology of police work', *International Journal of the Sociology of Law*, 7: 143–67.

Calhoun, C. (2000) 'Pierre Bourdieu', in G. Ritzer (ed.) *The Blackwell Companion to Major Social Theorists*. Oxford: Blackwell.

Canter, D., Comber, M., and Uzzell, D. L. (1989) *Football in its Place: An Environmental Psychology of Football Grounds*. London: Routledge.

Cashmore, E. (2002) 'Behind the window dressing: ethnic minority police perspectives on cultural diversity' *Journal of Ethnic and Migration Studies*, 28(2): 327–41.

Castle Communications, PLC. (1994) *Trouble on the Terraces* (video, viewed on 21 May 1998).

Chambliss, W. J. (1976) 'The Saints and the Roughnecks', in W. J. Chambliss and M. Mankoff (eds) *Whose Law? What Order? A Conflict Approach to Criminology*. New York: John Wiley.

Chan, J. (1996) 'Changing police culture', *British Journal of Criminology*, 36(1): 109–34.

Chan, J. (1997) *Changing Police Culture: Policing in a Multicultural Society*. Cambridge: Cambridge University Press.

Chatterton, M. (1976) 'Police in social control' in F. S. King (ed.) *Control Without Custody? Papers Presented to the Cropwood Round-Table Conference December 1975*. Cambridge: Institute of Criminology.

Chatterton, M. (1979) 'The supervision of patrol work under the fixed points system', in S. Holdaway (ed.) *The British Police*. London: Edward Arnold Press.

Chatterton, M. (1989) 'Managing paperwork' in M. Weatheritt (ed.) *Police Research: Some Future Prospects*. Aldershot: Avebury.

Coalter, F. (1985) 'Crowd behaviour at football matches: a study in Scotland', *Leisure Studies*, 4: 111–17.

Cohen, S. (1980) *Folk Devils and Moral Panics: The Creation of the Mods and Rockers*. Oxford: Martin Robertson.

Comeron, M. (2002) *Prevention of Violence in Sport*. Strasbourg: Council of Europe Publishing.

Cosgrove, S. (1991) *Hampden Babylon: Sex and Scandal in Scottish Football*. Edinburgh: Canongate Press PLC.

Csikszentmihalyi, M. (1975) *Beyond Boredom and Anxiety*. San Francisco: Jossey-Bass.

Davis, R. C., Ortiz, C. W., Dadush, S., Irish, J., Alvarado, A., and Davis, D. (2003) 'The public accountability of private police: lessons from New York, Johannesburg, and Mexico City', in *Policing and Society*, 13(2): 197–210.

The Department of Education and Science (1968) *Report of the Committee on Football*. London: HMSO.

Douglas, M. (1986) *How Institutions Think*. London: Routledge & Kegan Paul.

Dunning, E., Murphy, P., and Waddington, I. (2002) 'Towards a sociological understanding of football hooliganism as a world phenomenon', in E. Dunning, P. Murphy, I. Waddington, and A. E. Astrinakis (eds) *Fighting Fans: Football Hooliganism as a World Phenomenon*. Dublin: University College Dublin Press.

Dunning, E., Murphy, P., and Williams, J. (1988) *The Roots of Football Hooliganism: An Historical and Sociological Study*. London: Routledge & Kegan Paul.

Eisenhart, R. W. (1975) 'You can't hack it little girl: A discussion of the covert psychological agenda of modern combat training', *Journal of Social Issues*, 31(4): 13–23.

Ellis, S. (1984) *Attitudes Towards and Judgements of Incidents Which Occur Among Spectators and Football Matches*. Unpublished dissertation, University of Reading.

Emerson, R. M., Fretz, R. I. and Shaw, L. L. (2001) 'Participant observation and fieldnotes', in P. Atkinson, A. Coffey, S. Delamont, J. Loftland and L. Loftland (eds) *Handbook of Ethnography*. London: Sage.

Fielding, N. G. (1988) *Joining Forces: Police Training, Socialization, and Occupational Competence*. London: Routledge.

Fielding, N. G. (1994) 'Cop canteen culture' in T. Newburn and E. Stanko (eds) *Just Boys Doing Business? Men, Masculinities and Crime*. London: Routledge.

Fielding, N. G. and Fielding, J. (1992) 'A comparative minority: Female recruits to a British constabulary force', *Policing and Society*, 2: 205–18.

Finn, G. P. T. (1994) 'Football violence: A societal psychological perspective' in R. Giulianotti, N. Bonney, and M. Hepworth (eds), *Football, Violence, and Social Identity*. London: Routledge.

Foucault, M. (1977) *Discipline and Punish: The Birth of the Prison*. Translated by A. Sheridan. London: Allen Lane, Penguin Books Ltd.

Fyfe, N. R. (1992) 'Space, Time, and Policing: Towards a contextual understanding of police work', *Environment and Planning D: Society and Space*, 10: 469–81.

Garland, D. (2001). *The Culture of Control: Crime and Social Order in Contemporary Society*. Oxford: Oxford University Press.

Garland, J. and Rowe, M. (1999) 'Policing racism at football matches: An assessment of recent developments in police strategies', *International Journal of the Sociology of the Law*, 27: 251–66.

Garland, J. and Rowe, M. (2000) 'The hooligan's fear of the penalty', *Soccer and Society*, 1(1): 144–57.

Gilman, M. (1996) 'Football – the theft of a game', *Criminal Justice Matters*, 23: 7–8.

Giulianotti, R. (1991) 'Scotland's tartan army in Italy: The case for the carnivalesque', *Sociological Review*, 39(3): 503–27.

Giulianotti, R. (1994) 'Social identity and public order: Political and academic discourses on football violence', in R. Giulianotti, N. Bonney, and M. Hepworth (eds) *Football, Violence, and Social Identity*. London: Routledge.

Giulianotti, R. (1995) 'Football and the politics of carnival: An ethnographic study of Scottish fans in Sweden', *International Review for the Sociology of Sport*, 30(2): 191–219.

Giulianotti, R. (1996) *A Sociology of Scottish Football Fan Culture*. Unpublished PhD thesis, University of Aberdeen.

Giulianotti, R. (1999) *Football: A Sociology of the Global Game*. Cambridge: Polity Press.

Giulianotti, R. (2002) 'Supporters, followers, fans, and flâneurs: A taxonomy of spectator identities in football', *Journal of Sport and Social Issues*, 26(1): 25–46.

Giulianotti, R. and Armstrong, A. (2002) 'Avenues of contestation: Football hooligans running and ruling urban spaces', *Social Anthropology*, 10(2): 211–38.

Giulianotti, R. and Gerrard, M. (2001) 'Cruel Britannia? Glasgow Rangers, Scotland and "hot" football rivalries' in Gary Armstrong and Richard Giulianotti (eds) *Fear and Loathing in World Football*. Oxford: Berg.

Goffman, E. (1959) *The Presentation of Self in Everyday Life*. London: Penguin.

Goffman, E. (1961a) *Asylums: Essays on the Social Situation of Mental Patients and other Inmates*. London: Penguin.

Goffman, E. (1961b) *Encounters: Two Studies in the Sociology of Interaction*. Indianapolis: Bobbs-Merrill.

Goffman, E. (1963a) *Behaviour in Public Places: Notes on the Social Organisation of Gatherings*. New York: The Free Press.

Goffman, E. (1963b) *Stigma: Notes on the Management of Spoiled Identity*. London: Penguin Books.

Goffman, E. (1967) *Interaction Ritual: Essays on Face-to-Face Behaviour*. New York: Pantheon Books.

Goffman, E. (1969) *Strategic Interaction*. Philadelphia: University of Philadelphia Press.

Goffman, E. (1971) *Relations in Public: Microstudies of the Public Order*. London: Lane.

Goffman, E. (1974) *Frame Analysis: An Essay on the Organisation of Experience*. New York: Harper and Row.

Gordon, G. H. (1996) *Renton and Brown's Criminal Procedure* (6th ed.). Edinburgh: W. Green/Sweet & Maxwell.

Hale, C. (1996) 'Fear of crime: a review of the literature', *International Review of Victimology*, 4(2): 79–150.

Hammersley, M. and Atkinson, P. (1995) *Ethnography: Principles in Practice* (2nd ed.). London: Routledge.

Harman, H. (1982) 'Civil liberties and civil disorder', in D. Cowell, T. Jones and J. Young (eds) *Policing the Riots*. London: Junction Books.

Harper, C. Inspector (1990) *A Study of Football Crowd Behaviour*. Police Research Group: The Home Office.

Harrington, J. A. (1968) *Soccer Hooliganism: A Preliminary Report*. Bristol: John Wright & Sons Ltd.

Heidensohn, F. (1992) *Women in control? The Role of Women in Law Enforcement*. Oxford: Clarendon Press.

Heidensohn, F. (1994) '"We can handle it out here": Women officers in Britain and the USA and the policing of public order', *Policing and Society*, 4: 293–303.

Hester, S. and Eglin, P. (1992) *A Sociology of Crime*. London: Routledge.

Hobbs, D. (1988) *Doing the Business: Entreprenuership, The Working Class, and Detectives in the East End of London*. Oxford: Oxford University Press.

Hobbs, D., Hadfield, P., Lister, S. and Winlow, S. (2002) '"Door Lore": the art and economics of intimidation', *British Journal of Criminology*, 42: 352–70.

Hobbs, D. and Robins, D. (1991) 'The boy done good: Football violence, changes and continuities', *Sociological Review*, 39: 551–79.

Holdaway, S. (1983) *Inside the British Police: A Force at Work*. Oxford: Blackwell Press.

Holdaway, S. (1989) 'Discovering structure. Studies of the British police occupational culture', in M. Weatheritt (ed.) *Police Research: Some Future Prospects*. Aldershot: Avebury.

Holdaway, S. and Barron, A. (1997) *Resigners? The Experience of Black and Asian Police Officers*. Basingstoke: Macmillan Press Ltd.

Holdaway, S. and O'Neill, M. (2004) 'The development of Black Police Associations: changing articulations of race within the police', *British Journal of Criminology*, 44(6): 854–65.

The Home Office (1972) *Report of the Inquiry into Crowd Safety at Sports Grounds*. By The Rt. Hon. Lord Wheatley. London: HMSO.

The Home Office (1986) *Committee of Inquiry into Crowd Safety and Control at Sports Grounds: Final Report*. Chaired by Mr. Justice Popplewell. London: HMSO.

The Home Office (1990) *The Hillsborough Stadium Disaster: Final Report*. Inquiry by the Rt. Hon. Lord Justice Taylor. London: HMSO.

The Home Office (1997) *Guide to Safety at Sports Grounds (The Green Guide)* Fourth edition. London: HMSO.

The Home Office (2001) *Working Group on Football Disorder: Report and Recommendations*. Chaired by Lord Bassam. London: HMSO. <<http://www.homeoffice.gov.uk/docs/ftblwgrp.pdf>>

Horne, J. (1998) 'Football Hooligans: Knowing the Score (review of Gary Armstrong)', *The Sociological Review*, 46(4): 877–82.

Howard, W. Chief Inspector (1979) 'Soccer hooliganism', *Bramshill Journal*, Autumn: 35–43.

Hughson, J. (1998a) 'Among the thugs: The "New Ethnographies" of football supporting subcultures', *International Review for the Sociology of Sport*, 33(1): 43–57.

Hughson, J. (1998b) 'Soccer support and social identity: Finding the "thirdspace"', *International Review for the Sociology of Sport*, 33(4): 403–9.

Hughson, J. (1999) 'The Boys in Blue and the Bad Blue Boys: A case study of interactive relations between the police and ethnic youth in western Sydney', *The Australian Journal of Social Issues*, 34(2): 167–82.

Hughson, J. (2002) 'Australian soccer's "ethnic" tribes: a new case for the carnivalesque', in E. Dunning, P. Murphy, I. Waddington, and A. E. Astrinakis (eds) *Fighting Fans: Football Hooliganism as a World Phenomenon*. Dublin: University College Dublin Press.

Hunt, J. (1990) 'The logic of sexism among the police', *Women and Criminal Justice*, 1(2): 3–30.

Ingham, A. G., and Smith M. D. (1974) 'Social implications of the interaction between spectators and athletes', *Exercise and Sport Science Reviews*, 2: 189–224.

Jefferson, T. and Grimshaw, R. (1982) 'Law, democracy and justice: The question of police accountability', in D. Cowell, T. Jones and J. Young (eds) *Policing the Riots*. London: Junction Books.

Jenkins, R. (1992) *Pierre Bourdieu*. London: Routledge.

Johnston, L. (1999) 'Private policing in context', *European Journal on Criminal Policy and Research*, 7: 175–96.

Jones, T. and Newburn, T. (1998) *Private Security and Public Policing*. Oxford: Clarendon Press.

Kempa, M., Carrier, R., Wood, J. and Shearing, C. (1999) 'Reflections on the evolving concept of "private policing"', *European Journal on Criminal Policy and Research*, 7: 197–223.

Kempa, M., Stenning, P. and Wood, J. (2004) 'Policing communal spaces: a reconfiguration of the "mass private property" hypothesis', *British Journal of Criminology*, 44(4): 562–81.

Kerr, J. (1994) *Understanding Soccer Hooliganism*. Buckingham: Open University Press.

King, A. (1995) 'Outline of a practical theory of football violence', *Sociology*, 29(4): 635–51.

King, A. (1999) 'Football hooliganism and the practical paradigm', *Sociology of Sport Journal*, 16: 269–73.

King, A. (2001a) 'Violent pasts: Collective memory and football hooliganism', *The Sociological Review*, 49(4): 568–85.

King, A. (2001b) 'Abstract and engaged critique in sociology: on football hooliganism' *British Journal of Sociology*, 52(4): 707–12.

LeBon, G. (1895) (1960) *The Crowd: A Study of the Popular Mind*. New York: Viking Press.

Lewis, J. M. (1982) 'Crowd control at English football matches', *Sociological Focus*, 15(4): 417–23.

Lister, S., Hadfield, P., Hobbs, D. and Winlow, S. (2001) 'Accounting for bouncers: occupational licensing as a mechanism for regulation', *Criminal Justice*, 1(4): 363–84.

Livingstone, K. and Hart, J. (2003) 'The wrong arm of the law? Public images of private security', *Policing and Society*, 13(2): 159–70.

Loader, I. (1997a) 'Policing and the social: questions of symbolic power', *British Journal of Sociology*, 48(1): 1–18.

Loader, I. (1997b) 'Private Security and the demand for protection in contemporary Britain', *Policing and Society*, 7: 143–62.

Loader, I. (1997c) 'Thinking normatively about private security', *Journal of Law and Society*, 24(3): 377–94.

Loader, I. (1999) 'Consumer culture and the commodification of policing and security', *Sociology*, 33(2): 373–92.

Loader, I. (2000) 'Plural policing and democratic governance', *Social and Legal Studies*, 9(3): 323–45.

Lukes, S. (1974) *Power: A Radical View*. London: Macmillan Press Ltd.

Macpherson, Lord. (1999) *The Stephen Lawrence Inquiry*. Cm 4262-I. London: HMSO.

McArdle, D. (2000) *From Boot Money to Bosman: Football, Society and the Law*. London: Cavendish Publishing.

McBarnet, D. J. (1979) 'Arrest: The legal context of policing', in S. Holdaway (ed.) *The British Police*. London: Edward Arnold Press.

McLaughlin, E. and Murji, K. (1997) 'The future lasts a long time: Public police-work and the management paradox', in P. Francis, P. Davies and V. Jupp (eds) *Policing Futures: The Police, Law Enforcement and the Twenty-First Century*. Basingstoke: Macmillan.

Mack, R. W. (1954) 'The prestige system of an Air Force Base: Squadron rankings and morale', *American Sociological Review*, 19(3): 281–87.

Malcolm, D., Jones, I. and Waddington, I. (2000) 'The People's Game? Football spectatorship and demographic change', *Soccer and Society*, 1(1): 129–43.

Manning, P. (1992) *Erving Goffman and Modern Sociology*. Cambridge: Polity Press.

Manning, P. K. (1980) *The Narcs Game: Organisational and Informational Limits on Drug Law Enforcement*. Cambridge, Massachusetts: The MIT Press.

Manning, P. K. (1997) *Police Work: The Social Organisation of Policing* (2nd ed.). Prospect Heights: Waveland Press.

Marsh, P. (1982) 'Social order on the British soccer terraces', *International Social Science Journal*, 34(2): 247–56.

Marsh, P., Rosser, E. and Harré, R. (1978) *The Rules of Disorder*. London: Routledge.

Martin, C. (1996) 'The impact of equal opportunities policies on the day-to-day experiences of women police constables', *British Journal of Criminology*, 36(4): 510–28.

Martin, S. (1979) 'POLICEwomen and policeWOMEN: Occupational role dilemmas and choices of female officers', *Journal of Police Science and Administration*, 7(3): 314–23.

Martin, S. (1994) '"Outsider within" the station house: The impact of race and gender on black women police', *Social Problems*, 41(3): 383–400.

Marx, G. T. (1988) *Undercover: Police Surveillance in America*. Berkley: University of California Press.

Messinger, S., Sampson, H. and Towne, R. D. (1962) 'Life as theatre: Some notes on the dramaturgic approach to social reality', *Sociometry*, 14(2): 141–63.

Metcalfe, J. E. Chief Superintendent (1984) *Football Hooliganism: Police Methods to Deal With the Persistent Offender*. Bramshill Police Staff College, Twenty-first Senior Command Course.

Middleham, N. Inspector (1993) *Football: Policing the Supporter*. Police Research Group: The Home Office.

Moorhouse, H. F. (2000) 'Football Hooligans: Knowing the Score (review of Gary Armstrong)', *Urban Studies*, 37(8): 1463–64.

Morris, D. (1981) *The Soccer Tribe*. London: Jonathan Cape.

Muir, W. K. Jr. (1977) *Police: Streetcorner Politicians*. Chicago: University of Chicago Press.

Murphy, P., Williams, J., and Dunning, E. (1990) *Football on Trial: Spectator violence and development in the football world*. London: Routledge.

Murray, B. (1984) *The Old Firm: Sectarianism, Sport and Society*. Edinburgh: Jon Donald Publishers Ltd.

Noaks, L. (2004) 'Diversification of British policing: the citizen experience', *Policing: An International Journal of Police Strategies and Management*, 27(2): 264–74.

Norris, C. (1993) 'Some ethical considerations on field work with the police', in D. Hobbs and T. May (eds) *Interpreting the Field: Accounts of Ethnography*. Oxford: Clarendon.

Norris, C. and Armstrong, G. (1999) *The Maximum Surveillance Society: The Rise of CCTV*. Oxford: Berg.

Norris, C., Moran, J., and Armstrong, G. (1998) *Surveillance, CCTV, and Social Control*. Ashgate: Aldershot.

Nylen, L. Chief Constable (1994) 'Policing major soccer events', *Police Chief*, 61: 42–5.

O'Connor, D., Lippert, R., Greenfield, K. and Boyle, P. (2004) 'After the "Quiet Revolution": the self-regulation of Ontario contract security agencies', *Policing and Society*, 14(2): 138–57.

O'Neill, M (2004) 'Policing football in Scotland: the forgotten team', *International Review for the Sociology of Sport*, 39(1): 95–104.

O'Neill, M. and Holdaway, S. (*forthcoming*) 'Examining "Window Dressing": the views of Black Police Associations on recruitment and training', *Journal of Ethnic and Migration Studies*.

Phillips, D. (1988) 'New developments in policing football', in *Football into the 1990s*. Proceedings of a conference held at the University of Leicester, 29–30 September. Sir Norman Chester Centre for Football Research: University of Leicester.

Punch, M. (1993) 'Observation and the police: The research experience', in M. Hammersley (ed.) *Social Research: Philosophy, Politics and Practice*. London: Sage.

Redhead, S. (1991) 'Some reflections on discourses on football hooliganism', *Sociological Review*, 39(3): 479–86.

Redhead, S. (1997) *Post-fandom and the Millennial Blues: The Transformation of Soccer Culture*. London: Routledge.

Reiner, R. (1997) 'Policing and the police', in M. Maguire, R. Morgan and R. Reiner (eds) *The Oxford Handbook of Criminology* (2nd ed.). Oxford: Clarendon Press.

Reiner, R. (2000a) *The Politics of the Police* (3rd ed.). Oxford: Oxford University Press.

Reiner, R. (2000b) 'Police research' in R. D. King and E. Wincup (eds) *Doing Research on Crime and Justice*. Oxford: Oxford University Press.

Reuss-Ianni, E. (1983) *Two Cultures of Policing: Street Cops and Management Cops*. New Brunswick, New Jersey: Transaction Books.

Roman, L. G. (1993) 'Double exposure: The politics of feminist materialist ethnography', *Educational Theory*, 43(3): 279–308.

Roy, D. F. (1960) 'Banana Time: Job satisfaction and informal interaction', *Human Organisation*, 18: 156–68.

Rubinstein, J. (1973) *City Police*. New York: Ballantine Books.

Scottish Executive (2005) *Supporting Police, Protecting Communities: Proposals for Legislation*. Edinburgh: Scottish Executive.

Security Industry Authority website, viewed 3 August 2004. << http://www.the-sia.org.uk>>

Sharp, D. and Wilson, D. (2000) '"Household Security": Private policing and vigilantism in Doncaster', *The Howard Journal*, 39(2): 113–31.

Shearing, C. D. and Stenning, P. C. (1983) 'Private security: Implications for social control', *Social Problems*, 30(5): 493–506.

Silvestri, M. (2003) *Women in Charge: Policing, Gender and Leadership*. Devon: Willan Publishing.

Skolnick, J. H. (1966) *Justice Without Trial: Law Enforcement in Democratic Society*. New York: John Wiley & Sons, Inc.

Sloan, A. K. (1989) 'Ver Heyden de Lancey Medico-Legal Lectures 1988–1989: Chief Constable Strathclyde Police', *Medicine, Science and the Law*, 29(1): 14–25.

Smith, D. J. and Gray J. (1985) *Police and People in London: The PSI Report*. Aldershot: Gower.

Smith, T. (2000) '"Bataille's boys": Postmodernity, Fascists and football fans', *British Journal of Sociology*, 51(3): 443–60.

Soja, E. (1996) *Thirdspace: Journeys to Los Angeles and Other Real-and-Imagined Places*. Oxford: Blackwell.

Stenning, P. C. (2000) 'Powers and accountability of private police', *European Journal on Criminal Policy and Research*, 8: 325–52.

Stott, C. (2003) 'Police expectations and the control of English soccer fans at "Euro 2000"', *Policing: An International Journal of Police Strategies and Management*, 26(4): 640–55.

Stott, C., Hutchison, P., and Drury, J. (2001) '"Hooligans" abroad? Inter-group dynamics, social identity and participation in collective "disorder" at the 1998 World Cup Finals', *British Journal of Social Psychology*, 40: 359–84.

Stott, C. and Reicher, S. (1998a) 'How conflict escalates: the intergroup dynamics of collective football crowd "violence"', *Sociology*, 32 (2): 353–77.

Stott, C., and Reicher, S. (1998b) 'Crowd action as intergroup process: introducing the police perspective', *European Journal of Social Psychology*, 28(4): 509–29.

Stouffer, S. A., et al (1965) *The American Soldier: Combat and its Aftermath*, Vol. II. London: Geoffrey Cumberledge, Oxford University Press.

Strachan, G. (1999) 'Its not that you're not welcome...', *The Observer*, September 19.

Taylor, I. (1971) 'Soccer Consciousness and Soccer Hooliganism', in S. Cohen (ed.) *Images of Deviance*. Harmonsworth: Penguin.

Taylor, I. (1982) 'On the sports violence question: Soccer hooliganism revisited', in J. Hargreaves (ed.) *Sport, Culture and Ideology*. London: Routledge and Kegan Paul.

Taylor, I. (1983) 'The Soccer Tribe (review of Desmond Morris)', *Theory, Culture and Society*, 1(3): 163–66.

Taylor, I. (1987) 'Putting the boot into working class sport: British soccer after Bradford and Brussels', *Sociology of Sport Journal*, 4(2): 171–91.

Trivizas, E. (1980) 'Offences and offenders in football crowd disorders', *British Journal of Criminology*, 20(3): 276–88.

Trivizas, E. (1981) 'Sentencing the "Football Hooligan"', *British Journal Criminology*, 21(4): 342–49.

Van Maanen, J. (1978) 'Epilogue: On watching the watchers', in P. K. Manr and J. Van Maanen (eds) *Policing: A View from the Street*. New York: Ran House.

Van Maanen, J. (1988) *Tales of the Field: On Writing Ethnography*. Ch University of Chicago Press.

Waddington, P. A. J. (1996) 'Public order policing: Citizenship and mora guity', in F. Leishman, B. Loveday and S. P. Savage (eds) *Core Issues in* London: Longman.

Waddington, P. A. J. (1999) 'Police (canteen) sub-culture: an appreciation', *British Journal of Criminology*, 39(2): 287–309.

Wakefield, A. (2003) *Selling Security: The Private Policing of Public Space*. Devon: Willan Publishing.

Walker, A. (2000) 'Police may be charged over riot tape'. *The Scotsman*, 3 October, p. 1.

Walklate, S. (1996) 'Equal opportunities and the future of policing' in F. Leishman, B. Loveday and S. P. Savage (eds) *Core Issues in Policing*. London: Longman.

Weber, M. (1968) *Wirtschaft und Gesellschaft*, translated as *Economy and Society: An Outline of Interpretive Sociology*. G. Roth and G. Wittich (eds). New York: Bedminster Press.

Weed, M. (2001) 'Ing-ger-land at Euro 2000: How "handbags at 20 paces" was portrayed as a full-scale riot', *International Review for the Sociology of Sport*, 36(4): 407–24.

Westley, W. A. (1970) *Violence and the Police: A Sociological Study of Law, Custom, and Morality*. Cambridge, Massachusetts: The MIT Press.

Westmarland, L. (2000) 'Taking the flak: Operational policing, fear and violence', in G. Lee-Treweek and S. Linkogle (eds) *Danger in the Field: Risks and Ethics in Social Research*. London: Routledge.

Westmarland, L. (2001) *Gender and Policing: Sex, Power and Police Culture*. Devon: Willan Publishing.

West Yorkshire Metropolitan Police Authority (1977) *Violence and Vandalism at Football Matches and Public Gatherings in West Yorkshire – Involvement of Police Manpower*. A report by a special sub-committee of the West Yorkshire Metropolitan Police Authority: West Yorkshire Metropolitan County Council and West Yorkshire Metropolitan Police.

White, J. (1984) *A Socio-Legal Approach to 'Football Hooliganism'*. Unpublished PhD thesis, University of Edinburgh.

Williams, J. (1980) 'Football hooliganism: Offences, arrests and violence – A critical note', *British Journal of Law and Society*, 7(1): 104–11.

Williams, J. and Taylor, R. (1994) 'Boys keep swinging: Masculinity and football culture in England', in T. Newburn and E. Stanko (eds) *Just Boys Doing Business? Men, Masculinities and Crime*. London: Routledge.

Winlow, S., Hobbs, D., Lister, S. and Hadfield, P. (2001) 'Get ready to duck: Bouncers and the realities of ethnographic research on violent groups', *British Journal of Criminology*, 41: 536–48.

Young, K. (2002) 'A walk on the wild side: exposing North American sports crowd disorder', in E. Dunning, P. Murphy, I. Waddington, and A. E. Astrinakis (eds) *Fighting Fans: Football Hooliganism as a World Phenomenon*. Dublin: University College Dublin Press.

Young, M. (1991) *An Inside Job: Policing and Police Culture in Britain*. Oxford: Clarendon Press.

Zerubavel, E. (1979) *Patterns of Time in Hospital Life*. Chicago: The University of Chicago Press.

Zhao, J., Herbst, L., and Lovrich, N. (2001) 'Race, ethnicity and the female cop: Differential patterns of representation', *Journal of Urban Affairs*, 23(3–4): 243–57.

Index

LIVERPOOL JOHN MOORES UNIVERSITY
Aldham Robarts L.R.C.
TEL. 051 231 3701/3634